SUPREME INJUSTICE

The Nathan I. Huggins Lectures

SUPREME INJUSTICE

SLAVERY IN THE NATION'S HIGHEST COURT

PAUL FINKELMAN

Harvard University Press

Cambridge, Massachusetts
London, England
2018

First printing

Library of Congress Cataloging-in-Publication Data

Names: Finkelman, Paul, 1949– author.

Title: Supreme injustice : slavery in the nation's
highest court / Paul Finkelman.

Other titles: Nathan I. Huggins lectures.

Description: Cambridge, Massachusetts : Harvard University
Press, 2018. | Series: The Nathan I. Huggins lectures |
Includes bibliographical references and index.

Identifiers: LCCN 2017021771 | ISBN 9780674051218 (alk. paper)

Subjects: LCSH: Marshall, John, 1755–1835. | Taney, Roger Brooke,
1777–1864. | Story, Joseph, 1779–1845. | Slavery—Law and legislation—
United States—History—19th century. | Judicial opinions—United States—
History—19th century. | United States. Supreme Court—History—19th
century. | Judges—United States—Attitudes—History—19th century.

Classification: LCC KF4545.S5 F567 2018 | DDC 342.7308/7—dc23

LC record available at https://lccn.loc.gov/2017021771

For my sister, Triss Stein, who brilliantly weaves history into her novels, and for my brother-in-law, Bob Stein, who always provides wise counsel in my publishing endeavors.

CONTENTS

**SUPREME
INJUSTICE**

Introduction

THIS BOOK EXPLORES the slavery jurisprudence of the three most important justices on the antebellum Supreme Court—Chief Justice John Marshall, Associate Justice Joseph Story, and Chief Justice Roger Brooke Taney. All three believed that slavery—or more precisely, opposition to slavery—threatened national unity and political stability. Modern scholars understand that, as the historians Harold M. Hyman and William M. Wiecek put it, slavery was the "nemesis of the Constitution."[1] The justices I discuss in this book would have argued that *anti*-slavery was the nemesis of the Constitution. Their goal was to prevent opposition to slavery (and the moral disgust slavery engendered among many Americans) from undermining the nation's constitutional and political arrangements.

These three were leaders on the Court and highly respected public men. In their judicial opinions, publications, public speeches, and private correspondence, they might have played a role in mediating between slavery and freedom in American law. Had this happened, they might have helped the nation eventually find a political solution to the problem of slavery. Even if nothing could have induced the South to accept a peaceful (and probably gradual) end to slavery, a different jurisprudence would have had significant consequences. Some southern black men and women would have lived in freedom rather than slavery because the Supreme Court had upheld their claims to liberty. Blacks in the North would not have lived in constant fear of being seized and dragged into bondage. Free blacks would have had some legal rights and protections under the Constitution. Some northern abolitionists—white and black—would not have gone to jail or been heavily fined for helping fugitive slaves. Some Africans kidnapped and illegally brought to the United States might have been able to return to the continent of their birth, even to their home countries. Most significantly, with a different jurisprudence the Supreme Court, and the jurists in this book, would have left the nation with a legacy of liberty and justice, rather than one of slavery, racism, and oppression.

Such a jurisprudence would have been consistent with the nation's founding ideals, that "all men are created equal" and "endowed" with the "unalienable rights" of "life, liberty, and the pursuit of happiness," and with the Constitution's goal "to form a more perfect Union, establish Justice, insure domestic Tranquility, provide for the common defence, promote the general Welfare, and secure the Blessings of Liberty to ourselves and our Posterity."[2] Virtually all Americans understood that slavery was a threat to national defense and domestic tranquility. Most Americans, even some southern slave owners, understood that slavery was inconsistent with "equality," with "life, liberty, and the pursuit of happiness," and with "justice." In 1818, Mississippi's highest court had ruled that in close cases, "in matters of doubt," it was "an unquestioned rule, that courts must lean '*in favorem vitae et libertatis*'"—in favor of life and liberty. That early slave-state court asserted: "Slavery is condemned by reason and the laws of nature. It exists and can only exist, through municipal regulations."[3] Unfortunately, the leading justices of the Supreme Court in the period before the Civil War did not embrace this reasoning.

These jurists almost always failed to consider liberty or justice in cases involving slavery and race. To the contrary, with only a few exceptions in their many years on the bench, they continuously strengthened slavery in the American constitutional order. They cast opposition to slavery as unpatriotic, undermined the possibility of a political solution to America's "peculiar institution," and helped set the stage for the final antebellum crisis that ultimately led to secession, the Civil War, and the death of some 630,000 young Americans. Out of that carnage came an end to slavery and what Abraham Lincoln called "a New Birth of Freedom." But this outcome would surely have surprised these justices, and at least two of them—the two chief justices, John Marshall and Roger B. Taney—probably would have found this outcome outrageous and wrong. They certainly would have emphatically opposed the post-war constitutional amendments making blacks citizens of the United States and giving them the right to vote on the same basis as whites.[4]

The Supreme Court did not cause sectionalism or secession. Nor did any single decision, even *Dred Scott* v. *Sandford* (1857), cause the Civil War. Northern frustration over the Court's continuous support for slavery, however, helped create an electorate that was no longer willing to tolerate a proslavery government nurtured by a proslavery Supreme Court. The Court's assault on American liberty that culminated in *Dred Scott* helped catapult Abraham Lincoln to the White House. Lincoln's election, in turn, led to secession and war.

In the four decades before the Civil War, the Court narrowed the political options, removing possibilities for compromise and encouraging southern extremists to expect judicial support in every political and legal issue concerning slavery. Along with Democratic Party leaders, the Court helped dismantle the older political compromises on slavery, inadvertently setting the stage for the ascendancy in the 1850s of a new, northern-based political party that successfully ran against the Supreme Court's proslavery jurisprudence.

Marshall, Taney, and Story personally disagreed about slavery. Marshall and Taney were lifelong slave owners. Both were personally and politically hostile to the presence of free blacks in the United States. Neither looked to a time when slavery would be ended. In both their private and public lives, they supported slavery. Marshall was personally involved in buying (and sometimes selling) significant numbers of slaves. Story, on the other hand, never owned a slave, personally found slavery abhorrent, and made that clear in his early decisions and comments on the African slave trade. But, after 1822, Story did little to challenge slavery or the African slave trade. When issues of fugitive slaves arose, Story abandoned his earlier antislavery principles. In *Prigg* v. *Pennsylvania* (1842) he wrote an opinion that was as proslavery as anything Chief Justice Taney would conjure up in the *Dred Scott* case.[5] Indeed, in *Prigg*, Story went out of his way to offer a proslavery interpretation of the Constitution. Despite different personal and professional relationships to slavery, all three justices supported and protected slavery at almost every turn.

John Marshall's father, Thomas Marshall, was not wealthy, but through hard work and shrewd land purchases he rose to political prominence in his community and enjoyed a comfortable life as a small-scale planter, owning more than twenty slaves after the Revolution. Young John grew up on the frontier, had very little formal education, and watched his father work to increase the family's wealth and social status. After the war, John emulated his father, purchasing vast quantities of land and ultimately owning hundreds of slaves throughout his lifetime. In 1830, five years before his death in 1835, Marshall owned about one hundred and fifty slaves, and by this time he had also given substantial numbers of slaves to his adult children.

Throughout his thirty-four years on the Court (1801–1835), Marshall avoided as much as possible discussions of the substance of slavery, the nature of slaveholding, or the rights of slave owners. He *never* wrote an opinion supporting a claim to liberty brought by a slave. Nor did he ever write an opinion punishing someone for illegal participation in the African slave trade. The Marshall Court did uphold freedom claims by some slaves, and did support sanctions against some slave traders, but other justices *always* wrote the opinions. Off the bench, in his private and public statements, Marshall opposed the presence of free blacks in the country, arguing that they were "pests" and criminals. But on the bench, Marshall avoided discussions of blacks in most of his opinions, and refrained from making the kind of racist assertions that mark his Indian law jurisprudence.[6] Marshall was a master craftsman of opinions and a persuasive leader who usually controlled the outcome of cases in his first three decades on the Court. He successfully prevented his Court from confronting slavery directly or talking about the place of blacks in American society. Marshall wanted to preserve and protect slavery without appearing to do so—much like the Founders who wrote a proslavery Constitution in 1787.[7] He tried to contain issues of slavery and race in his circuit court duties and urged his fellow justices to do the same. Reliably protecting the interests of slave owners, Marshall showed virtually no concern for the rights or liberties of black people—whether born in the United States or Africa. Always protecting slavery, Marshall shrewdly avoided language that would enflame the passions of northerners. The result is that scholars who write about race, slavery, and the law often have little to say about Marshall, and Marshall scholars have little to say about his relationship to slavery.

Joseph Story, who served on the court for thirty-three years (1811–1845), never owned a slave or profited from slavery. He was born in 1779, a year before his native Massachusetts prohibited slavery in its Constitution. By the time he entered Harvard, in 1795, there were no slaves in Massachusetts and free blacks there had almost complete legal equality, including the right to vote on the same basis as whites. Story personally abhorred slavery and, early in his career, spoke out against it. But like his two slaveholding colleagues, in his Supreme Court opinions Story never supported liberty and he justified his proslavery jurisprudence as a matter of Constitutional obligation, history (which he sometimes distorted to support the opinions he wrote for the Court), and political necessity.

In 1819, while riding circuit, Story condemned slavery, urging grand juries to vigorously investigate violations of the federal laws prohibiting the African slave trade. During the debates over the Missouri Compromise, Story spoke out, off the bench, against the extension of slavery in the West. But on the high court he failed to exert his energy and influence in slave trade cases, and in some critical cases he said nothing. He was similarly silent when slaves with impressive claims to liberty brought their freedom suits to the Court. When confronted with cases involving fugitive slaves or free blacks claimed as fugitive slaves, he failed to support freedom. Abolitionists vilified him as the "SLAVE-CATCHER-IN-CHIEF

FOR THE NEW ENGLAND STATES" because of his unwavering support for the fugitive slave law of 1793.[8] His opinion in *Prigg* v. *Pennsylvania* (1842) made every black in the North, even if born free, vulnerable to being seized as a fugitive slave without any due-process hearing. However much he disliked slavery, his jurisprudence supported and protected the institution.

Roger Brooke Taney succeeded John Marshall as chief justice in 1836 and remained on the Court until his death in 1864. Unlike Marshall, who was of more humble origins, Taney came from a wealthy and powerful family whose fortune rested on slaves and land. He grew up in comfort with all the advantages of an elite planter's son and attended Dickinson College, graduating in 1795. He owned slaves all his adult life, but unlike many politicians of the era—such as Thomas Jefferson, Henry Clay, John C. Calhoun, Andrew Jackson, Zachary Taylor, Jefferson Davis, and his predecessor John Marshall—Taney did not actively buy and sell human beings, or make a substantial portion of his living through slavery or land speculation.

As a young lawyer Taney manumitted most (but not all) of his slaves, presumably because as an urban lawyer and politician he needed only a few personal servants. The fact that he freed some slaves—rather than selling them—suggests that the young Taney was uncomfortable treating people as merchandise. But the fact that he kept some slaves indicates that he never separated himself from slaveholding or the system of slavery. In 1819, he successfully defended the Reverend Jacob Gruber, who was prosecuted for allegedly inciting slaves to revolt by preaching a public sermon that questioned the morality of slavery. Historian Timothy Huebner argues that as a young man Taney was "a moderately antislavery lawyer" because of this defense and the few slaves he freed. This is not entirely clear, but Huebner is absolutely correct in noting that Taney later became "a zealous proslavery judge."[9]

Taney is most remembered for his painfully racist, pro-slavery opinion in *Dred Scott* v. *Sandford* (1857). His assertion that blacks, even when free, "had no rights which the white man was bound to respect" shocked many Americans in 1857 and still does today. But this was not the first time he expressed views that blacks, even if free, had no rights under the U.S. Constitution. In 1832, as Andrew Jackson's attorney general, Taney told the president that blacks in the United States had no rights, except those they were able to "enjoy" at the "sufferance" and "mercy" of whites, and that blacks, "even when free," were a "degraded class" whose "privileges" were "accorded to them as a matter of kindness and benevolence rather than right."[10] His opinion in *Dred Scott* reaffirmed this position. During the Civil War he did all he could to obstruct President Lincoln's attempts to hold the Union together. He even drafted an opinion in anticipation of an opportunity to strike down the Emancipation Proclamation.

Many Supreme Court scholars avoid any discussion of slavery when talking about Marshall and Story, and downplay it when talking about Taney. A recent study of the influence of chief justices does not mention slavery at all. It is hard to imagine talking about Chief Justice Roger B. Taney's influence without even a passing reference to *Dred Scott*.[11] Most scholars are not so extreme, but nevertheless their persistent failure to analyze slavery in their scholarship on the Court is striking. G. Edward White's influential *The American Judicial Tradition* explains why Marshall and Story are two of our greatest justices, but never mentions their slavery jurisprudence. White claims Marshall "had a strong and consistent commitment to the general inalienability of natural rights."[12] But, he ignores Marshall's consistent refusal to enforce the bans on the illegal African slave trade and his many opinions overturning trial court verdicts where slaves had won their freedom. White never considers Story's problematic opinion in the *Amistad* case and his aggressively proslavery opinion in *Prigg* v. *Pennsylvania*. The comprehensive *Holmes Devise History of the Supreme Court* for the period 1801 to 1815 does not have the terms "slavery" or "African slave trade" in the index and does not discuss any of the Marshall Court's cases on the African trade or freedom suits. A study of Marshall's chief justiceship asserts that the Marshall Court "did not deal with the domestic institution of slavery."[13] Such conclusions can only be reached by ignoring the Court's many cases on slavery.

Slavery does not fit comfortably in the narrative of the Supreme Court, where Marshall and Story are called great and heroic. Scholars often try to explain away *Dred Scott* by claiming it was a mistake or an aberration and by ignoring most of Taney's other slavery jurisprudence. But slavery does not disappear just because scholars ignore it. Support for human bondage and persistent hostility to the rights of free blacks were important components of the Court's jurisprudence from 1801 until the Civil War.

These three jurists interpreted a Constitution that protected slavery in a variety of ways. The abolitionist leader William Lloyd Garrison argued it was a proslavery "covenant with death," and refused to vote because the Constitution protected slavery and the political system was rigged against opponents of slavery. This analysis led Garrison to argue for disunion, with the free states seceding. The Garrisonians were mostly correct in their analysis that the Constitution was proslavery. But the Constitution and the political system still allowed for numerous ways to hem in slavery, to prevent its expansion, to suppress the African slave trade, and to protect free blacks. These justices might have read the Constitution in a way that would have allowed that. Some justices, like John McLean of Ohio and Smith Thompson of New York, read the Constitution with an eye toward liberty. But these three leading jurists did not. They leaned toward slavery and discrimination—and, in doing so, were supremely unjust.

1

The Antebellum Constitution
and Slavery

THE GREAT NINETEENTH-CENTURY abolitionist William
Lloyd Garrison described the Constitution as a proslavery
compact—a "covenant with death" and "an agreement with
Hell." Under the slogan "No Union with slaveholders," he rejected electoral politics because voting implied support for
"the proslavery, war sanctioning Constitution." He wanted the
union dissolved or the North to secede to create a truly free
country.[1]

Garrison's position in part grew out of his perfectionism
and his desire to avoid the moral taint of slavery that supporting a proslavery Constitution would entail. But the Garrisonians also had pragmatic reasons for rejecting politics. If
they were correct—that the Constitution was proslavery and
that the political system was rigged to protect slavery—then
political action was a waste of time. They were far better off
trying to persuade northerners to avoid the moral taint of
slavery than debating which candidate was the least evil in his
relationship to human bondage. Traditional political activity
created popular support for the constitutional order, which in
turn strengthened the stranglehold slavery had on America.

The Garrisonian critique of the Constitution rested on the specific provisions in the document that explicitly or implicitly protected slavery and on the political structure those provisions created. The Constitution written in 1787 does not contain the words slavery or race.[2] Still, Garrisonians identified numerous clauses that protected or favored slavery and allowed for racial discrimination. At the Constitutional Convention, the framers had debated the place of slavery under the new system of government, openly talking about slaves, blacks, and Negroes. But in the final document, the framers avoided the terms in deference to some northerners who feared their constituents might oppose the Constitution if the document specifically talked about slaves or Negroes.[3] Throughout the main body of the Constitution, slaves are referred to as "other persons," as "such persons," or in the singular as a "person held to Service or Labour."

Direct Protections of Slavery in the Constitution

Despite the careful circumlocution, various constitutional provisions directly protected slavery. A number of other clauses provided strong protections for slavery even though they were not only designed for that purpose. The three-fifths clause, for example, provided for counting three-fifths of all slaves for purposes of representation in Congress.[4] This clause gave the slave states a huge bonus in their representation in Congress. Without the extra representatives created by counting slaves it is unlikely that such proslavery bills such as admitting Missouri as a slave state or the Fugitive Slave Law of 1850 could have passed the House of Representatives.

This clause also provided that the three-fifths rule would be applied to direct taxation, implying that southerners would have to pay for the political power they gained from counting slaves for representation. In practice, however, no direct taxes were ever imposed before the Civil War, and when the Constitution was being considered no one actually expected such taxes to be imposed. At the Constitutional Convention, the wealthy Gouverneur Morris scoffed at the idea that there could ever be a direct tax because it was "idle to suppose that the General Government can stretch its hand directly into the pockets of the people scattered over so vast a Country." Thus the South gained extra representation in Congress by virtue of its slaves and had to pay nothing in return. In this debate Morris declared he "would sooner submit himself to a tax for paying for all the Negroes in the United States than saddle posterity with such a Constitution."[5] But this antislavery outburst did not affect the final outcome of the debate.

The slave trade clause prohibited Congress from banning the "Migration or Importation of such Persons as any of the States now existing shall think proper to admit" before 1808.[6] Awkwardly phrased, this clause prevented Congress from ending the African slave trade before 1808, but did not require Congress to ever ban the trade.

During the Revolutionary War, every state had banned the slave trade because most imported slaves came on British ships. In 1787, when the Constitution was written, the slave trade remained dormant, although Georgia and North Carolina technically allowed it. Nevertheless, delegates from the Deep South insisted on this explicit protection for the trade because they fully expected to reopen the trade as soon as their economies were stronger. They feared that without the clause Congress would immediately ban the trade. Because of this clause, at least forty thousand new slaves would be imported into the United States between 1803 and 1808, when Congress prohibited the trade.[7]

Most Convention delegates believed the South was growing faster than the North, and the South Carolina and Georgia delegates expected that by 1808 they would have the political clout to prevent an end to the trade. Fortunately, the North grew faster than the South, and in 1808 Congress banned the trade. President Thomas Jefferson supported the ban because he thought the slave trade was immoral and he feared having too many blacks in the nation. Jefferson and other Virginians also understood that closing the trade enhanced the value of their slaves.[8]

Under the Constitution, Congress could immediately regulate all foreign commerce *except* the African slave trade. At the Convention, Gouverneur Morris denounced the immorality of the trade and noted in particular that allowing more slaves to be brought from Africa, while also counting slaves for representation, led to the terrible irony that:

> the inhabitant of Georgia and South Carolina who goes to the Coast of Africa, and in defiance of the most sacred laws of humanity tears away his fellow creatures from their dearest connections and damns them to the most cruel bondages, shall have more votes in a Government instituted for protection of the rights of mankind, than the Citizen of Pennsylvania or New Jersey who views with a laudable horror, so nefarious a practice.[9]

The slave trade clause led some antifederalists to oppose the Constitution. A New Yorker complained the Constitution condoned "drenching the bowels of Africa in gore, for the sake of enslaving its free-born innocent inhabitants." A Virginian sarcastically noted the slave trade provision was an "excellent clause" for "an Algerian constitution: but not so well calculated (I hope) for the latitude of America."[10]

As noted above, the three-fifths clause also applied to taxation. Article I, Section 9, contained a second tax clause which applied the three-fifths clause to any "capitation" or other "direct tax." Thus, if a head tax were ever levied, slaves would be taxed at three-fifths the rate of free people.[11] In theory this provision harmed slavery, but the national government never imposed a direct tax.

The creation of the Electoral College was also directly tied to slavery. At the Convention, James Madison argued that "the people at large" were "the fittest" to choose the president. But Madison ultimately opposed election by the people because the "Southern States . . . could have no influence in the election on the score of the Negroes." In order to guarantee that the nonvoting slaves could provide political power for the South in presidential elections, Madison proposed the Electoral College, with each state having a number of electors equal to its total congressional representation. This meant that the three-fifths clause would help determine the outcome of presidential elections.[12]

Many northerners complained that this clause helped elect southerners, who dominated the presidency from 1789 to 1861. In 1800, John Adams would have been reelected had it not been for the presidential electors created by counting slaves for representation. In 1812, many northerners believed that James Madison was reelected only because of this clause, although a careful analysis of the election suggests this was not true.

The fugitive slave clause prohibited the states from emancipating runaway slaves and required that slaves fleeing to another state be returned to their owners "on demand."[13] Added to the Constitution near the end of the Convention with almost no debate, this became one of the most divisive proslavery provisions of the Constitution. It led to two federal statutes and numerous cases in state and federal courts.

Without this clause the northern states could have freed any fugitive slaves. Such a result would have been consistent with the English precedent, *Somerset* v. *Stewart* (1772), which was part of American common law at the time of the Revolution. In that case Chief Justice Lord Mansfield ruled that the slave Somerset could not be held in bondage against his will in England because "[t]he state of slavery is of such a nature, that it is incapable of being introduced on any reasons, moral or political, but only by positive law, which preserves its force long after the reasons, occasion, and time itself from whence it was created, is erased from memory. It is so odious, that nothing can be suffered to support it, but positive law."[14] Under *Somerset* the northern states could have emancipated fugitive slaves. But the fugitive slave clause overrode this concept by preventing northern states from determining the status of fugitives in their jurisdictions. Southerners understood this, and praised the clause. General Charles Cotesworth Pinckney told the South Carolina legislature, "We have obtained a right to recover our slaves in whatever part of America they may take refuge, which is a right we had not before."[15]

Article V of the Constitution prohibited any amendment to the slave trade provision before 1808. Even if every state had supported an immediate end to the trade, the Constitution prohibited an amendment to stop the trade.[16] This again indicated the extent of the direct protection the Constitution afforded slavery.

Taken together, these constitutional protections gave the South a strong claim to "special treatment" for its peculiar institution. The three-fifths clause also gave the South extra political muscle—in the House of Representatives and in the Electoral College—to support that claim.

Indirect Protections of Slavery in the Constitution

In addition to specific slavery-related clauses, the Constitution provided enormous support for slavery through federal aid to suppress slave revolts; a ban on export taxes, which prevented the indirect taxation of slaves; the impossibility of amending the constitution to harm slavery; and the creation of a government of limited powers, which prevented the national government from ending slavery, or ever regulating the institution, in the states where it existed. While not explicitly about slavery, some of these provisions, like the ban on export taxes, were included at the insistence of slaveholding southern delegates.

In two places the Constitution authorized the national government to suppress "insurrections" and "domestic Violence," including slave rebellions. Article I of the Constitution empowered Congress to pass special laws "for calling forth the Militia" to "suppress Insurrections," while Article IV obligated the national government to "protect" the states "against domestic Violence." While these clauses are not explicitly or only about slavery, Southerners correctly understood that they guaranteed federal aid to suppress slave rebellions. The abolitionist leader Wendell Phillips considered them to be among the key proslavery provisions of the Constitution.[17]

Gouverneur Morris complained that the insurrections and domestic violence clauses would compel the northern states "to march their militia for the defence of the Southern States; for their defence against those very slaves" that the southerners wanted to continue to import. In Massachusetts three antifederalists complained that under the Constitution everyone in the nation was "under obligation . . . reciprocally to aid each other in defense and support of every thing to which they are entitled." As members of the state militia they feared they would be called to suppress a slave revolt. They believed "this lust for slavery [was] portentous of much evil in America."[18] Under these clauses the national government helped suppress the Nat Turner rebellion in 1831; used northern militias and the army and navy to help return fugitive slaves in the 1850s; and in 1859 sent federal troops to suppress John Brown's raid at Harpers Ferry. Eventually, Massachusetts men would march south to suppress a treasonous insurrection started by white slaveholders, and in the process end slavery. But that was not on the horizon in 1787 or at any time before 1861.

The American Revolution had been in part a taxpayers' revolt, as reflected in the rallying cry of "taxation without representation is tyranny." At the Convention the southerners feared that the new national government, or the northern states, would indirectly tax slavery by taxing the export products slaves produced: tobacco, rice, and indigo. Cotton and sugar would become important crops after the Constitution was written. Caving into southern demands, the Convention prohibited both the states and the national government from taxing exports. While theoretically applicable to exports having nothing to do with slavery, the Convention adopted bans on export taxes to placate Southerners.[19] These two clauses, along with the Electoral College, remain to this day as legacies of the proslavery Constitution.

By requiring a three-fourths majority of the states to ratify any amendment to the Constitution, Article V ensured that the slaveholding states would have perpetual veto power over any constitutional changes.[20] In 1787 there were six southern slave states, and of the remaining seven states, two were free (Massachusetts and New Hampshire), three were in the process of becoming free (Pennsylvania, Connecticut, and Rhode Island), and two were likely to become free (New York and New Jersey). Americans expected that the Old Northwest would produce a number of free states, and that the Old Southwest would be carved up into slave states. Thus, there would continue to be an almost equal number of slave and free states. But even if there had been a few more free states than slave states, by requiring that an amendment be ratified by three-fourths of the states, the Constitution gave the South what amounted to a permanent veto over any constitutional change. In 1861 there were fifteen slave states. To this day, in the early twenty-first century, those fifteen states could block a constitutional amendment in a fifty-state union.

The structure of the Constitution prevented any Congressional interference with slavery where it already existed. Virtually everyone in 1787—and thereafter until the Civil War—fully understood that Congress could not interfere with the "domestic institutions" of the states, absent a specific grant of power in the Constitution. Indeed, the only federal interference with slavery or race relations in the states allowed under the Constitution was the fugitive slave clause that prevented the northern states from applying their laws on personal status and liberty to fugitive slaves. Most southerners, even those who opposed the Constitution for other reasons, agreed with General Charles Cotesworth Pinckney of South Carolina, who bragged to his state's

House of Representatives: "We have a security that the general government can never emancipate them, for no such authority is granted and it is admitted, on all hands, that the general government has no powers but what are expressly granted by the Constitution, and that all rights not expressed were reserved by the several states."[21]

This understanding of the Constitution prevailed until the Civil War. In his first inaugural address Abraham Lincoln reaffirmed this aspect of American constitutional law, noting that "I have no purpose, directly or indirectly, to interfere with the institution of slavery in the States where it exists. I believe I have no lawful right to do so, and I have no inclination to do so."[22]

These proslavery provisions helped create a nation where slavery flourished between 1787 and 1861. In 1845 Wendell Phillips accurately noted that, in the years since the Constitution's adoption, Americans had witnessed "the slaves trebling in numbers—slaveholders monopolizing the offices and dictating the policy of the Government—prostituting the strength and influence of the Nation to the support of slavery here and elsewhere—trampling on the rights of the free States, and making the courts of the country their tools." This experience, Phillips argued, proved "that it is impossible for free and slave States to unite on any terms, without all becoming partners in the guilt and responsible for the sin of slavery."[23]

Phillips might have added that, since the founding, slave owners and their northern allies had dominated American politics and the government. From 1801 to 1861, with the sole exception of John Quincy Adams, presidents were slave owners, former slave owners, or northern doughfaces—northern men with southern principles. No opponents of slavery served in presidential cabinets in this period, whereas a number of aggressive proslavery politicians were cabinet officials. With the exception of a few years towards the end of Marshall's chief justiceship, there was a southern majority on the Court from 1801 to 1861. This majority was complemented by numerous doughface northern justices who always voted with their southern colleagues on matters involving slavery. Throughout the first six decades of the nineteenth century, southern slave owners also dominated leadership positions in Congress and the army.[24] The history of the nation confirmed the Garrisonian understanding, that the Constitution had created a slaveholders' republic.

Alternatives to the Proslavery Constitution

The Garrisonian critique of the Constitution was on the mark. But even within the proslavery Constitution there was room to expand freedom, sometimes protect black liberty, and even hem in slavery. From the beginning of the nation, Congress passed some legislation that reined in slavery or at least limited its expansion. Acting under its authority to "make all needful Rules and Regulations respecting the Territory or other Property belonging to the United States," the first Congress reenacted the Northwest Ordinance, banning slavery in the territories north and west of the Ohio River. In the Missouri Compromise, in 1820, Congress barred slavery in the northern part of the Louisiana Purchase. Congress similarly prohibited slavery in the Oregon Territory.[25] Congress could have used this clause to limit slavery and prevent its spread across the continent. In *Dred Scott* v. *Sandford* (1857), however, Chief Justice Taney would find that despite this Constitutional language, Congress had no power to regulate slavery in the territories. Starting in 1794 Congress passed laws to restrict the African slave trade, prohibiting Americans from participating in slave-trading ventures as sailors or investors, or building or refitting ships for the trade. Congress banned the trade completely as of January 1, 1808.[26] But the Supreme Court was often unwilling to vigorously enforce these laws. Article I empowered Congress to "exercise exclusive Legislation" over the national capital.[27] This provision might have been used to end slavery in the District of Columbia, and when hearing slavery-related cases from Washington, D.C., the court might have leaned towards freedom. Neither possibility came to pass, however, before the Civil War.

Slavery affected the process of making new states. In 1791 Vermont entered the Union as a free state, with blacks having the same political rights as whites. In 1796 Tennessee entered the Union as a slave state, but with suffrage available to free black men. In 1820 Congress banned slavery in the territories north and west of Missouri, and admitted Maine as a free state, even as it admitted Missouri as a slave state. Clearly there was room, even under the proslavery Constitution, for some legislation and public policies that leaned toward freedom.

The ratification of the Bill of Rights offered other possible routes to challenge slavery. The Fifth Amendment provided that under federal law no one could be deprived of "life, liberty, or property without due process of law." The Court might have interpreted this provision to prohibit slavery in the District of Columbia and federal territories because bondage deprived slaves of their liberty without due process of law. But in *Dred Scott*, Chief Justice Taney would use this clause to prohibit Congress from banning slavery in the territories.

In 1793 Congress passed the first fugitive slave law, which provided virtually no due-process protections to prevent the kidnapping of free blacks. Justices inclined towards freedom might have applied the provisions of the Fifth and Sixth Amendments to give alleged slaves meaningful due-process rights before they could be returned to their masters. The Supreme Court might even have held that the 1793 law was unconstitutional, because of its denial of a jury trial to alleged slaves.

The Court also might have determined that Congress lacked the power to pass this law, as well as the 1850 law. The authority to pass a fugitive slave law is not found in the enumerated powers of Article I, Section 8, of the Constitution, and under General Pinckney's theory of the Constitution, "the general government has no powers but what are expressly granted by the Constitution, and that all rights not expressed were reserved by the several states."[28] The structure of the Constitution, and the language of Article IV, could have been interpreted to mean that the states were solely responsible for regulating the return of fugitives, or that masters had to act on their own, bringing alleged slaves before state judges to vindicate a common law right (which the Constitution protected) to their property.

Other provisions of the Constitution might also have been used to protect the rights of free blacks and opponents of slavery. Article IV of the Constitution required that the "citizens of each State shall be entitled to all Privileges and Immunities of Citizens of the United States."[29] At the time the Constitution was ratified, free blacks voted in at least six states, and were clearly considered citizens in those places.[30] In the 1790s, Vermont and Tennessee would provide similar rights to free blacks. The justices might have used the privileges and immunities clause of the Constitution to protect the rights of free blacks and northern opponents of slavery when they visited slave states. The First Amendment protected freedom of speech and the press, the right of assembly, and the right to petition the government. The Supreme Court might have extended these protections to free blacks and opponents of slavery in federal jurisdictions.

Beyond these potentially antislavery constitutional provisions, the courts could have applied traditional notions of liberty embedded in Anglo-American common law and precedents when dealing with slave cases. The Supreme Court might have accepted the ideology of the early Mississippi Supreme Court that it is "an unquestioned rule, that courts must lean *in favorem vitae et libertatis*."[31] This approach would have been especially useful when interpreting the many acts regulating and then banning the African slave trade, the fugitive slave laws of 1793 and 1850, the local laws governing the District of Columbia, and the statutes affecting slavery in federal territories. Similarly, the Court might have used this theory of law when adjudicating civil cases involving slavery brought into federal courts by citizens of different states—that is, when exercising the "diversity jurisdiction" granted to it.[32]

Starting in the 1830s, antislavery lawyers and politicians including Salmon P. Chase of Ohio, John P. Hale of New Hampshire, William H. Seward of New York, and Charles Sumner of Massachusetts made arguments along these lines in public speeches, in political campaigns, and before judges. Such arguments, especially when presented to the U.S. Supreme Court, fell on deaf ears. The Court showed no inclination to limit the reach of slavery. Even when statutes seemed to indicate that the courts should reach an antislavery result, the Supreme Court often ended up supporting bondage. With very few exceptions, the U.S. Supreme Court from 1801 to

1861 was a constant friend of slavery and almost never a friend of liberty.

These decisions were not preordained. Even under a proslavery Constitution—Garrison's "covenant with death"—there was room for protecting the liberty of free blacks, liberating some slaves, providing due process for alleged fugitive slaves, enforcing the federal suppression of the African slave trade, or preventing slavery from being established in federal territories. But the Supreme Court rarely sided with liberty. The most prominent members of the court in this period—Chief Justice John Marshall, Associate Justice Joseph Story, and Chief Justice Roger Brooke Taney—invariably voted against liberty and in favor of slavery.

2

John Marshall:
Slave Owner and Jurist

WITH GOOD REASON John Marshall is considered our greatest chief justice. He is central to our constitutional development and an icon of our constitutional history. A imposing, six-foot bronze statue of him sits outside the Supreme Court building while a smaller, marble one sits inside the building. He has been on four U.S. postage stamps, a commemorative silver dollar, the $20 Treasury note in 1890 and 1891, and the $500 Federal Reserve note in 1918. Four law schools have been named for him.[1] The scholarship on him is universally admiring.

For nearly three and half decades—longer than any other chief justice in our history—he led the Court. More than any other justice, he shaped our constitutional law. Two centuries later, Marshall's opinions are still read and cited. Five of the ten opinions most cited by the Court itself are Marshall's.[2]

Marshall scholars have mostly ignored his personal and judicial relationship with slavery. Jean Edward Smith's mammoth biography never considers Marshall's decisions on black freedom or all his early decisions on the African slave trade. The comprehensive multivolume Oliver Wendell Holmes

Devise History of the Supreme Court has two separate books on the Marshall Court. The first Marshall book, covering the period 1801 to 1815, ignores all his cases involving black freedom and the African slave trade, and does not even have the words slave, slavery, or slave trade in the index. In the second Marshall volume, covering the last two decades of the Marshall Court, the author, G. Edward White, shockingly reports that "John Marshall was not a slave owner." White makes this erroneous assertion even as he discusses slaveholding by other members of the Marshall Court. Such a claim in this monumental history of the Marshall Court underscores the failure of scholars to come to terms with Marshall's slavery jurisprudence and his role as a slaveholder. In his influential book *The American Judicial Tradition,* White finds that "Marshall had a strong and consistent commitment to the general inalienability of natural rights." Again, White never mentions Marshall's massive personal investment in slaves or any of his slave cases.[3]

Marshall's biographers somehow do not see his slavery cases, even though his court heard more than fifty cases involving slavery and Marshall wrote numerous opinions in freedom suits and on the African slave trade. Slavery does not accord with the narrative of "the Great Chief Justice," and so, with the exception of Kent Newmyer, biographers simply ignore it or offer a cursory analysis. Charles Hobson says Marshall heard "relatively few freedom suits," but "relatively" is clearly a relative term. The Marshall Court heard fourteen cases involving black freedom.[4] The chief justice decided seven between 1806 and 1830, and the slaves lost in every one. The Jeffersonian William Johnson rejected freedom in the eighth case in 1827. In the remaining six cases, between 1829 and 1835, Justices John McLean, James Wayne, Gabriel

Duvall, and Smith Thompson upheld black freedom. Given the narrow scope of the Court's jurisdiction at the time, and the cost and difficulty of appealing to the Court, especially for a slave, we might conclude that fourteen was actually a large number of cases. But whether "relatively few" or "relatively many," these cases add up to a striking outcome: Chief Justice Marshall *never* wrote an opinion supporting black freedom. Significantly, Marshall ruled against freedom before the advent of antislavery politics, the abolitionist movement, and the nullification crisis, whereas other justices—including two slaveholders, Wayne and Duvall—ruled in favor of freedom after antislavery emerged as a significant political issue. Thus, we cannot explain Marshall's hostility to black freedom and to the suppression of the slave trade as a response to southern proslavery politics.

Marshall was a great justice because he was creative and courageous. He challenged presidents, popular feelings (such as opposition to the Bank of the United States during the Panic of 1819), and powerful state politicians—particularly the anti-nationalists in his home state of Virginia.[5] He infuriated Thomas Jefferson with rulings that derailed Jefferson's attempt to have Aaron Burr hanged for treason. He withstood vicious attacks from numerous states' rights politicians in his home state for his nationalist opinions in *M'Culloch* v. *Maryland* (1819) and *Cohens* v. *Virginia* (1821). Whether they loved Marshall or hated him, no one ever accused him of being shy, timid, or narrow in his jurisprudence. Marshall is remembered as the Great Chief Justice because he was bold, brilliant, forceful, and often fearless.

But in slavery cases, Marshall's opinions were cautious, narrow, legalistic, and hostile to freedom.[6] Constitutional history requires more than an analysis of key constitutional principles and precedents. Justices come to the Court with political, social, economic, and personal views and interests. Marshall was an active politician before going on the bench and was appointed for partisan reasons by a lame-duck president trying to preserve his party's ideology through the Court. We cannot separate Marshall's nationalist jurisprudence from his life as a Revolutionary War officer, diplomat, and Federalist politician. Nor can we separate his commercial and economic jurisprudence from his huge landholdings and investments in banks, canals, railroads, and slaves.

Such an analysis considers Marshall's life as slave owner, his hostility to free blacks, and his deep personal and professional commitment to private property. Marshall's early life, his pre-Court career, his fierce nationalism, his personal investment in and relationship to human bondage in his private life, and his nonjudicial public life help us understand his slavery jurisprudence.

It is important to note that the Marshall Court's slavery cases never threatened the system of slavery. Marshall heard no slavery cases on such politically charged issues as the return of fugitive slaves. Marshall's most famous slave case, *The Antelope* (1825), which involved the illegal African slave trade, did not become a *cause célèbre*. Until his last half-decade on the bench, there was not even a significant abolitionist movement in the nation.

Marshall's slavery jurisprudence was *not* shaped by the need to preserve the Union or fend off proslavery southerners' claims of states' rights. In Virginia, states' rights leaders like Representative John Randolph and Judge Spencer Roane vilified Marshall for his nationalist opinions, which they feared might somehow allow the national government to end slavery in the states. But they were mostly concerned with Marshall expanding the power of Congress to regulate the economy or charter a national bank, or the power of the Court to hear appeals from state courts. They feared his nationalist opinions might allow the federal government to end slavery in Virginia, but none of Marshall's slavery cases raised such issues. The Virginia states' rights crowd could hardly have been unhappy if Marshall had applied Virginia or Maryland law to cases involving freedom claims in the District of Columbia. Nor would they have been concerned with a strict enforcement of the ban on the African slave trade, since most Virginians conceded Congress had the power to end the trade. Furthermore, closing the trade increased the value of the slaves already in the country, which many Virginians were selling to the gulf coast states and territories.

Marshall's best biographer, Kent Newmyer, says Marshall's slavery jurisprudence is "painful to observe," but asserts Marshall "adhered to the law of slavery" only "because his system of federalism deferred to the states on questions of slavery." Most of Marshall's slave cases, however, had nothing to do with federalism or conflicts between the national government and state laws.[7] Most of the freedom suits Marshall heard involved appeals from the District of Columbia courts, which were federal courts. In many of these cases, Marshall reversed decisions of local District of Columbia courts where juries of southern white men had granted freedom to slaves. It might be comforting to explain Marshall's habit of deciding against freedom as a function of his desire to respect the states or his fear of radical proslavery sectionalists, but the opposite is true. At the time, local law in the District of Columbia was based on Virginia and Maryland statutes. Thus, when Marshall ignored the statutes and precedents of those states to deny freedom to black plaintiffs in the District of Columbia, he actually disrespected Virginia and Maryland law. Ironically, many of these slaves would have won their freedom if they could have sued in the Virginia or Maryland courts instead of federal courts in the District of Columbia.

Marshall also heard a number of cases involving the African slave trade. At the time, no one denied the national government's plenary power to regulate the African slave trade. In some cases a lower federal court, with a local jury, ruled against a slave trader, and Marshall reversed. The lower court cases enforcing the slave trade bans hardly infringed on the rights of the states or threatened slavery within the states.

Finally, it is important to see Marshall's jurisprudence in the context of his personal relationship with slavery. All of Marshall's biographers assert that he had relatively few slaves as "house servants" at his home in Richmond. The received wisdom is that Marshall was never involved in the business of slavery or earning money from human bondage. We are told he was the "owner of a modest number of slaves" or that he "maintained a small holding of slaves" throughout his life, or that he "experienced slavery primarily as an urban slave owner," with about a dozen slaves in his house in Richmond.[8] A dozen slaves in an urban setting was in fact a large number. But Marshall actually owned hundreds of slaves during his life. He also owned a number of plantations around the state and clearly profited from them. In 1830, five years before his death, he had about 150 slaves.[9] By this time he had given substantial numbers of slaves to his sons, and perhaps to other relatives. Unlike his distant cousin Thomas Jefferson, Marshall did not inherit these slaves; rather, he bought them throughout his life.

Frontier Boyhood to National Leadership

Marshall was born in 1755 in what is today Fauquier County, Virginia, about forty-five miles west of present-day Washington, D.C. His father, Thomas Marshall, was never rich but by 1780 he owned twenty-two slaves and some two thousand acres of land, including a plantation at Oak Hill. He served as a sheriff, justice of the peace, vestryman, and delegate in the House of Burgesses. When the Revolution began, Thomas Marshall was a major, commanding the county militia, and by the war's end he was a full colonel.[10] Through his mother, Mary Randolph Keith Marshall, John was related to the Randolph and Lee families as well as to Thomas Jefferson. Mostly educated at home, Marshall on the eve of the Revolution was reading William Blackstone's *Commentaries on the Laws of England* in preparation for a legal career.

Marshall was a junior militia officer when the Revolution began, but he quickly transferred to the 15th Virginia Regiment, which was part of the Continental Army, and was eventually promoted to Captain. Marshall fought at the battles of Germantown, Brandywine, and Monmouth; marched through Maryland, Delaware, New York, New Jersey, and Pennsylvania; and served under George Washington at Valley Forge.[11] His close contact with men from other states and his service outside Virginia led him to appreciate the necessity of cordial relations with Americans whose economic interests, religions, social values, and accents differed from his own. His military experience made him a committed nationalist for the rest of his life.

Marshall returned to Virginia during a lull in the War, briefly studying law under George Wythe at the College of William and Mary before being admitted to the bar in the summer of 1780. In 1782 Fauquier County elected him to the Virginia legislature. In 1783 he married Mary "Polly" Ambler, whose father, Jaquelin Ambler, was the state treasurer. For a wedding present Marshall's father gave him one slave, Robin Spurlock, who was about eighteen at the time, and three horses. By 1784 he had moved to Richmond and was elected to the Virginia ratifying convention in 1788, where he vigorously supported the Constitution. After ratification he built an enormously successful law practice, helped organize the state's Federalist Party, and again served in the legislature. In 1792 Marshall began acquiring vast lands, including at least 215,000 acres from the estate of the late Thomas, Lord Fairfax.[12] These and other land acquisitions would make Marshall a very wealthy man. During this period Marshall began purchasing slaves in significant numbers.

In 1797 Marshall was an envoy in France, negotiating with the French foreign minister Talleyrand to reduce tensions between the two nations. The negotiations failed, but Marshall emerged as a national figure after his dispatches exposed the demands of French officials for bribes in the XYZ Affair. Marshall returned home a hero, won a seat in Congress in 1798, became secretary of state in May 1800, and assumed the chief justiceship in March 1801.

Thus before going on the Court, Marshall had unusually broad experiences as a soldier, lawyer, land speculator, state politician, diplomat, congressman, and secretary of state. Marshall's pre-Court years exposed him to a larger world of ideas, viewpoints, and economic interests that were quite different from those found in Fauquier County or even his new home in Richmond, a tiny provincial backwater.[13] His Revolutionary War service had made him an ardent and forceful nationalist.

Marshall's background contrasts sharply with the parochialism of his successor, Roger Brooke Taney. Except for attending Pennsylvania's Dickinson College, Taney spent all of his pre-Court years in Maryland and Washington, D.C. He never served in Congress and so never had to work with men who were not from slave states; he never shared a campfire meal or a state dinner with people who were fundamentally different from him. He never traveled overseas, and had no diplomatic experience.

But John Marshall was different. He grew up on the Virginia frontier, wearing a fur cap and carrying a tomahawk, and later ate state dinners in France. With his broad experience, brilliant mind, well-honed legal skills, and uncompromising commitment to a strong national government, Marshall was well suited for the Court.

As chief justice from 1801 until his death in 1835, Marshall wrote 58 percent of the Court's opinions: 508 majority opinions, 25 concurrences, and a mere 6 dissents. Until the late 1820s he dominated the Court.[14] During that period Marshall wrote almost every decision on slavery, shaping a jurisprudence that was hostile to free blacks and surprisingly lenient to people who violated the federal laws banning the African slave trade. Starting in the late 1820s the Court was more supportive of freedom claims by blacks and more hostile to slave traders. This is precisely when Marshall was losing his dominance. Marshall wrote none of these decisions.

Marshall vigorously supported a strong national government, the power of Congress to regulate the economy, and the supremacy of the Constitution. He challenged states' rights politicians, military officials who exceeded their authority, opponents of the Bank of the United States, and presidents Thomas Jefferson and Andrew Jackson. Marshall was savvy, shrewd, and often brilliant. He never sought political confrontation, but neither did he shy away from interpreting the Constitution and federal law to support his nationalism.

Some of his decisions were enormously unpopular. In *Fletcher* v. *Peck* (1810) he upheld land purchases from the Yazoo land fraud under traditional property and contract law. In *M'Culloch* v. *Maryland* (1819) he upheld the constitutionality of the Bank of the United States, despite its unpopularity during the nation's first significant recession. In *Cohens* v. *Virginia* (1821) he infuriated Virginia's states' rights politicians simply because he accepted jurisdiction in an appeal from a state criminal conviction. Thomas Jefferson fumed that his distant cousin was leading an "irresponsible body." In the end, Marshall upheld the original verdict, leaving the Virginians to rant because Marshall had heard the case, even though Virginia actually won the case.[15]

While riding circuit he derailed Jefferson's transparently vengeful efforts to hang Aaron Burr for treason, preventing Jefferson from bringing to the United States the arbitrary ideas of constructive treason that had so long been used to punish political opponents of the Crown in England.[16] Marshall had no sympathies for Burr, a self-serving huckster and fraud, but the chief justice proved to be a fierce advocate for substantive justice, insisting on an exact application of the Constitution's treason clause.

This very brief summary of Marshall's jurisprudence illustrates how this Revolutionary War veteran fearlessly challenged powerful political forces. Given Marshall's deft hand, sharp mind, and courage, he might very well have shaped American jurisprudence to uphold freedom claims of black petitioners and to vigorously suppress the illegal African slave trade. But he did not take this road. Instead, his slavery jurisprudence was clumsy and uninspired. He could find justice for the scoundrel Aaron Burr, but not for individuals whose only "crime" was their race.

Master John Marshall: Slaveholder in the New Nation

Marshall's slavery jurisprudence must be seen in the context of his personal ties to slavery. Unlike his kinsman Thomas Jefferson, Marshall did not spout fine phrases about equality while buying and selling human beings. Marshall occasionally criticized slavery, such as by stating in *The Antelope* (1825) that it was "contrary to the law of nature" because "every man has a natural right to the fruits of his own labour."[17] But in his personal life Marshall bought and sold slaves, gave them to relatives, and actively participated in the business of human bondage. His jurisprudence, moreover, suggested no discomfort with slavery. An ardent patriot and soldier in the struggle for American liberty, he opposed black freedom. He was constantly buying slaves, accumulating more than one hundred and fifty by 1830, while also giving about seventy slaves to two of his sons between 1819 and 1830. In the Virginia constitutional convention he vigorously supported counting slaves for representation in the state legislature, to preserve the power of the planter aristocracy. When he died, he did not free the dozen or so personal slaves who had loyally served him for so long, much less any of those toiling on his plantations.

Sometimes Marshall recognized the humanity of his slaves. In the first version of his will, in 1827, Marshall stipulated that when his slaves were divided among his heirs it should be done "preserving the families together as near as may be except young men and young women." Such concern for keeping families together was rare among slave owners. This contrasts with Thomas Jefferson, whose slaves were sold off after his death without regard to families. But Marshall bought and sold slaves throughout his life, which meant many of his slaves were exiled from family and friends. This is a kind of cruelty that exceeds physical punishment. For example, in 1787 Marshall recorded buying a woman and her child without commenting on whether the purchase forced her to leave her husband and perhaps other children or family members.[18]

If Marshall had possessed *only* a dozen slaves while living in Richmond this would have been a measure of his wealth and his considerable commitment to owning other human beings. But Marshall was far more than an urban master with a "modest number of slaves" taking care of his family's daily needs.[19] In 1830 he owned more than 125 slaves in Henrico and Fauquier Counties, in addition to more than a dozen slaves in Richmond. His holdings would have been well over two hundred slaves by this time, had he not given about seventy to his sons Jaquelin and Edward between about 1819 and 1830.

John Marshall's father gave him one slave as a wedding present, and a few more when Thomas Marshall moved to Kentucky in 1784. Marshall's early account books show his ongoing acquisition of slaves, but the numbers are imperfect because the records are often vague and incomplete. The account books mostly cover his day-to-day life in Richmond and indicate little about his slaves and land in Fauquier County and his growing landholding in Henrico County. In October 1783 Marshall bought Moses for £74 and purchased shoes for Hannah. On July 1, 1784, he paid just over £90 for Ben. Three days later, on the Fourth of July—ironically, the first anniversary of the signing of the Declaration of Independence since the Treaty of Paris ended the Revolution—he bought two slaves for £30, probably children named Edey and Harry. He also paid £20 "in part for two servants." In September he paid another £25 for unnamed and uncounted "servants." In November he bought Kate and Esau. In 1784 he also purchased Harry, but did not record the purchase price.[20] Thus in the twelve months from October 1783 to October 1784 Marshall bought nine named slaves plus some unnamed and uncounted "servants." These were in addition to a few other slaves he already owned. For a relatively young man, just recently married with only a few years of law practice under his belt, this was a significant investment in slaves.

Some of these slaves were in his house in Richmond, although he rented out Moses. He also owned nine slaves in Henrico County and he owned "other slaves ... on his Fauquier County plantation."[21] By this time he also owned the Oak Hill Farm in Fauquier County, which his father had deeded to him in March 1785, where eventually he would have scores of slaves. There are no records that Marshall bought more slaves in 1785, but in November 1786 he paid £50 for two slaves. In April 1787 he bought Israel for £55 and in May paid another £55 for "a Woman bought in Gloster." On June 3 he made a down payment of just under £11 for two more slaves and paid for the burial of Sam; there is no record of when he acquired Sam.

As he had in 1784, on July 4, 1787, Marshall spent Independence Day buying slaves—this time a woman and her child, both of whom he passed on to his father-in-law Jaquelin Ambler. That day he paid money he owed on another slave he had purchased. In August he paid another £30 on slaves he had bought in Gloucester and he also bought an unnamed "negroe man" for £47.[22]

The entries in his account book for this period show he purchased at least fifteen slaves for himself, and a few for others, over a four-year period. But there are also purchases with no specific number of slaves attached. Initially he recorded the names of these slaves when he purchased them and sometimes noted their names when he bought them clothing. But by the end of this period the slaves ceased to have names. He bought a "woman," a "negroe man," and "two slaves," and purchased clothes for "negroes." In December 1788, he bought "Sundries at Mr. Drinkals for Negroes," and "shoes for negroes." In October 1789 he paid £38 for "a negroe woman." In November 1790 he bought "Shoes for house servants" who went nameless even though they served him daily.[23] Occasionally he still noted names for specific expenditures such as blankets for Ben and Moses and the purchases of Hannibal for £70 in March 1789 and "Negro Bob" for £50 in January 1790. Perhaps emblematic of the naming and not naming of slaves was the outlay of £130 in June 1790 "for Dick and others." The editors of the Marshall papers surmise that the "others" were two or three more slaves.[24] In 1789 and 1790 Marshall bought at least six more slaves.

Marshall's Richmond property records give us some sense of the total numbers of slaves he had in that city, but they do not quite add up. Nor do they tell us how many slaves he had in Henrico or Fauquier. Tax records show that in June 1788 he owned six adult slaves in Richmond, but this was at the end of a buying spree when he bought at least fifteen slaves. In March 1789 he owned "7 tithable [taxable adult] slaves and 2 slaves below the age of 16" in Richmond. This suggests that he purchased an adult slave that year, or that an unrecorded slave turned sixteen. In October 1789 he purchased another Negro woman. By 1791 he had ten adult slaves and one child.

In 1792 he had only nine adult slaves with no children mentioned. In 1794 he was down to eight adult slaves with no children listed, and in 1795 he was back up to nine adult slaves, again with no children listed.[25] The records are incomplete as to how many slaves under age sixteen he owned, and these records do not indicate how many slaves he had outside of Richmond. What we do know is that his holdings in Richmond gradually rose, from six adults in 1788 to nine in 1795 with perhaps uncounted or unlisted children.

Marshall's account books and the Richmond property records, incomplete as they are, illustrate that Marshall owned a substantial and growing number of slaves and that he was deeply engaged in the economic activities of slavery. In the early 1780s, just married and with no children, he was buying far more slaves than he needed to run his household. By the 1790s he had purchased many more slaves than the Richmond property records counted. At this time he was populating his estates in Henrico and Fauquier with slaves. Marshall was well on his way to being a wealthy southern gentleman with a significant number of slaves.

There are no account books for Marshall after the late 1790s. Thus the evidence of his more extensive slaveholding comes from census records and the wills he wrote, rewrote, and then rewrote again. In his first will, written in 1827, Marshall named twelve slaves in Richmond to be given to his wife along with the unnamed "children born and to be born" of his slave Sally.[26] We do not know how many children Sally had at the time or later. But Marshall also mentions slaves in a number of other places in the will.

Marshall's son John Jr. was living in Fauquier County on land the chief justice owned. John Jr. was a troubled and troubling man. In 1815 he was expelled from Harvard for "immoral and dissolute conduct." He returned to Fauquier County, living on his father's Mont Blanc plantation. John Jr. had some modest success in politics. But he was often in debt and frequently intoxicated. Marshall noted it had been his "intention" to give John Jr. the land and "all the negroes and stock" on that land. But, he explained, "indiscretions on his part in the management of his pecuniary affairs extremely painful to me" forced a change of plans. Instead, "all the land and all the slaves" were to be placed in trust for the benefit of John Jr.'s wife and children. We do not know how many slaves this constituted, but three years later the 1830 census found thirty-one slaves at Mont Blanc. He also bequeathed land and "all my slaves and property of every description usually on the said lands" to his son Edward Carrington Marshall, who had moved to Fauquier County after he graduated from Harvard in 1826. We do not know how many slaves were on these lands, but in 1830 the twenty-five-year-old Edward owned twenty-seven slaves, while living on land still owned by his father. These twenty-seven slaves are almost certainly the slaves the Chief Justice had in mind in his 1827 will.[27]

In this 1827 will Marshall also divided the slaves on his "tract of land on chiccahominy" among various heirs. The Chickahominy plantation was a nearby exurban retreat for the Marshalls. An 1830 codicil to this will provided that "my slaves at Chiccahominy" should "be divided into two moieties preserving the families together as near as may be except young men and young women." In 1830 the U.S. Census recorded sixty-two slaves at Chickahominy.[28]

The 1830 codicil was a significant recognition of the fundamental humanity of Marshall's slaves, and would have been reasonably easy to implement by his heirs. This was something many slave owners never did. In the end the codicil was unnecessary because in his final will Marshall placed all the Chickahominy slaves in a trust for his daughter, Mary Harvie.

Marshall rewrote his will in 1831, bequeathing to his wife "during her natural life" twelve named slaves plus the un-named (and unnumbered) "children" of his slave Becky. He also gave his wife bank and turnpike stock, and his "estates" in Hampshire County. He now gave his son John Jr. the land at "Mont blanc" where he was living at the time, "together with all the negroes and other property in his possession." He gave the same lands to his son Edward that he had promised in the 1827 will, but he now noted that the "slaves on the said land are already given to him."[29] These were the twenty-seven slaves the census counted on the land in 1830.[30] Marshall also reworked the distribution of the Chickahominy slaves. Marshall's detailed provisions illustrate his active engagement in the business of plantation slavery.

> I give to my Nephew Thomas M. Ambler my tract of land on chiccahominy, (reserving to my beloved wife for her life the house and field on which the house stands as a quiet retreat from the town whenever she may find it convenient, also reserving to her as much hay and firewood as she may desire) with all the slaves[,] stock[,] and plantation uten-sils thereon . . . in trust to apply the annual profits to the maintenance of my daughter Mary Harvie and her family and to the education of her children.[31]

In 1832 Marshall rewrote his will (for what would be the final time) following the death of his wife. By this time he owned about 150 slaves, excluding the twenty-seven he had recently given to his son Edward. Marshall reconfirmed various gifts of land to his sons Thomas, James Keith, and Jaquelin and bequeathed to his son Edward the land that he was already living on, again noting the "slaves on the land are already given to him." He once more changed his mind about John Jr., now directing that "all the negroes and other property in my son John's possession" be held in trust for John Jr.'s wife and children. He continued to have his nephew Thomas Ambler control "a tract of land on Chickahominy, with all the slaves[,] stock, and plantation utensils, thereon" to provide income for his daughter, Mary Harvie. He also directed Ambler to hold his "real property, slaves and household furniture in the City of Richmond," in trust for Mary.[32]

In a codicil to the will added in August 1832 Marshall declared it was his "wish to emancipate my faithful servant Robin."[33] Robin Spurlock had been given to Marshall as a wedding present in 1783, when Robin was about eighteen years old, which meant he was close to seventy years old when Marshall changed his will to manumit Spurlock. Marshall also owned Spurlock's daughter, Agnes Spurlock, but did not offer to free her. Some might see this offer of freedom as an indication of his paternalism and humanity, but emancipating one slave among so many is hardly compelling evidence of that. Even Thomas Jefferson emancipated more slaves than that, although all of them were members of the Hemings family and thus related to him.[34]

Robin Spurlock would in fact never gain his freedom. The codicil promised him fifty dollars if he accepted freedom and went to some other state, one hundred dollars if he moved to Liberia, but nothing if he remained in Virginia, close to his family and friends. As Marshall well knew, Virginia law required any manumitted slave to leave the state or "apply" to a local court "for permission to reside within such county or corporation."[35] To become free and remain in Virginia, Robin Spurlock needed the intervention of a white patron, probably a lawyer. Furthermore, even if he gained his freedom, Spurlock would be penniless. Consistent to the end in his obsession with not having free blacks in the state, Marshall offered money to his "faithful servant" only if he left Virginia. The options for the elderly Spurlock were hardly attractive. He could gain freedom (and a little money) only by abandoning all his friends, his daughter Agnes whom Marshall owned, and any other relatives, to live in another state or Africa. The codicil also allowed him to choose an owner from among Marshall's children. Not surprisingly, Spurlock chose to stay in Richmond, becoming the property of Marshall's daughter, Mary Harvie.

Marshall, the wealthy lawyer and planter, could easily have provided for his elderly "faithful servant Robin" to stay in Richmond, living among his friends, with enough money to spend his remaining years as a free man.[36] But Marshall offered nothing to Spurlock if he remained in Virginia, took no steps to free Spurlock when he was alive, and failed to direct his executors to hire counsel to petition the court on Spurlock's behalf. This codicil, which came to nothing, speaks volumes about his "paternalism," his views on race, and his lifelong support for slavery. The "greatness" of the chief justice is apparent when we parse his opinions; he is less great when we parse this part of his will.

One more event intervened between the writing of Marshall's final will and his death. In 1833 John Jr. died, leaving a wife, children, and many debts. Marshall's 1832 will had directed that the land and slaves at his Mont Blanc plantation be held in trust to provide for his son's wife and children. His son's death with pressing debts changed everything. Ever the dutiful father, the chief justice felt obligated to pay off John Jr.'s creditors.[37]

At this time Marshall held stock in banks, turnpikes, and other companies, owned land all over the state, and regularly collected interest on money he had loaned out. But he chose not to use these assets to settle his son's estate. Instead, he directed his son James Keith to sell the Mont Blanc slaves to pay the debts. Marshall knew that John Jr.'s widow would need some of the slaves to run her household, and so told James Keith "that the servants intended to be reserved for the family should be sold with the others and purchased in my name."[38]

Marshall wanted to protect his daughter-in-law, his grandchildren, and the family name. It would be embarrassing if his daughter-in-law and grandchildren were thrown into poverty by creditors. But he achieved the admirable goal of protecting his own family by increasing the misery of the slaves who had worked for years to support his son's family. The auction would inevitably destroy slave families—separating husbands from wives and children from parents. Marshall's actions here contrast with his hero, George Washington, who famously refused to buy or sell slaves "as you would do cattle at a market."[39] Marshall, the first great biographer of Washington, learned little from the experience about how a true hero of the Republic—even a slaveholder's republic—should treat people, including slaves.

How many slaves did Marshall own? How many were sold at Mont Blanc to pay the debts of his dissolute son? He gave twenty-seven slaves to his son Edward sometime before 1830, but how many did he give to his other children? In 1810 his son Dr. Jaquelin Marshall was apparently living in Richmond (or out of state) as a single young man. In 1820 he was recently married, owned forty-seven slaves, and lived on Marshall's land at Prospect Hill, in Fauquier County. It is hard to imagine this thirty-three-year-old ne'er-do-well, with a virtually non-existent medical practice, acquiring such a large number of slaves on his own. The only plausible explanation is that Jaquelin, like Edward, acquired his slaves as a gift from his father, probably as a wedding present.[40] We cannot know if Marshall gave slaves to his other sons, but this certainly seems likely. Marshall seems to have been concerned with treating all his children equally and making sure all of them were financially secure. He may also have given slaves to his siblings in Fauquier County, since they too seemed to accumulate large numbers rather quickly. His son Thomas Marshall had sixty-four slaves at the Oak Hill plantation. John gave him the plantation sometime before 1827, and as with his other sons, it seems reasonable that some slaves were conveyed as well. His son James K. Marshall had forty-seven slaves on the Leeds plantation in Fauquier. This, too, was land that Marshall had owned before giving it to his son. In 1830 Marshall owned more than 150 slaves in Richmond, Henrico, and Fauquier, after giving many to his sons. In 1830 Marshall and his sons collectively owned more than 250 slaves in Fauquier and Henrico Counties.

It is impossible to know how many slaves Marshall owned at any one time, or in his lifetime. Many tax and probate records no longer exist. The census records were never entirely accurate and are sometimes vague about who actually owned slaves on particular parcels of land. Nevertheless, the 1830 census shows that there were over sixty slaves on the Chickahominy plantation and thirty-one at Mont Blanc (where John Jr. lived), twenty-one held for him by his overseer Thomas Hilary in Fauquier, and twenty-two at his "quarters" in Henrico. The 1830 census listed eight slaves in Marshall's house in Richmond.[41] This is likely an undercount, however, because his will written a year later listed fifteen slaves in Richmond plus Becky's unnamed and unnumbered "children."[42] This does not include the twenty-seven slaves he had just given to Edward or the forty-five Jaquelin owned in 1820, which Marshall had probably given him—perhaps as a present when he got married in 1819.

It is simply wrong to claim that Marshall "experienced slavery primarily" as an urban slave owner or "was never involved in large-scale agriculture" or "had no significant holdings" of slaves. Nor can we accept the claim that "it is doubtful that he traded in slaves."[43] His own record books and letters show he did trade in slaves. In the 1780s and 1790s he regularly bought slaves and in the 1830s he auctioned off slaves to pay John Jr.'s debts. He held scores of his slaves at Chickahominy, working the fields and adding to his wealth. He also kept tabs on slaves on at least three plantations in Fauquier County. The Great Chief Justice was constantly in the business of buying, giving away, and sometimes selling slaves.

Nor can we actually know how these slaves were treated. We have no evidence that Marshall whipped his slaves in Richmond, and such treatment coming directly from him seems unlikely. But we also have no evidence of how Marshall's overseers, sons, nephews, and other men in his family treated the vast majority of Marshall's slaves, living in the countryside. The fastidious Jefferson never personally whipped slaves, but always left that unpleasant business to underlings. Marshall simply did not leave a documentary record of how he treated his slaves, or what his relatives, agents, and overseers did to his slaves. The fact that John Jr. was often drunk might suggest that he could be angry, violent, and out of control around the slaves he borrowed from his father, but we cannot know how he behaved.

Because Marshall never wrote much about slavery, he avoided leaving a paper trail of insensitivity and hypocrisy like Jefferson's or of grotesque racism, at least on the Court, like Chief Justice Taney's. But the fact of Marshall's vast slaveholding forces a reconsideration of his personal feelings on slavery. Kent Newmyer notes: "He neither condemned nor defended slavery itself, but simply accepted it, along with racial prejudice and social inequality, as a part of the 'actual state of the world.'"[44] But Marshall more than "accepted it." He actively participated in slavery on a very personal level. Unlike Jefferson, who inherited his hundreds of slaves, Marshall aggressively bought—and sometimes sold—slaves throughout his life. Some prominent Virginians—among them Robert Pleasants, Edward Coles, Robert Carter, and George Washington—freed their slaves in Marshall's lifetime.[45] Marshall just bought more slaves, gave them to his children, and occasionally sold some, "as you would do cattle at a market."[46] Slaves were a constant factor in his personal life, his economic success, and his children's future. He was personally fully invested in slavery. This seems to have affected his jurisprudence and his public activities off the bench.

John Marshall and the Problem of Slavery in the New Nation

Marshall became chief justice before slavery had begun to emerge as a central issue—eventually becoming *the* central issue—of American politics.[47] Near the beginning of his chief justiceship Congress restricted and then banned the African slave trade, while all of the northern states either had already abolished slavery or were in the process of doing so. In the middle of his Court career, Congress spent two years debating whether Missouri should come into the Union as a slave state or a free state, and South Carolina saw the arrest and hanging of Denmark Vesey for plotting what would have been the largest slave revolt in American history. Near the end of Marshall's Court career, William Lloyd Garrison initiated the modern abolitionist movement and Nat Turner led the bloodiest slave rebellion in United States history.

During the Marshall years, slavery expanded across the South and disappeared in the North through state constitutions and gradual emancipation acts. In 1800, just before Marshall went on the Court, there were more than 37,000 slaves in the North. By 1840 (just a few years after Marshall's death) only about 1,100 slaves remained in the North.[48] Meanwhile, Congress ended the African slave trade on January 1, 1808, and members of the Revolutionary-era antislavery organizations devoted their energies to local post-emancipation projects, such as schools for blacks and filing lawsuits to prevent people from being illegally held in bondage.

Slavery remained robust in the South, with no end in sight. There were about 900,000 slaves in the U.S. when Marshall came on the Court and about 2,250,000 when he died. In 1816 prominent political leaders and philanthropists formed the American Colonization Society (ACS) to remove blacks to settlements in Africa, in what eventually became the country of Liberia. Some ACS founders opposed slavery and believed that helping blacks move to Africa would encourage private manumissions. Other ACS members were active slave owners who saw Liberia as a place to send unwanted free blacks. But even these members were not aggressively proslavery, since the ACS did help individual masters disengage from slaveholding by transporting their manumitted slaves to Africa. From its founding until the Civil War the ACS sent about 13,000 blacks—almost all of them recently manumitted slaves—to Liberia.

Marshall was a life member of the ACS, the president of its Richmond branch, and the leader of the society in Virginia. He supported colonization with his time, prestige, and occasional lobbying efforts. But he never considered manumitting his own slaves and resettling them in Liberia. His colleague Justice Bushrod Washington was the national president of the ACS from its founding until his death in 1829. While president of the ACS, Washington sold many of his own slaves to raise money for the upkeep of Mount Vernon, which he had inherited from his uncle George Washington.

Marshall's leadership in the ACS was not inspired by any personal discomfort with slavery. Rather, it stemmed from his fear of slave rebellions and his hostility to free blacks. He argued that the entire nation "could be strengthened" by the "removal of our colored population." He believed the "danger" from free blacks "can scarcely be estimated."[49] The ACS was safe, comfortable, and conservative, led by Federalists and future Whigs, like Marshall, Bushrod Washington, and Henry Clay. Its goal was to remove American free blacks to Africa, not to end slavery. It was at most mildly antislavery, given that it helped some masters manumit their slaves while never challenging slavery on moral or political grounds.

Black and white opponents of slavery soon denounced the ACS, leading to the emergence of the new, more radical abolitionist movement. In 1829 the black activist David Walker attacked colonization in his *Appeal to the Colored Citizens of the World,* which frightened the South with its radical demands for emancipation or revolution. In January 1831 William Lloyd Garrison began publishing *The Liberator*, signaling the beginning of a new abolitionist movement and demanding immediate steps by Americans to end slavery. That summer, Nat Turner's rebellion in Virginia left at least fifty-five whites and at least two hundred blacks dead.

Marshall watched these events with horror but they did not stir him to question slavery or reduce his commitment to the institution. After the Turner Rebellion, he never suggested that Virginia should take gradual steps to end slavery or even pass new laws to ameliorate bondage by giving slaves some protections, such as legal recognition of their marriages. Rather, as the state leader of the ACS, he petitioned the Virginia legislature for funds to send the state's free blacks to Liberia because of the "urgent expedience of getting rid in some way, of the free coloured population of the Union." Marshall declared that free blacks in Virginia were worthless, ignorant, and lazy and that in Richmond half the free blacks were "criminals." Marshall suggested that the presence of free blacks led to the Turner rebellion, "the awful scenes in Southampton a few months ago," a claim consistent with his hostility to free blacks.[50] In fact, there were very few free blacks in Southampton County, and there was no evidence they participated in the Turner revolt.

Like Jefferson, Marshall argued free blacks were "pests" who should be removed from the state.[51] Marshall did not believe in promoting even gradual emancipation. He thought all emancipation schemes were impractical. If there ever were an emancipation program he believed in, it would have to include sending all the former slaves to Africa. He told the Marquis de Lafayette that this was the "only secure asylum" that would be "beneficial for them and safe for us."[52] Marshall's most aggressive racism and hostility to free blacks never appeared on the pages of U.S. Reports or in a book like Jefferson's *Notes on the State of Virginia,* but he carried these ideas to the bench when he heard cases involving slavery.

As chief justice, Marshall heard roughly fifty cases involving slavery. This number excludes cases where slavery was mentioned but not important to the case, such as *Fairfax's Devisee* v. *Hunter's Lessee* (1813) and cases like *Gibbons* v. *Ogden* (1824) and *Cohens* v. *Virginia* (1821), where the importance of slavery was stressed in arguments of counsel or in the opinions of the court, even though the case had nothing to do with slavery.[53] In his many opportunities to rule on slavery and to rule in ways that would have favored freedom, Marshall always favored slavery, even when there were strong legal and policy arguments to side with freedom. He also adjusted his jurisprudence when slavery cases came before the Supreme Court. For example, Marshall used natural-law arguments to defend property rights, to protect the inviolability of contracts, and to condemn bankruptcy laws.[54] In *The Antelope* (1825), which involved a large number of Africans illegally brought to the United States, Marshall conceded that the African slave trade was "contrary to the law of nature."[55] But in contrast to his opinions in cases involving property, he emphatically rejected the legitimacy of using natural law to decide the case.

From the Founding until the ratification of the Thirteenth Amendment, most day-to-day legal issues involving slavery— contracts for the sale of slaves, wills and inheritances involving slaves, criminal prosecutions of slaves or of free people who harmed them—were heard in state courts. Federal jurisdiction was generally limited to cases involving constitutional provisions, treaties, legal disputes between citizens of different states (known as "diversity" suits because of the parties' diverse state citizenships), and cases involving the few

federal laws touching on slavery, such as the statutes regulating and then ending the African slave trade. The one major
exception involved cases from the District of Columbia.
Because Washington, D.C., was entirely under Congressional
jurisdiction, every trial or lawsuit was a "federal case" which
could be appealed to the U.S. Supreme Court. Through these
routes the Marshall Court heard three kinds of slave cases.

The first involved mundane cases that filtered up to the Supreme Court (or that Marshall heard while riding circuit),
involving such matters as contracts, settlements of estates
and disputed wills, sales of slaves, divorce settlements, debts,
and other private law matters. These cases dealt with the day-
to-day business of slavery, but usually did not directly involve
politics or focus on the status of slaves. These cases don't tell
us much about how Marshall or the Court viewed slavery, and
I do not discuss them here. It is important to mention them
because they remind us that slavery was often before our nation's highest court and in the lower federal courts.[56] These
cases illustrate that for Marshall, slaves were another form of
property subject to litigation, which also reflected his own life
as a slave owner and as a purchaser and seller of slaves.

The second kind consisted of freedom suits by slaves or
contested wills involving slave manumissions in the District
of Columbia, and sometimes in other places. These cases did
not raise large political issues, but mattered a great deal to
the individuals involved, since they determined if someone
would be a slave for life or live as a free person. They were at
the crossroads of freedom and bondage. Often the cases were
not clear-cut, and the justices had various options. Facts read
one way, a statute interpreted another way, or the application
of a procedural rule would determine whether a slave became
free or whether a master kept a valuable piece of property.

Illustrative of the complexities of these cases was Marshall's admission in one case that the statute at issue was "certainly ambiguous, and the one construction or the other may be admitted, without great violence to the words which are employed."[57] How he read that "ambiguous" act would determine whether an African-American spent his life in slavery or freedom.

The last kind were cases involving illegal participation in the African slave trade. Federal laws of 1794, 1800, 1803, and 1807 prohibited all American involvement in the trade and, after January 1, 1808, the importation of any African slaves.[58] Later acts increased enforcement and regulated penalties.[59] Marshall heard some slave-trade cases while riding circuit and the Supreme Court heard a number of cases on appeal. As with the freedom cases, the statutes and the facts were sometimes ambiguous and open to conflicting interpretations. How Marshall read these acts and examined the factual record determined whether slave traders lost their ships and their investments in Africans, or profited from the commerce in human flesh. Similarly, after 1819, how the Court read the laws and viewed the evidence determined whether hapless Africans were returned to the continent of their birth or spent the rest of their lives on southern plantations. I discuss the cases involving the African slave trade in the next chapter of this book.

Black Freedom and the Marshall Court

Most American slaves were doomed to a lifetime of bondage. For some, however, there were legal routes to freedom. In rare instances, state legislatures manumitted a slave for some patriotic or worthy act.[60] Some masters voluntarily took their slaves to free jurisdictions, formally manumitting them. Famously, in 1817, Edward Coles, who was both a neighbor of Thomas Jefferson and President James Madison's private secretary during the War of 1812, took his seventeen inherited slaves to Illinois where he freed them. Other masters manumitted slaves in the states where they lived, sometimes during their lives and sometimes in their wills.[61]

Slaves could also gain their freedom if their masters voluntarily took them to non-slave states or foreign countries where slavery was illegal. Before 1830, courts in Louisiana, Mississippi, Kentucky, and Missouri emancipated slaves because their masters had taken them to live or reside in the Northwest Territory, where the Northwest Ordinance prohibited slavery. Freedom claims based on residence or sojourn in free states or foreign countries continued until the eve of the Civil War.[62] Some slave states, moreover, including Maryland and Virginia, had strict laws regulating the importation of new slaves. A 1785 Virginia law freed any slave brought into the state and kept there more than a year unless the owner was either a bona fide migrant who registered his slave within ten days of arriving in the state or had inherited the slave in another state. Migrants bringing slaves into the state had to file certificates proving they had taken the oath of citizenship, or had the intention to become citizens of the state.[63]

Finally, slaves could become free if they could prove a maternal ancestor was white, Indian, or a free black. These claims were difficult to prove, but not impossible. Just a year after Marshall became chief justice, the North Carolina Supreme Court ruled that a young slave boy was free because he appeared to be of mixed ancestry and his owner could not prove he was descended from a slave mother. Similarly, in 1806, Virginia's highest court liberated a family of slaves on grounds of appearance and the reputation that their maternal ancestor was a free Indian woman and not a black slave.[64]

Cases involving the status of alleged slaves were generally regulated by state law unless they involved claims of freedom based on the Northwest Ordinance or other federal laws. Freedom suits or contested wills involving residents of different states might also end up in federal courts. District of Columbia cases could always be appealed to the U.S. Supreme Court, which also served as the District's highest court. The laws of the District were oddly complicated. The District was created by cessions of land from Virginia and Maryland. Virginia gave Alexandria County (present-day Alexandria, Virginia) to the nation, and Alexandria remained part of the District until it was returned to Virginia in 1846. Maryland gave the nation Washington County, which constitutes present-day Washington, D.C. Congress had full constitutional power to enact laws for the District, but Congress left many state laws in place; during Marshall's chief justiceship Alexandria County was mostly governed by Virginia law, and Washington County was mostly governed by Maryland law.

The Marshall Court heard fourteen cases involving freedom claims. The chief justice wrote an opinion in seven cases; in each of these, the slave plaintiff lost.[65] All but one of the seven cases Marshall decided involved the application of either Virginia or Maryland law to slaves living in the District of Columbia. In these cases Marshall often ignored Maryland or Virginia law or precedent on slavery to rule against black plaintiffs, and he never rigorously enforced statutes if doing so would have led to black freedom. His very first case on this issue as a chief justice reveals this.

In *Scott* v. *Negro London* (1806) Marshall reversed a jury verdict in favor of black freedom.[66] London sued for his freedom in the District of Columbia under a Virginia law prohibiting the importation of slaves. Under this law, anyone bringing a slave into Virginia (and by extension that section of Washington, D.C., governed by Virginia law) had to take an oath of citizenship and file the relevant certificate with the clerk of the court.[67] Here a jury of twelve white men, some of whom were probably slave owners, concluded that London was free because he had been imported into the District and kept there for more than a year without his master's taking the requisite oath indicating an intention to move to the Alexandria section of the District of Columbia. The trial court also found that London was sent into Alexandria *before* the master moved there and before the master expressed any intention to move there. In finding that London had been illegally imported into Washington and was free, the trial court rigorously adhered to the law of slavery in Virginia.

This result was consistent with other decisions from American state courts of the period that strictly applied statutes regulating slavery and at the same time liberally construed the common law in favor of liberty. For example, in 1797, the Pennsylvania court freed slaves because of the failure of a slave owner to comply with the technical requirements of keeping a slave in the state. A decade after London's case, Mississippi's highest court ruled that the Northwest Ordinance—a federal law—required that Mississippi free a slave who had been taken to Indiana.[68]

Similarly, in *Wilson* v. *Belinda* (1817), Pennsylvania's chief justice William Tilghman liberated the slave Belinda because her master had failed to follow the technical requirements of registering a slave under Pennsylvania's Gradual Abolition Act of 1780.[69] Significantly, Tilghman was a conservative Federalist like Marshall and he was also one of the very few political leaders in Pennsylvania who still owned slaves. The Pennsylvania Gradual Abolition Act of 1780 required that all slave owners register their slaves, providing each slave's name, age, and gender. Tilghman declared that Belinda was free because her master had not indicated her gender on the registration form. The master argued that the slave's name, "Belinda," was a sufficient indication of her gender, but Tilghman would have nothing to do with that argument:

> [I]t is said that the sex is implied in the name. . . . The answer is not satisfactory. It may be very true that every one who hears the name of Belinda would suppose at once that the person was a female. The name, however, is not a certain criterion of sex; for men are sometimes called by the names generally given to women, and vice versa. But we are not left to argument on this matter; the law is express that the name shall not be the criterion of sex, because it requires that the name, together with the age and sex, shall be set forth.

Thus he held "that the registry is fatally defective."[70]

Marshall might easily have upheld London's freedom using the same sort of analysis that the slaveholding conservative Tilghman would later use in Belinda's case. A distinguished federal judge in the slave jurisdiction of the District of Columbia had already concluded that London was free under Virginia law. Such a decision would not have threatened slavery or even been seen as "antislavery." Rather, it would have been consistent with jurisprudence in a number of slave states and with enforcement of Virginia's own statutes. But Marshall chose to read the statute in favor of slavery and not freedom, stating in part that his interpretation was consistent with the "spirit" of the law.[71] This case took place well before sectional tensions over slavery were on the political horizon, so the outcome could not have been dictated by any political concerns Marshall had about placating the South on slavery. Furthermore, it would be hard to argue that strictly reading a Virginia state law could possibly threaten slavery or the South. A different decision would simply have allowed one man to live his life in freedom and dignity while upholding the laws of Virginia.

Just a few years before this, Marshall had strictly construed the Constitution to overturn a part of the Judiciary Act of 1789 in *Marbury* v. *Madison*.[72] A year after London's case Marshall would require a strict and narrow interpretation of the law of treason in *Ex parte Bollman* and in Aaron Burr's trial.[73] But in this freedom suit of a slave, Marshall found great room for flexibility in determining that freedom had not vested for the benefit of London.

Marshall continued his anti-freedom jurisprudence in *Scott* v. *Negro Ben* (1810). Ben had been brought to Washington County, which was governed by Maryland law. He sued for freedom under a Maryland law that required a migrant to register his slaves with "the naval officer, or collector of the tax." The jury determined that Ben's owner failed to follow these rules and declared Ben to be free.[74]

Marshall reversed the jury verdict, asserting that "it would be a singular and very extraordinary provision that a naval officer, or the collector of the tax, should be made the sole judge of the right of one individual to liberty, and of another to property."[75] This analysis was disingenuous and counter to the statute. The statute tasked these officials with determining if the person importing that slave into the District complied with the requirements of the law. It was purely an

administrative task the legislature had given to appropriate public officials. A jury (or a judge) would still determine the case on the basis of the evidence. The defendant
was still free to dispute these facts, as Scott had unsuccessfully done at trial.

As in London's case, Marshall refused to interpret a law to
emancipate a slave. Here the lower court, in a slave jurisdiction, found in favor of freedom and Marshall reversed. Significantly, in his opinion Marshall admitted that: "The act, in
its expression, is certainly ambiguous, and the one construction
or the other may be admitted, without great violence to the
words which are employed."[76] He might easily have given the
act a construction that would have led to freedom, upholding the lower court and resolving the ambiguity in favor
of liberty. Instead, Marshall resolved the ambiguity of the law
in favor of slavery.

Two years later, Marshall's hostility to free blacks and
freedom suits led to the outcome in *Hezekiah Wood* v. *John
Davis and Others* (1812).[77] A Maryland jury had concluded
that John's mother, Susan Davis, had *never* legally been a
slave. Thus, Davis and his siblings argued that they were born
free and they had never been slaves. This was consistent
with the law of *every* slave state. Since the 1660s American
law had held that the children of free women were free.
Because their mother was never a slave, Davis and his siblings
won their case in the circuit court with Justice Gabriel Duvall,
who was from Maryland, presiding. Duvall noted that in
similar cases in Maryland the rule was always the same. If
the mother was proven to be free from birth then the
children "were only bound to prove their descent."[78]

On appeal Wood argued that he had purchased the Davis
children before their mother proved her freedom and thus

their claim to freedom was not governed by the case that led to Susan Davis's freedom. Wood's lawyer, Francis Scott Key, argued that Wood "was not a party, nor privy to any party, to the suit of Susan Davis" for her freedom.[79] This argument should have been a nonstarter for Marshall, since if Susan Davis was *always free* and had never been a slave, then her children were not slaves when Wood bought them. Under this theory, Wood would have had a valid suit against the person who sold Davis to him. During the oral argument, Justice Duvall "stated in open court that when he had been in practice in Maryland he had filed petitions to establish freedom" for a number of slaves, and that after their freedom had been proved, "the descendants of the petitioners had only to cite the judgment and prove their descent."[80]

Marshall ignored Duvall's knowledge of Maryland practice, concluding that the Davis children were not free, even though he knew their mother had always been a free person. This result was completely at odds with the universally accepted American rule that the children of a free woman were always born free. Marshall, obsessed with property rights, was more concerned about the nature of contract law than about the settled law of every slave jurisdiction in the country or the freedom of a handful of African Americans.

Marshall asserted that the judgment giving Susan Davis her freedom "was not conclusive evidence in the present case" because there was "no privity" between Wood and the man who had claimed to own Susan Davis.[81] This was a non sequitur, because the case had nothing to do with Susan's owner. If Susan had never been a slave, then under the law of *every* state in the nation, the children were also free, no matter how they ended up in the hands of others who illegally claimed them as slaves. A court in the District of Columbia, which was governed by Maryland law, legitimately accepted the finding that Susan was free. Marshall might have concluded that the D.C. courts, when applying Maryland law in the District, were obliged—under a concept akin to full faith and credit—to accept the rulings of the Maryland courts. Alternatively Marshall might have held that, because Susan Davis's freedom had been confirmed by another court, the burden of proof had shifted to Wood, who had to prove that John Davis and his siblings were slaves. But he did not.

Marshall ought to have held that once Susan Davis established she was free from birth, there was no legal theory under which her children could be enslaved. This was Duvall's position at trial. But Marshall rejected it without any discussion. Here Marshall divorced himself from the law of slavery, and instead introduced an irrelevant contract theory to a case that should have turned on the free birth of the mother. Marshall may have laid the "foundations of power" for the Court and the national government, but here he abused his power to deny liberty to a family of African Americans who were considered free under the laws of every state in the nation.

Marshall's callous attitude toward back freedom was confirmed a year after *Davis,* in *Mima Queen and Child* v. *Hepburn* (1813).[82] Mima Queen claimed her freedom on the basis of her ancestry. The only proof offered, however, was the testimony of a number of neighbors whose statements were clearly a form of hearsay. At the trial she tried to present affidavits proving the freedom of her great-grandmother, Mary Queen. Francis Scott Key, representing the slaves, argued that if this kind of evidence were excluded in a civil case, *especially* a freedom suit, it would "be impossible to prove any antient fact."[83] The lower court in the District of Columbia rejected this testimony, while allowing the white man who claimed her to present affidavits that her mother was in fact a slave.[84] The lower court also rejected a juror who expressed some antislavery sympathies. Marshall sustained the rejection of the hearsay evidence that favored the slaves. He also found it was appropriate for the trial court to strike a juror who opposed slavery, while jurors who supported slavery were allowed to serve. Marshall's biases were clear. Because opposition to slavery was sometimes based on religion—Quakers and Methodists often opposed slavery on religious grounds—Marshall was in effect establishing a religious test for federal jurors in violation of the Constitution's absolute prohibition on religious tests.

On the hearsay issue, Marshall rejected Maryland practice, even though the case was decided under Maryland law. He also ignored legal understandings that hearsay evidence might be appropriate in civil cases and was often used to determine boundaries in real estate. Key's co-counsel argued: "Such evidence as this is always admitted in the Courts of Maryland, under whose laws this case was tried, and its use had been sanctioned by the authority of the highest court of that state. The case cited by the opposite counsel shows that it is admitted not only in cases of prescription, custom and pedigree, but in all cases of the like nature."[85]

But Marshall could not "perceive any legal distinction between" a claim of freedom and "any other right" and thus he refused to allow the court even to hear the voluminous evidence that Mima Queen's great-grandmother was free. Reflecting his concerns with the ownership of private property, his persistent acquisition of slaves, and his hostility to the presence of free blacks in his society, Marshall concluded: "If the circumstance that the eye witnesses of any fact be dead should justify the introduction of testimony to establish that fact from hearsay, no man could feel safe in any property, a claim to which might be supported by proof so easily obtained."[86] This statement ignored the use of hearsay in other property matters and civil cases, such as where land boundaries might lie. More importantly, Marshall ignored the context of the case. This case would determine if someone was condemned to a lifetime of bondage or allowed to live a life of freedom.

Marshall's opinion was at odds with the law in Maryland, Virginia, and other slave states, where judges often recognized the distinction between freedom suits and other kinds of cases. Only a few years before this case, in *Hudgins* v. *Wrights* (1806), the Virginia Court of Appeals had upheld the freedom of an enslaved family based in part on hearsay evidence. The lower court decision in that case had been written by Marshall's former law professor George Wythe, and it was upheld by one of the state's leading jurists, St. George Tucker, the author of the first American edition of Blackstone's *Commentaries*.[87] Marshall could easily have found an exception to hearsay rules in freedom suits, because they were special kinds of cases.

Justice Gabriel Duvall, who had previously served as chief justice of Maryland, wrote the only dissent of his Supreme Court career, "demonstrating . . . a firm grasp of Maryland law."[88] Duvall argued that the trial court should have applied Maryland rules in this case, and that under Maryland law hearsay was admissible in a freedom suit involving a long-dead ancestor. Marshall should have shown some deference to Duvall's superior knowledge and experience with Maryland law. Duvall, who owned many slaves, was hardly a radical opponent of slavery. But he did accept the idea that courts might lean toward freedom when appropriate. Duvall noted that in Maryland freedom suits "hearsay evidence was admitted upon the same principle upon which it is admitted to prove a custom, pedigree, and the boundaries of land—because from the antiquity of the transactions to which these subjects may have reference, it is impossible to produce living testimony." He noted that "the reason for admitting hearsay evidence upon a question of freedom is much stronger than in cases of pedigree or in controversies relative to the boundaries of land. It will be universally admitted that the right to freedom is more important than the right of property." Duvall ended by offering a dose of reality, as well as fundamental justice, to counter Marshall's refusal to allow a group of slaves to prove their freedom:

> And people of color, from their helpless condition under the uncontrolled authority of a master, are entitled to all reasonable protection. A decision that hearsay evidence in such cases shall not be admitted cuts up by the roots all claims of the kind and puts a final end to them unless the claim should arise from a fact of recent date, and such a case will seldom, perhaps never, occur.[89]

But Marshall would have none of this. An active purchaser of slaves on his way to owning hundreds of human beings over his lifetime, Marshall fully understood the "uncontrolled authority of a master" and the importance of property. Marshall claimed he feared that allowing hearsay in freedom suits—as Maryland law allowed—would threaten property everywhere, although that conclusion was patently absurd. Marshall might have easily limited the use of this evidence to freedom suits in the District of Columbia.

Had Marshall reversed in this case, Mima Queen would not necessarily have become free; she would only have been given an opportunity to prove her freedom, perhaps with a jury that did not include only supporters of slavery. Mima Queen might have lost before a jury of white men in Washington, D.C., but she would have had her day in court with the *only* evidence available to her. Marshall prevented this from happening. Significantly, in Mima Queen's case Marshall departed from a jurisprudential rule he had followed a few years before, in a case not involving a freedom claim. In *Telfair* v. *Stead's Executors* (1805) Marshall decided a complicated case involving slaves, land, and pre–Revolutionary War debts, based on Georgia law. In affirming a lower court ruling, Marshall noted the Court had "received information as to the construction given by the courts of Georgia" and so he followed the Georgia rule.[90] Thus, Marshall was ready to defer to state law on suits over the ownership of land and slaves. But in a case involving human freedom, Marshall refused to defer to the relevant state law. Property and the settlement of debts mattered a great deal to Marshall; freedom was less important.

In 1816, three years after *Mima Queen,* John Davis once again brought his quest for freedom before Marshall's court. Here Marshall reaffirmed his opinion in *Mima Queen* that freedom claims based on hearsay evidence would not be entertained by his Court. As before, Davis claimed freedom because a Maryland court had declared his mother to have been a free person by birth. But Marshall had rejected that argument. Davis now also claimed, with substantial hearsay evidence, that his maternal ancestor Mary Davis was a white woman born in England. If that was true, then Davis was free. But Marshall would not allow this hearsay evidence. Nor would he reconsider whether Davis was free because his mother had proved she was born free. He concluded that the Maryland decision declaring Susan Davis free did not apply

to her son and his owner because "verdicts are evidence between parties and privies" and the court "does not feel inclined to enlarge the exceptions to this general rule." That
same day, Marshall denied a freedom claim to another slave
who had been imported into Washington, D.C., in violation
of Maryland law.[91]

Significantly, the year he rejected freedom claims in these
two cases Marshall became a leader of the American Colonization Society, which was dedicated to removing free blacks
from the South. Marshall's jurisprudence ensured there would
be fewer free blacks to remove.

In 1827 the Court once again denied a freedom claim, with
Justice William Johnson speaking.[92] The Washington, D.C.,
trial court had ruled that the slave Matilda and her children
were free because there was no evidence that the owner had
taken an oath indicating his intention to reside in Washington
within sixty days after moving to Alexandria, as required by
Virginia law. The move had happened thirty years before, but
as in many freedom suits, slaves often discovered their right
to freedom long after it had vested. There was no record
that the defendant slave owner had taken the proper oath—
apparently no paperwork was actually filed if the oath had
been taken—and all of the magistrates from thirty years earlier
were dead. The slave owner argued that the Court should presume he had taken the oath, and let him keep Matilda and her
children. The trial court rejected this presumption and a jury of
white men in Washington, D.C., declared the slaves to be free.

This case was almost a mirror image of Mima Queen's case.
Here the slave owner wanted to use something even weaker
than hearsay evidence—a mere presumption that the court
should favor him. If the Marshall Court had been consistent,
it would have upheld Matilda's freedom, perhaps citing *Mima*

Queen to support this result. But this did not happen. Instead, the Court reversed, asserting that there was a Virginia case which held that, in situations like this, Courts should presume the oath was taken. But here again, the Marshall Court was inconsistent. In both *Wood* v. *Davis* and *Mima Queen*, Marshall refused to apply Maryland precedent, which would have freed Davis and his siblings and allowed Mima Queen to present evidence of her freedom. In this case, however, the Court asserted that it was "a relief to us to find that there has been an express adjudication on" the issue, and thus, by following this Virginia precedent, the Court could find for the slave owner.[93] Once again the slaves in the District of Columbia saw freedom snatched from their hands by a decision of the Marshall Court.

In 1829 the Court heard *Le Grand* v. *Darnall,* a diversity case involving a free black from Maryland. The defendant, Darnall, was born a slave but his owner, who was also his father, had emancipated him. He inherited land from his father, which Le Grand wanted to purchase. The case was brought to determine if Darnall was legally free and legally held the land in question. The Court asserted that the outcome turned on "one question only": whether "at the time of the death of the testator" Darnall "was entitled to his freedom under the will and deeds of manumission." If he was, then "his title to the land sold was unquestionable." The Court found Darnall was free, and the sale of the lands could then proceed. This is apparently the first case in which the Supreme Court affirmed that a former slave was free. Significantly, the opinion was not by Marshall, but by Justice Gabriel Duvall. Here Marshall acquiesced to Duvall's expertise in Maryland law, and thus the Court acknowledged that one of the parties was a free black. One other aspect of this case bears mentioning. This case was brought in federal court as a diversity suit, with Le Grand suing Darnall in his capacity as a citizen of Maryland. Le Grand's lawyer was Roger B. Taney, who would assert in *Dred Scott* that no black person could ever be considered a citizen of the United States or sue in diversity. As the last chapter of this book demonstrates, by the time of Darnall's case, Taney already believed that free blacks could never be considered citizens of the United States, and thus he believed they could not be parties to a diversity suit, which involved citizens of different states. As a good advocate, however, Taney did not raise this issue. Instead, he told the Court he had "submitted the case without argument," stating that it "had been brought up merely on account of its great importance to the appellee; which rendered it desirable that the opinion of the supreme court should be had on the matters in controversy."[94]

In *LaGrange* v. *Choteau,* in 1830, the Marshall Court heard its first freedom suit based on a federal statute, rather than a law of Maryland or Virginia.[95] In 1817 Pierre Menard had taken his slave LaGrange (also known as Isadore) from Missouri to the Illinois territory, where slavery was illegal under the Northwest Ordinance, a federal statute. Menard later sold LaGrange to Pierre Chouteau, one of the wealthiest men in St. Louis. LaGrange claimed his freedom under the Northwest Ordinance. While the Missouri courts often freed slaves who had lived or worked in Illinois, in this case the trial court did not emancipate LaGrange, because he had spent only a few days in Illinois. In 1828 the Missouri Supreme Court upheld this outcome, noting that any sort of "residence contrived or permitted by the legal owner . . . to defeat or evade the [Northwest] ordinance, and thereby introduce slavery *de facto* would doubtless entitle a slave to freedom, and should be punished by a forfeiture of title to the property." Here, however, the Missouri court explained that the mere presence of a slave in Illinois for a few days did not constitute such an attempt "to defeat the ordinance." The Missouri court spelled out *its* interpretation of the Ordinance: "This court has decided that it will not be tied down to the particular exceptions contained in the ordinance, but will look at its spirit and object, and a case cannot be well conceived that could fall more fully without the spirit of its provisions." Bringing LaGrange to Illinois did not violate the spirit and the object of the Ordinance, which the Missouri court asserted "was intended as a fundamental law for those who may choose to live under it, rather than as a penal statute to be construed by the letter against those who may choose to pass their slaves through the country." But the Missouri court also made clear that "if the residence had otherwise been sufficient" LaGrange would be entitled to his freedom.[96]

LaGrange appealed to the U.S. Supreme Court, arguing that the Missouri Supreme Court incorrectly interpreted the Northwest Ordinance and that he became free the moment his master voluntarily took him into the territory. This was consistent with English law dating from *Somerset* in 1772, and by this time a number of southern state courts had upheld freedom claims based on residence in the Northwest Territory, in free states, or in foreign countries. Here was an opportunity for Marshall, who strongly supported a powerful central government, to implement the supremacy clause of the Constitution and the power of Congress by applying the Northwest Ordinance to LaGrange's case. Marshall concluded, however, that the Court had no jurisdiction in the case because the pleadings did "not show that any act of congress was drawn into question."[97] Marshall implied that

LaGrange's trial attorney, in asserting that Illinois did not allow slavery, failed to specifically state that this was under the Northwest Ordinance.

But none of this should have mattered because LaGrange was not appealing the trial verdict. In fact, the Supreme Court would not have had jurisdiction to hear an appeal from the state trial court. But the U.S. Supreme Court did have jurisdiction to hear appeals from state supreme courts. Thus, LaGrange appealed the Missouri Supreme Court decision, which offered a detailed interpretation of the Northwest Ordinance. Furthermore, in the trial, LaGrange's lawyers argued that he was free because he was taken to the federal territory of Illinois in 1817—a fact that was not in dispute—and that he was thus free because slavery was illegal in the Illinois territory at that time. This illegality was based on the Northwest Ordinance, which was an act of Congress, and based on Illinois territorial laws which were technically also federal laws. Therefore, when the Missouri courts failed to emancipate LaGrange, the courts were construing—or according to LaGrange, misconstruing—federal law. The Missouri Supreme Court decision shows that no one involved in this case doubted that it turned on the interpretation of federal laws. Marshall could claim he lacked jurisdiction only by ignoring the opinion of the Missouri court.[98]

Clearly Marshall did not want to decide this case and be compelled to consider the implications of the Missouri Supreme Court's narrow reading of the Northwest Ordinance. In his short, almost impatient opinion, the chief justice concluded: "It is not perceived that any act of congress has been misconstrued. The court is therefore of opinion that it has no jurisdiction of the case."[99] This analysis simply ignored the status of Illinois as a federal territory, the Northwest

Ordinance, and the Missouri Supreme Court's long discussion of the Ordinance.

A year later, *Menard* v. *Aspasia* (1831) once again brought the Northwest Ordinance and slavery along the Mississippi before the Supreme Court. Here the federal issues were clear. Aspasia was born in the Illinois territory after 1787.[100] If the Northwest Ordinance meant anything, it meant no one could be born a slave in a place where there could be "neither slavery nor involuntary servitude." The Missouri Supreme Court upheld Aspasia's freedom. His owner, Pierre Menard, appealed to the U.S. Supreme Court on the grounds that:

1. Slaves in the northwestern territory, before and at the time of the adoption of the ordinance of 1787, were not liberated by that instrument, but continued slaves.
2. That the offspring of such slaves follow the condition of the mother, and are also slaves . . . . By the treaty of peace, concluded in 1763, between England and France, the latter ceded to the former the country out of a part of which the state of Illinois was formed. In the colonies of both France and England, it is well known that slavery is tolerated.[101]

The Court answered these claims with a long and detailed history of the Revolution, the Confederation period, the Northwest Ordinance, and subsequent federal laws. The bottom line was that after the adoption of the Ordinance all people in Illinois were born free. The Court dismissed Menard's suit for lack of jurisdiction because the Ordinance did not give him any title to a slave in Illinois. This was the first time the Marshall Court had ever upheld a lower court decision giving freedom to slaves. It was the first time the Court rejected an appeal by a master, trying to recover his slaves after a state or lower federal court had freed them.

This was not, however, the work of Chief Justice Marshall. John McLean of Ohio, Andrew Jackson's first nominee to the Court, wrote this historically detailed, careful, and scholarly opinion. It reflected McLean's decisions as a state judge in Ohio.[102] We have no way of knowing whether Marshall agreed with this result or, having been outvoted on the court, simply acquiesced in the outcome.

In the six years after the *Menard* case, the Marshall Court heard four more cases involving black freedom. Smith Thompson, a James Monroe nominee from New York with moderate antislavery views, upheld freedom claims in two of them. The Court upheld freedom in two others, with opinions by James Wayne, a Georgia slave owner nominated to the Court by Andrew Jackson in 1835. Wayne was a moderate on slavery issues and in 1861 would remain on the bench when his home state seceded.[103] There was nothing earth-shattering about these cases; none threatened the institution of slavery in any way. They simply upheld manumissions by wills, voluntary manumissions, and the laws liberating slaves illegally imported into the District of Columbia. Significantly, Marshall was silent in these cases.

It was only in Marshall's last years on the bench that the Court sided with slaves seeking freedom. Some scholars argue that Marshall's slave jurisprudence was necessary to preserve the Union, to preserve national harmony, and to placate the South. That analysis might arguably be true in the *LaGrange* case where Marshall did not compel Missouri to strictly apply the Northwest Ordinance. But in all the other cases involving black freedom, such an argument is unpersuasive. In some of those cases Southern white jurors and judges had determined that slave plaintiffs deserved to be free, but Marshall overturned them to side with the master. In some cases—like those of John Davis and Mima Queen—Marshall rejected slave-state jurisprudence to *prevent* slaves from gaining freedom. These were not cases brought by abolitionists; there was not even an abolitionist movement at the time. The freedom claims from the District of Columbia, which Marshall consistently denied, did not threaten slavery or the South.

Had Marshall accepted Justice Duvall's analysis and the spirit of his lower-court opinion in the *Davis* case, or his explication of Maryland law in his dissent in *Mima Queen*, the results would not have undermined slavery or property in the District of Columbia. Slaves who claimed freedom would still have had to find white witnesses to testify to their freedom. All-white juries would have been able to judge the veracity of the evidence. White judges (usually slave owners) would have presided over such trials. But the result would have been that some slaves—perhaps Mima Queen and her children and certainly John Davis and his siblings—would have gained their liberty. Marshall's jurisprudence showed him as deeply committed to slavery as he was in his personal life, and opposed to black freedom, which dovetailed with his role in the American Colonization Society.

Even when he offered freedom to his personal slave, Robin Spurlock, Marshall forced him to choose exile in Liberia, freedom in some other state far from his friends and family, or life in Virginia with no money (if the laws allowed it, which was hardly certain). Marshall must have known Spurlock would not be able to accept freedom under these conditions. So, while claiming to "wish to emancipate my faithful servant

Robin," he also provided that Spurlock could choose a master from among his children.

Marshall's offer of freedom to Robin Spurlock, with its impossible conditions, recalled his idiosyncratic jurisprudence in freedom suits—insisting on strict rules in one case, ignoring them in another, and admitting ambiguity in another—but always supporting slavery and blocking freedom. Dealing with the African slave trade, his jurisprudence was similar.

3

John Marshall and the
African Slave Trade

B<small>Y THE LATE</small> eighteenth century, many people in the Atlantic world were thoroughly horrified by the barbaric cruelty of the African slave trade. Even before the American Revolution, a few people in England and the American colonies denounced the trade. Great Britain dominated the trade and, as the Revolution began, all the colonies prohibited the trade as part of their general boycotts of trade with Britain. The postwar depression, revolutionary ideology, and general revulsion with the trade kept it closed or dormant. When the Constitutional Convention met, slave importations were technically legal in North Carolina but a prohibitive tax made them uneconomical. The African trade was also legal in Georgia, but inactive.

At the Constitutional Convention the delegates from Georgia and South Carolina successfully insisted on a clause to prevent the new Congress from immediately banning the trade. Article I, Section 9, of the Constitution prohibited Congress from interfering with the trade to the "states now existing" until 1808. After that, Congress had the power, if it chose to exercise it, to abolish the trade. In the meantime, under its commerce clause jurisdiction, Congress regulated the trade.[1]

Congress passed laws in 1794, 1800, and 1803 prohibiting American participation in the African trade and banned the use of American ports, vessels, and shipyards for the trade. Under these laws Americans involved in the trade faced significant fines, possible imprisonment, and confiscation of their ships. Portions of the fines and of the value of confiscated ships would go to informants. Slaves could still legally be imported into states that allowed the African trade, but only on foreign ships with foreign crews. Between 1803 and 1808, Georgia and South Carolina imported at least forty thousand slaves.[2]

An 1807 law absolutely banned all slave importations after January 1, 1808. Fines under this law ranged from eight hundred dollars for buying an illegally imported slave (who would be confiscated and sold) to twenty thousand dollars for anyone building a ship for the trade or fitting out an existing ship for the trade. Americans participating in the trade faced jail terms of five to ten years. Slave ships of any nation found in American ports or hovering off the American coast could be seized and forfeited, and their captains fined and imprisoned. The law allowed the United States Navy to interdict ships involved in the illegal trade. Acts of 1818, 1819, 1820, and 1823 strengthened enforcement of the original ban on the trade.[3]

Under the 1819 act, illegally imported slaves were to be returned to Africa rather than sold in the United States.[4] The United States used Liberia as a destination for Africans rescued from intercepted slavers. The 1820 law, reaffirmed in 1823, declared that any American citizen engaging in the African slave trade and any American or foreigner bringing slaves into the United States "shall be adjudged a pirate; and on conviction thereof before the circuit court of the United States for the district wherein he shall be brought or found, shall suffer death."[5]

The African Slave Trade and the Marshall Court:
1803 to 1825

Like most elite Virginians, Marshall found the African trade to be offensive—"one of the foulest stains on the character of Christendom."[6] But on the bench Marshall muted the moral implications of the trade—even in the face of statutory language roundly condemning it. Writing cramped opinions that were often intellectually inconsistent with his jurisprudence unrelated to slavery, Marshall seemed to work hard *not* to enforce the bans on the trade.

Illegal slaving was particularly difficult to stop because ships left U.S. ports looking like normal merchant vessels, were refitted elsewhere to take on slaves, and then did not return to the United States for months or years. Federal law enforcement at this time was extraordinarily weak and gathering evidence for a criminal case was difficult unless an American ship was actually caught with illegal slaves on board. The 1794 law encouraged private citizens to help stop American participation in the trade, with significant financial incentives for those who provided evidence of illegal slaving.

Adams, qui tam v. *Woods* (1805) was such a case. Adams provided evidence of Woods' having illegally participated in the trade, and this was a civil action under the 1794 law, which would allow Adams to collect one half of the two thousand dollar fine that Woods would have to pay. This was not a criminal prosecution and thus the standard for winning was lower. The informant in this case (Adams) had a huge financial incentive to gather evidence of illegal involvement in the trade. Given that federal resources for such investigations were limited, this system of private incentives was critical to suppressing illegal American involvement in the trade. This case illustrates Marshall's reluctance to enforce its suppression.[7]

The defendant, Woods, claimed that the action failed to meet a statute of limitations under a different federal law which provided that no one could be subject to "any fine or forfeiture under *any* penal statute, unless the *indictment or information* for the same shall be found or *instituted* within *two* years from the time of committing the offence. . . ." Attorney General Levi Lincoln, on behalf of Adams, argued that this provision applied only to prosecutions for criminal activity—and that this was not a criminal action, but a civil action to recover money.[8]

Lincoln further argued that the interpretation offered by the defendant would be "a total annihilation of the penalties of the act" because a slave trade voyage was "always circuitous, and generally takes more than the two years to perform it." Such voyages went "from the United States to the West-Indies—from thence to Africa—thence back to the West-Indies or South America, and thence home."[9] His point was that the two-year statute of limitations made the 1794 ban virtually impossible to enforce *if* the statute meant that the two-year limitation began on the day the ship sailed from the United States. Lincoln gave Marshall strong policy arguments for upholding the suit against Woods. He also gave Marshall useful precedents—citing Chief Justice Lord Mansfield and Sir William Blackstone for the proposition that "there is no distinction better known, than the distinction between *civil* and *criminal* law; or between *criminal prosecutions* and *civil actions*."[10]

Marshall might also have upheld the action without re-jecting the idea of a two-year statute of limitations. Viola-tions of the 1794 law were ongoing. The slave trade was not like a robbery which took place at a single moment and was then over. Marshall might have interpreted the time of "com-mitting the offence" to include the entire voyage of the ship, and thus the two-year statute of limitations began to run only when the ship returned to the United States and the illegal voyage came to an end.

The strongest argument for such an interpretation was that the offense did not actually begin in the United States, because in cases like this one, the ship was refitted as a slaver after it left the United States. Thus no one could know that it was a slaver when it left the country, because it was not yet a slaver. Once the ship left the U.S., it would be impossible to file an action against the ship until it returned. Furthermore, new offenses were committed throughout the journey. Marshall might have explained that there were a long series of offenses in a voyage like this, including sailing from the United States, refitting the ship (later), taking on slaves in Africa (still later), transporting them across the Atlantic (much later), selling them in the Caribbean, and then returning to the United States with money obtained through illegal activity. There might even have been a violation that began when the slavers landed in the United States in possession of their ill-gotten gains—the fruits of their criminal activity.

Marshall is famous for his creative solutions to legal prob-lems. Here he could certainly have either explained why the two-year statute did not apply, or found that the ongoing il-legal activities kept extending the statute of limitations. This case furthermore provided Marshall with an opportunity to give a strongly nationalist opinion, which dovetailed with his lifelong support for a powerful central government. Instead he weakened the national government and federal law enforcement. Marshall's reading of the two-year statute of limitations, and his application of it to a civil case, effectively eviscerated the 1794 law. Under Marshall's interpretation, an American ship could continuously trade in slaves as long it had been out of the United States for more than two years. Under Marshall's unrealistic analysis, a ship on a voyage from Africa, with a full cargo of slaves, would be immune from any federal action if that ship had left the United States more than two years before it was captured.

Marshall held that the 1790 law limited the civil claim under the 1794 law. He argued that the application of the 1790 law to all subsequent laws was "stronger because not many penal acts were at that time in the code." But this argument could just as easily cut in the opposite direction: because there were so few penal acts at the time, it was equally plausible that the law was not meant for civil cases. In embargo cases Marshall famously declined to apply "technical niceties" of procedure in common law to admiralty courts.[11] But in slave trade cases Marshall's rigid application of technical niceties protected slave traders from suffering for their illegal and immoral commerce.

Adams presented Marshall with an opportunity to strike a blow against the African slave trade. Instead he eviscerated a key statute designed to suppress illegal American participation in the trade. Compared to Marshall's creative decisions in other cases and his strong nationalism, his opinion here seems particularly cramped and uninspired. Given a chance to strike a blow against the African slave trade, he chose to protect slave traders rather than to help rein them in.

In *The Brigantine Amiable Lucy* v. *United States* (1810) the Marshall Court overturned the conviction of a ship for illegally importing a slave from the West Indies.[12] The decision was *per curium,* with no detailed opinion and no justice listed as the author of the opinion—however, given Marshall's almost total dominance of the Court at this time, it is likely that he either wrote this opinion or directed its thrust. The Court offered no analysis of its reasoning, but the end result was clear. The *Amiable Lucy* had brought a slave to the United States from the West Indies. The U.S. District Court in Louisiana found this violated the 1803 act which prohibited bringing blacks into the United States except to states that allowed such importation. The Marshall Court reversed this outcome.

The case turned on the fact that Louisiana was not a *state,* but a federal territory. The constitutional provision protecting the African slave trade applied only to states—the provision prevented Congress from ending the trade before 1808 to "any of the States now existing."[13] Thus Congress was presumably free to ban importations into territories. The *Amiable Lucy* had been prosecuted under the 1803 Act, which prohibited importing slaves into states, unless those states specifically allowed such importations. In 1804 Congress banned bringing foreign slaves into the territory, and explicitly made the 1803 law applicable to Louisiana. An 1805 law which created a territorial legislature explicitly provided that existing laws (including the 1804 act), would remain in force. All this should have settled the issue. Congress could have allowed slaves to be imported into territories, but it did the opposite. Thus, on both statutory and constitutional grounds, the Court should have held, as the U.S. District Court did, that the 1803 ban on importing slaves into states also applied to the Louisiana Territory, unless there was a specific congressional action or perhaps a specific territorial law to the contrary.

The Marshall Court apparently accepted the defendant's argument that the federal law banning importations did not apply to a federal territory unless the federal territory explicitly adopted the federal law. This narrow reading of the law is inconsistent with the Marshall Court's usually expansive view of congressional power. Since Congress had plenary power over the territories, there was no need for the territorial legislature to explicitly adopt congressional laws passed before the territorial legislature existed. This was the high point of Marshall's dominance of the Court and he would have had little difficulty bringing the Court along in upholding the prosecution for slave trading. But, consistent with his record of supporting slavery and protecting those who imported slaves, Marshall's Court reached a different result, and the owners of the *Amiable Lucy* remained unpunished for importing slaves into the Louisiana Territory.

Three years after the Court released the owners of the *Amiable Lucy*, Marshall reversed the conviction of *The Caroline* (1813) for illegal slaving.[14] The federal prosecutor in Charleston, South Carolina, brought a libel—a legal action to recover the value of a ship or to physically take possession of a ship—against *The Caroline* both for violating the 1794 federal act prohibiting American ships from participating in the African slave trade and for violating the 1807 act banning the importation of slaves to the United States. While in Charleston harbor, *The Caroline* received "fitments" and "articles calculated for the slave trade only."[15] Before this slave-trading equipment could be fully attached to the ship, this refitting was discovered and the owners quickly removed the slave-trade fitments and then sailed the ship to Havana where they sold it to Spanish subjects "who fitted her out for the African slave trade." The defense argued that the ship had not violated the law because it was only in the process of being fitted for the African trade and never actually was fitted for the trade in the United States. The prosecution argued that it was "not necessary that everything necessary to the voyage should be on board before the forfeiture accrues."[16] It was also clear that the owners had sailed to Cuba with the intention of selling the ship to be used in the illegal slave trade, which also violated various federal laws.

Here Marshall could not have been worried about offending the South, because he was reviewing a conviction won by southern prosecutors in a South Carolina court. Yet Marshall found that the libel was "too imperfectly drawn" to condemn the ship.[17] This commerce—nefarious, illegal, and universally condemned as immoral—was carried out in secret. The libel against the ship had clearly set out various offenses. In other aspects of criminal law the commencement of a crime was enough to warrant prosecution and conviction. The prosecution also rested on two separate statutes. But Marshall refused to allow this, asserting that the prosecutor had to choose under which statute he wanted to act, even though both statutes applied to the multiple offences in the case. Marshall remanded the case to the circuit court, to allow for an amended complaint and a retrial. The decision clearly undermined the ability of the U.S government to suppress the African trade. In a footnote to this case, the Court noted that it reached the same result in cases involving four other ships, including one called *The Emily*.

A few years after *The Caroline,* Chief Justice Marshall asserted in an embargo case that "technical niceties which the astuteness of ancient judges and lawyers" had "introduced into criminal proceedings at common law" were not "engrafted into proceedings in the courts of admiralty."[18] In the embargo cases and other admiralty cases Marshall was flexible. But he was not in the slave-trading cases. Had Marshall been flexible about "technical niceties," the outcomes in *Adams, The Amiable Lucy,* or *The Caroline* might have been entirely different. But in slavery cases, the Chief Justice developed a different standard of jurisprudence than when hearing other cases.

The prosecutors in South Carolina rewrote their libel against *The Caroline,* and the slavers were again convicted, and again they appealed. In 1824 the Court would uphold the convictions of *The Caroline* and *The Emily.* Marshall, however, did not write the opinion. Justice Smith Thompson of New York, who had recently been appointed and was probably the most significant opponent of slavery on the Court at that time, upheld the prosecution.[19]

A variation on the slave trade reached the Court in 1815 in *The Brig Alerta, and Cargo* v. *Blas Moran.*[20] In 1810 a French privateer, *L'Epine,* commanded by Captain Batigne, had seized the *Alerta,* a Spanish slaver owned by Moran, with about 170 slaves on board. Batigne seized the *Alerta* as a prize, since at the time France and Spain were at war. The *Alerta* was then caught in a gale, damaged and almost out of food, when an American ship under the command of a Captain Allen rescued her and brought her to New Orleans.[21] There the U.S. Courts denied Batigne his prize because some of his crewmen were U.S. citizens, which violated American law.

The ship and the slaves were then returned to Moran, after he paid salvage to Allen and his crew. Speaking for the Court, Justice Bushrod Washington upheld this decision, returning the *Alerta* and its cargo to the Cuban owner, according to generally recognized rules of war, privateering, and diplomacy. Oddly, no one on the Court pondered the status of the human cargo on the ship or the American law which banned the importation of slaves. Imported slaves were contraband. While the case was pending, some of the slaves had been sold to Americans, in violation of the slave-trade bans. No one on the Court seemed to be concerned by this. Nor was anyone apparently concerned that the American crewmen on the French privateer had violated federal bans on slave trading after *L'Epine* had captured the *Alerta*. For the Marshall Court, this was just a complicated maritime case centering on who owned the cargo; the Court was unconcerned with the fate of the human beings who made up that cargo. The Court might have remanded the case to consider the violations of the slave trade bans, but it did not do so.

In 1820, in *The Josefa Segunda,* the Supreme Court finally upheld a judgment against a slave trader.[22] The ship was originally Cuban, but had been seized by Venezuelan privateers. An American ship seized *The Josefa Segunda* "hovering on the coast of the United States" near New Orleans with its cargo of African slaves. Such "hovering" violated the slave-trade suppression laws. The Court held that when a ship was legitimately captured by a privateer, the ownership, including the cargo, transferred to the privateer. Thus the slaves on *The Josefa Segunda* were legally the property of the privateer, and not of the Cubans who had once owned them.[23]

Speaking for the Court, Justice Henry Brockholst Livingston, a New Yorker, concluded that the ship could provide no plausible reason for "hovering" off the coast of Louisiana other than planning to land its slaves illegally in New Orleans, where they might be worth as much as a thousand dollars each. The explanations of the captain, that he was attempting to reach a nearby island and had entered U.S. waters in distress, were patently fraudulent. Livingston bluntly concluded there was "no reasonable doubt of the whole story being a fiction."[24] Thus, for the first time, the Marshall court upheld the seizure and condemnation of a slaver and its cargo. Marshall, however, did not write this opinion.

In 1823 Marshall wrote another opinion in a slave trade case, and once again he failed to uphold the prosecution of a slaver. In March 1818 *The Mary Ann* surreptitiously departed from either New York City or Perth Amboy, New Jersey, without giving a proper manifest of its cargo to the collector of either port, as required by the 1807 slave-trade act. Under that law, any vessel of forty tons or more going from one part of the United States to another had to register all slaves on board. This was to prevent the illegal acquisition of slaves during the voyage, who would then be fraudulently landed at an American port as slaves from another part of the country. During the voyage, *The Mary Ann* had in fact taken on thirty-six slaves, either from the Spanish gulf coast or from an African trader while at sea.

The libel charged the ship with failing to provide the manifest at either port, because the prosecutor in New Orleans did not know which port the ship had actually used. In a very narrow opinion, Marshall held that the libel was void because the ship was only required to file paperwork at one port, not two. But this conclusion ignored the reality that the ship had not filed its manifest in *either* port. Marshall also ignored the reality that when slave traders were violating federal law, they would naturally be as surreptitious as possible.

Marshall also found that the libel was flawed because it did not assert that the ship was at least forty tons, the minimum weight for bringing the ship under the statute. This may have been an oversight, but it was hardly one that affected the illegality of importing slaves into the United States. The prosecutor was able to win his case in New Orleans because everyone involved in the case knew that a ship with that many slaves on it, embarking on a voyage from New York to New Orleans, would be over forty tons. Marshall actually conceded that it was "in general, true that it is sufficient for a libel to charge the offence in the very words which direct the forfeiture" and that therefore, by prosecuting the libel in order to have the ship forfeited, the prosecutor implicitly charged the ship with being over forty tons. Moreover, the defense could have showed the weight of the ship at trial if it was less than forty tons. But Marshall, who was so flexible in other cases, especially admiralty cases, still found the libel flawed because it failed to state the obvious—that the ship was over forty tons.

Marshall reversed the forfeiture, even as he noted that "there is much reason to believe that the offence for which the forfeiture is claimed has been committed." Marshall did remand the case, however, with instructions "to allow the libel to be amended." A new libel would have separate counts setting out the failure to give the manifest to authorities in each port, and also allege that the ship weighed more than forty tons.[25]

Marshall's technical ruling here was inconsistent with his great opinions in cases including *Marbury* v. *Madison, M'Culloch* v. *Maryland,* and *Cohens* v. *Virginia,* as well as inconsistent with his position that technicalities were less important in admiralty cases. His willingness to remand the case to allow a new libel appears to support the ban on the trade *and* to respect technical legal rules. But this is somewhat misleading. The ship had sailed for Louisiana in 1818. It took five years, until 1823, for the case to reach the U.S. Supreme Court. A new libel and a trial would have taken more time. By then witnesses might have disappeared or died. The owners of the ship would still have the use of the vessel, making money from it, while the new case was prepared. And of course the illegally imported slaves would continue to remain in the possession of those who purchased them. The case might never be renewed and then the slaves would never gain their freedom, despite the fact that there was "much reason to believe, that the offence for which the forfeiture is claimed has been committed."[26]

In 1824, a year after the decision in *The Mary Ann*, the Court's slave trade jurisprudence changed. The Court heard a series of slave trade cases, starting with the return of *The Caroline*. Here Justice Livingston, speaking for the Court, upheld that prosecution. Livingston also wrote for the Court in a complicated set of cases known as *The Merino*.[27] The traders in these cases claimed they were headed to Spanish colonies, where the trade was legal, and that any violations of the U.S. laws were due to weather or other unforeseen circumstances. The trial courts rejected these patently dishonest and fraudulent claims. The owners of these ships made various technical arguments about the forms of the libels and other proceedings, which the Court rejected. Justice Livingston asserted "that technical niceties of the common law, as to informations, which are unimportant in themselves, and stand only on precedents, are not regarded in Admiralty information."[28] After a very careful review of each of these cases, the Court upheld one of the sentences, remanded two of the cases for retrial with an amended libel, and returned one ship with its slaves to its Cuban owners, who were legally able to trade slaves into Cuba and then legally transship them to the Spanish colony at Pensacola.[29] The most important aspect of this case was the Court's willingness to accept that there should be flexibility in the application of "technical niceties of the common law" in slave trade prosecutions. Significantly, Marshall did not write any of these opinions.

In the same Court term, Justice William Johnson sustained the prosecution of a slaver in *The St. Jago de Cuba*. Here the Court reversed a lower court ruling that favored the defendants and supported the arguments of the United States government. Again, Marshall was not the author of this opinion, upholding a slave trade prosecution.

The Court had now begun to support the American suppression of the African slave trade, but the Chief Justice remained strangely silent. In his twenty-three years in the center chair he had *never* written an opinion supporting black freedom or attempts to punish slave traders. In every case where he wrote an opinion blacks were denied freedom and slave traders went unpunished. In his last decade on the bench the Great Chief Justice would continue this record.

The *Antelope* Case and the Last Years of the Marshall Court

The starkest example of Marshall's stubborn support for slavery was in the protracted litigation of *The Antelope*.[30] This complex slave trade case came before the Court three times, with Marshall writing the first opinion in 1825.

On December 19, 1819 an American ship, *The Columbia*, left Baltimore with a mixed crew that included some Americans posing as citizens of other countries. Supposedly the captain had a commission as a privateer from the Venezuelan admiral Luis Brión, but this was a ruse. After a month at sea the ship renamed itself the *Arraganta*, raised the flag of revolutionary Uruguay, and continued as a privateer under a commission from José Artigas, the "Protector of the Eastern Shore," as he called himself.[31] Artigas was leading revolutionary Uruguay in a war with both Spain and Portugal. Cruising the African coast, the *Arraganta* seized slaves from various Spanish and Portuguese ships as well as from an illegal American slaver, *The Exchange*, from Bristol, Rhode Island. Ultimately, the *Arraganta* captured *The Antelope*, which had just filled its hold with African slaves for a voyage to Cuba. Both ships sailed for Brazil, in order to sell the slaves.

When the *Arraganta* was wrecked off the coast of Brazil, the surviving crewmen and Africans moved to *The Antelope*, which now headed north, unsuccessfully attempting to sell its slaves at various Caribbean ports. Ultimately *The Antelope* reached the northeastern coast of Spanish Florida. The ship now flew an American flag so it would not be attacked by Spanish vessels. In June 1820, *The Dallas*, an American revenue cutter, seized *The Antelope*, with 281 slaves on board, off the northern coast of Florida. After arresting her American captain, John Smith under the 1807 and 1819 laws, Captain John Jackson of *The Dallas* took *The Antelope* to Savannah. The U.S. government successfully condemned the ship under the federal laws that prohibited slavers from lingering off the American coast. This was the beginning of an eight-year legal saga which included three Supreme Court decisions.

The status of the Africans on *The Antelope* remained unclear. Witnesses from Cuba armed with documents arrived to claim both the ship and its human cargo. If the Africans were slaves they were worth a small fortune. If free people, as the U.S. government contended, they had to be returned to Africa. By the time the case first went to trial there would be 212 Africans in the custody of the United States marshal. Some had died from illness and some had been stolen and were doubtless working on plantations in Georgia. Some may also have been illegally sold as slaves or in some other way conveyed to planters near Savannah.[32]

In December 1820 the prosecution of John Smith, the captain of *The Antelope*, came before U.S. District Judge William J. Davies. The prosecution charged Smith with piracy for his actions at sea. He would eventually be acquitted of this charge. Oddly he was not charged with violating the American ban on importing slaves, for which he might easily have been convicted.

This trial took place before slavery had become *the* central issue of American politics, before the rise of an aggressive abolitionist movement threatened southerners, and before the Nullification Crisis, which exacerbated feelings of sectionalism. Grand juries had indicted slave traders in both Charleston and New Orleans, and so it is not unreasonable to believe the same sort of indictment could have been obtained in Savannah. In addition, the prosecutor could have charged Smith with numerous violations of the many laws prohibiting the trade without seeking a death penalty. The piracy charge, without tying his actions to illegal slave trading, was particularly weak. The evidence (and many of the specific provisions of the indictment) focused on various items he had removed from the ships he had helped capture. Most of these were small items of little value and the jury may not have been impressed that acquiring such things really constituted piracy. In addition, Smith claimed that he was acting under a valid commission as a privateer, and thus seizing ships of the enemy and taking goods from them was legal.[33] As a privateer, however, he had no commission authorizing him to smuggle slaves into the United States or to "hover" outside US territorial waters with a ship full of slaves. Thus, it seems in retrospect that a slave trading charge would have been more effective. It certainly would have been more honest. After the jury acquitted him for piracy, the government did not attempt to charge him under the slave trade suppression laws, and Smith was eventually released from custody.

In January and February 1821 Judge Davies presided over a second trial where he ordered that the surviving Africans be divided into three groups: slaves belonging to Spanish (Cuban) owners; slaves belonging to Portuguese claimants; and Africans who had been taken from an American ship and were thus free under U.S. law. His allocations were arbitrary and transparently proslavery. Of the 212 Africans in the custody of the marshal, only 7—about 3 percent—were allocated to the American ship, and thus likely to be freed, even though originally 15 percent of the Africans had been taken from the American ship.[34]

Had Davies followed the precedent of *The Josefa Segunda* he might have determined that all the Africans were victims of the illegal slave trade because *The Antelope* had tried to smuggle them into the United States. In *The Josefa Segunda*, the Supreme Court determined that when a ship was captured by a legitimate privateer during wartime, ownership legally transferred to the privateer. Under such a ruling the privateers would have legally owned all the Africans on *The Antelope*, and because *The Antelope* was trying to smuggle them into the United States, all the Africans would have been forfeited and returned to Africa.

But the proslavery Davies ruled that John Smith was not a legitimate privateer because his commission was from a revolutionary government and thus his actions were more like piracy than a legitimate seizure in war time. This was truly an odd position for an American judge to take since, during the American Revolution, the revolutionary government of the United States had commissioned many privateers and no one, at least in the United States, had ever considered them to be pirates. Furthermore, in *The Josefa Segunda*, the Supreme Court had set a very low bar for determining if a ship was a legitimate privateer. In that case Justice Livingston found that the ship was legitimately a privateer because "Among the exhibits is a copy of a commission, which is all that, in such a case, can be expected, which appears to have been issued under the authority of the republic of Venezuela." It did not matter that the United States did not recognize the revolutionary government in Venezuela; it only mattered that "it is well known that open war exists between them and his Catholic Majesty, in which the United States maintain strict neutrality." Under such circumstances the United States had to "respect the belligerent rights of both parties; and does not treat as pirates, the cruizers of either, so long as they act under, and within the scope of their respective commissions."[35] This was exactly the same situation as the privateers who captured *The Antelope,* and therefore, its cargo had legitimately transferred to the privateers. Under this standard, *The Antelope* was a legitimate privateer—and in that case, because the slaves would then belong to the ship, Smith could easily have been convicted of trying to illegally import slaves into the United

States, and all the Africans would have been turned over to the president to be returned to the continent of their birth.

Davies was not interested in history, logic, or a recent Supreme Court precedent. He was, it seems, interested in turning freeborn Africans into slaves. Thus he determined that the Africans were in fact legitimately held as slaves by the Spanish and Portuguese slave traders, and that they were illegally removed from the Spanish and Portuguese ships contrary to international law because Smith was a pirate. This analysis seems surreal in light of the verdict earlier in December that Smith was not a pirate, but rather, under the precedent in *The Josefa Segunda,* a legitimate privateer.

The United States appealed these results to the circuit court, where Justice William Johnson affirmed the general outcome, although he ruled that sixteen, not seven, Africans came from an American ship and should be repatriated to Liberia. Johnson indicated that the claims of the Portuguese were not yet proved, but he gave the Portuguese vice counsel another bite at the apple—another opportunity to prove that someone from Portugal or Brazil had a legitimate and legal claim to these Africans. Without that proof more Africans would gain their freedom, but Johnson was quite lenient in allowing the Portuguese government to come up with someone who had a plausible claim to some of the Africans. Johnson also dealt with the complicated question of which Africans would go to Liberia and which would be turned into slaves, owned by Spanish and Portuguese claimants. His solution was for lots to be drawn. Sixteen lucky Africans would go to Liberia; the remaining unlucky Africans would be slaves for life. Johnson ignored the precedent of *The Josefa Segunda,* which could have been used to send all the Africans to Liberia.

The case ultimately went to the Supreme Court, by which time fewer than two hundred Africans were alive and in custody. Chief Justice Marshall ruled that some of the slaves on this ship were to be returned to the Spanish government because they had been lawfully owned by Spanish subjects when the ship was captured in American waters. Marshall ignored the recent precedent in *The Josefa Segunda* which pointed to an outcome of all the Africans going to Liberia. Marshall ruled that all the remaining Africans, those claimed by Americans and others, were to be turned over to the U.S. government as the fruit of the illegal trade. The Court rejected the Portuguese claims in part because no ship owners had stepped forward to make a claim.

In *The Antelope* Marshall asserted that "sacred rights of liberty and property come in conflict with each other."[36] This was only true if Marshall accepted the legitimacy of the African slave trade and, equally important, the legitimacy of the claims of the Cubans to the ship. If Marshall had applied the precedent in *The Josefa Segunda*, Marshall would have ruled that the Spanish owners lost their "rights of . . . property" when *The Antelope* was legally seized by a privateer, and the privateer lost his "rights of . . . property" when he tried to smuggle the slaves into the United States in violation of federal law. Here was a pro-freedom strategy that was consistent with international law, the law of privateers, and the Supreme Court's precedents.

But Marshall did not follow *The Josefa Segunda*, which was not a decision he had written. As he had in every case relevant to slavery or the slave trade in which he did write the opinion of the Court, he ruled that property rights stood higher than liberty or human rights. Marshall firmly supported the sacredness of property over liberty, even in the African slave trade.

Marshall admitted that the African trade was "contrary to the law of nature" but asserted it was "consistent with the law of nations" and "cannot in itself be piracy."[37] Under this analysis the Court recognized the right of foreigners to engage in the slave trade if their own nations allowed them to do so. This conclusion ignored the fact that Congress had prohibited any importation of African slaves into the United States and declared that slave trading was piracy. Marshall's analysis allowed the Court to uphold prosecutions of American traders because they violated the U.S. prohibition on the African trade, while also protecting the property rights of foreign nationals from lands where the trade was legal.

Marshall's rejection of natural law was problematic. Marshall had used natural-law arguments in contract cases including *Fletcher* v. *Peck* (1810) and *Dartmouth College* v. *Woodward* (1819). Two years after this case, he would make a strong natural-law argument in his dissent in *Ogden* v. *Saunders* (1827), the only dissent he ever wrote in a constitutional law case. This opinion "is notable for its extension of natural-law protection to contractual agreements."[38] His *Antelope* opinion contrasts with his *Saunders* dissent, where Marshall relied on a higher morality, natural law, to condemn a law that allowed insolvents to declare bankruptcy and not have to pay their debts. This dissent with its heavy emphasis on natural law was written only two years after he asserted that natural law was inapplicable to the Africans found on *The Antelope*.

In *Saunders* Marshall invoked natural law to bolster his view that New York's bankruptcy law was unconstitutional. He rejected positive law in the bankruptcy case because it conflicted with natural law: "If, on tracing the right to contract, and the obligations created by contract, to their source, we find them to exist anterior to, and independent of society, we may reasonably conclude that those original and pre-existing principles are, like many other natural rights, brought with man into society; and, although they may be controlled, are not given by human legislation."[39] He argued that his view of contract law "is, undoubtedly, much strengthened by the authority of those writers on natural and national law, whose opinions have been viewed with profound respect by the wisest men of the present, and of past ages."[40]

In *The Antelope* the Great Chief Justice had the opportunity to condemn slavery and the African trade and to uphold and enforce a series of federal laws, using natural law as well as the jurisprudence of many European jurists he admired. Marshall began by noting that:

> the course of opinion on the slave trade should be unsettled, ought to excite no surprise. The Christian and civilized nations of the world, with whom we have most intercourse, have all been engaged in it. However abhorrent this traffic may be to a mind whose original feelings are not blunted by familiarity with the practice, it has been sanctioned in modern times by the laws of all nations who possess distant colonies, each of whom has engaged in it as a common commercial business which no other could rightfully interrupt. It has claimed all the sanction which could be derived from long usage, and general acquiescence. That trade could not be considered as contrary to the law of nations which was authorized and protected by the laws of all commercial nations; the right to carry on which was claimed by each, and allowed by each.

He later noted: "Public sentiment has, in both countries [Britain and the U.S.], kept pace with the measures of government; and the opinion is extensively, if not universally entertained, that this unnatural traffic ought to be suppressed."[41]

Citing and quoting various British cases, Marshall observed it could "scarcely be denied" that slavery was "contrary to the law of nature." Even as the owner of at least one hundred-and-fifty slaves at this point in his life (after having conveyed about forty slaves to one of his sons), Marshall conceded that it was "generally admitted" that "every man has a natural right to the fruits of his own labour" and noted that the implication "that no other person can rightfully deprive him of those fruits, and appropriate them against his will, seems to be the necessary result of this admission."[42] This argument is akin to another he would make two years later, in *Ogden* v. *Saunders*. But these arguments did not lead to the liberation of the Africans. Being contrary to natural law did not make the slave trade contrary to international law.

Turning again to foreign law, Marshall's opinion relied on Sir William Scott of the British High Court of Admiralty to assert that slave trading was not piracy under international law: "The act of trading in slaves, however detestable, was not, he said, 'the act of freebooters, enemies of the human race, renouncing every country, and ravaging every country, in its coasts and vessels, indiscriminately.' It was not piracy." Marshall almost always respected and enforced federal statutes but, here, despite a federal law which in fact declared slave trading to be piracy, Marshall let international law and his own proslavery views trump American domestic law.[43]

Although American statutes provided that illegally imported slaves should be returned to Africa, Marshall was not ready to apply American law, in an American court, to slaves illegally smuggled into an American port on a ship under an American captain with a number of Americans in the crew. Similarly, while American law declared participation in the African slave trade to be piracy, Chief Justice Marshall refused to apply the American law of piracy in an American court. Instead, he asserted about the African slave trade: "If it is consistent with the law of nations, it cannot in itself be piracy. It can be made so only by statute; and the obligation of the statute cannot transcend the legislative power of the state which may enact it."[44] The problem with this argument is that U.S. law *had* declared slave trading to be piracy by statute and *The Antelope* had voluntarily entered U.S. waters.

Here, then, was an opportunity to apply American law in an American court to a great humanitarian issue. Kent Newmyer has described international law as the "least confining" tradition Marshall could draw on to fashion a body of law.[45] With the flexibility afforded by it, and his support for natural law, Marshall might have concluded that the law of the United States required that all the slaves aboard *The Antelope* be returned to Africa. He could even have done this without pushing the issue of capital punishment and piracy for the slave trader, since this was not before him.[46] This was an opportunity to use the liberating aspects of American law to overcome the older, repressive law of nations that allowed the African slave trade.

Alternatively, Marshall could have freed the slaves based on the Court's recent precedent on the law of privateers in *The Josefa Segunda*. This would not have undermined the Court's credibility with southerners or with foreign jurists. It would also have been consistent with America's own political traditions of recognizing revolutionary regimes. Marshall has been called a "child of the Revolution" because his politics and ideology largely stemmed from his experiences during the Revolution.[47] But *The Antelope* suggests he no longer recalled America's revolutionary tradition, at least in cases involving slavery.

Following this decision, the Court remanded the case to the circuit court to sort out which Africans were to be retained as slaves, and which were to be sent back to Africa as free people. In 1826 the Supreme Court sent a second mandate to the circuit court in response to the question of whether the slaves should be separated "by lot, or upon proof on the part of the Spanish claimant." The Supreme Court declared, in a one-paragraph "certificate to the Circuit Court," that it should be "by proof made to the satisfaction of that court."[48]

A year later, the case came back again to the Court. The circuit court had separated out the Africans, having determined that thirty-nine were owned by the Spanish claimant and should be returned to him. The other Africans were "to be delivered to the United States to be disposed of according to law." The circuit court was uncertain, however, whether it could deliver the Africans to the United States government when there were still remaining costs to be paid by it. The U.S. marshal who had been feeding and housing the Africans claimed to have spent a substantial sum of money and did not want to let the Africans out of his custody until he was reimbursed. Justice Robert Trimble, speaking for the Court, held that whatever the marshal was owed, it could not affect the status of the Africans who were to be repatriated to Liberia. Trimble also noted that originally the Spanish had owned ninety-three slaves, and were initially awarded fifty of the slaves who were still alive. But the Spanish could only offer proof of ownership for thirty-nine which the Court decreed should be returned to the Spanish clamant. The rest were to "be delivered to the United States, unconditionally" to be returned to Africa.[49] This opinion recognized the humanity of the remaining Africans and their right to be returned to Africa. Significantly, Chief Justice Marshall did not write this opinion.

In 1825, along with *The Antelope*, the Court heard two more slave trade cases. The Court revisited *The Josefa Segunda*, with Justice Story certifying the distribution of proceeds from the sale of the slaves illegally brought into the U.S. That ship had been prosecuted under the 1807 slave trade act, which required the sale of contraband slaves for the benefit of the U.S. government and the captors of the ship. *The Antelope*, on the other hand, had been adjudicated under the 1819 act which provided that illegally imported Africans be sent to Liberia.

Justice Story also upheld the condemnation of *The Plattsburgh*, an American-built ship used to transport Africans to Cuba. This ship had cleared Baltimore Harbor in 1819 under the command of an American captain. The Americans then fraudulently sold the ship to a Cuban named Marino, but the original American captain remained in command. Thus the ship was condemned, with Justice Story denouncing the notorious nature of fraudulent transactions in Cuba by Americans who persisted in trying to import slaves from Africa.[50] Once again, the Court affirmed the condemnation of a slaver, but Marshall did not write the opinion.

In 1830 the case of the *Josefa Segunda* returned to the Supreme Court. At issue were the proceeds from the sale of the Africans found on the ship. Louisiana officials had sold the Africans for about $83,000, which they planned to donate to the charity hospital of New Orleans. This sale was conducted under the 1807 law banning the slave trade, which provided for the sale of slaves illegally brought into the United States for the benefit of the state where the illegally imported slaves landed. By the time the sale took place, however, the laws had changed; now illegally imported Africans were to be delivered to the President of the United States for repatriation in Liberia. Justice William Johnson ruled that Louisiana was not entitled to the money because it had not been entitled to sell the slaves. But the Court did not order that the sales of the Africans be voided and the actual people be returned to Africa. Nor did the Court require that the state find the Africans and repurchase them, or take them in eminent domain proceedings, so they could be sent to Liberia. In clear disregard for the applicable federal laws, the Africans remained slaves in Louisiana and the United States gained some money.[51]

Marshall's last opinion in a slave trade case exhibited the confusion and sometimes bizarre results of his Court's slave trade jurisprudence. The caption of the case was confusing in itself: *Sundry African Slaves, The Governor of Georgia, Claimant, Appellant, v. Juan Madrazo; The Governor of Georgia, Appellant, v. Sundry African Slaves, Juan Madrazo Claimant* (1828).[52] The facts were equally confusing.

Juan Madrazo owned the *Isabelita,* a ship used in the legal slave trade between Africa and Spanish Cuba. In 1817, while returning from Africa, it was captured by the *Successor,* a privateer originally built in the United States, fitted and armed in the United States, and "commanded by one Moore, an American citizen."[53] Moore operated under the authority of Louis Michel Aury, who is variously described as both a pirate and a privateer serving various revolutionary groups in Mexico, Columbia, and Venezuela.[54] At the time, Aury was operating out of Amelia Island, just off the northeast coast of Florida, under

a privateer commission granted by the revolutionary government in New Grenada (Colombia). Aury condemned the *Isabelita* at a prize court hearing, and William Bowen then
bought the slaves and took them into Georgia, claiming that
he intended to bring them later to Spanish Florida for sale.
He claimed that he was forced to go to Georgia because of
military conflict in Florida, but of course the federal laws
banning the importation of slaves into the United States did
not allow an exemption for such circumstances. American officials confiscated the slaves under the 1807 act prohibiting
the African slave trade, and the governor of Georgia sold
some of the slaves "without any process of law, and the
proceeds paid over to the treasurer of Georgia."[55] The state
retained custody of the remaining slaves. Meanwhile, Moore
began using Madrazo's ship, but foolishly sailed it to George-
town, South Carolina, where customs officials seized it.
The United States District Court ultimately returned it to
Madrazo.

Bowen, Madrazo, and the state of Georgia all claimed the
slaves. The governor wanted the Court to certify his state's
right to the slaves and to the proceeds from the slaves who had
already been sold to people in Georgia. The governor indicated that the state was prepared to give the remaining
slaves to the American Colonization Society for resettlement
in Liberia. In his dissent in the U.S. Supreme Court, Justice
William Johnson explicitly described the case as having been
brought by the state on behalf of the Colonization Society.
Bowen claimed the slaves, arguing that he had not violated
the bans on the slave trade but had only entered Georgia to
avoid on-going military conflict in Spanish Florida, and that
he had no intention of keeping the slaves in Georgia. Madrazo
claimed the slaves on the grounds that Aury was a pirate, not

a legitimate privateer, and that the prize court he convened on Amelia Island was illegal (and thus Bowen could not have legally bought the slaves from Moore). Bolstering Madrazo's claim that the slaves should be returned to him was the fact that the District Court in South Carolina had already returned *The Isabelita* to him.

The District Court in Georgia dismissed the claims of Bowen and Madrazo and "directed that the slaves remaining unsold should be delivered" to Georgia's governor and that the proceeds of those sold should remain in the state treasury." On appeal, the U.S. Circuit Court reversed the dismissal of Madrazo's claim, and awarded him all the remaining slaves and the proceeds from those already sold.[56] This was probably a technically correct application of existing law because Moore, as an American, could not have legally been a privateer and thus his seizure of the *Isabelita* was illegal, and all transactions after that were illegal.

Both Georgia and Bowen appealed to U.S. Supreme Court, while Madrazo defended the circuit court ruling. Before the Supreme Court, Georgia suddenly argued that under the Eleventh Amendment the federal courts had no jurisdiction because, under the Eleventh Amendment, neither Bowen nor Madrazo could sue the state of Georgia without its permission. Thus, Georgia argued that the federal courts could not order the governor of Georgia to relinquish either the remaining slaves or the proceeds from those that had been sold.[57] Up to this point, Georgia had raised no jurisdictional issues and had willingly participated in the case. Nevertheless, Chief Justice Marshall held that this case was in effect a suit against the state of Georgia, in violation of the Eleventh Amendment. The result was that neither Bowen nor Madrazo could make a claim for the slaves.

The slaveholding Justice William Johnson from South Carolina, who had heard this case in the circuit court, bitterly dissented, setting out the real facts of the case, arguing that the outcome was deeply unjust. Johnson argued that the entire case had been initiated by Georgia, which had not only been a willing party to the case, but had actually initiated some of the proceedings—and thus Johnson argued Georgia had waived any Eleventh Amendment claim. "Where" he asked "is the provision of the Constitution, which disables a state from suing in the Courts of the Union?"[58] He argued that Georgia raised the jurisdictional issue before the Supreme Court only when it lost on the merits of the case before the circuit court.

Johnson explained that many of the "facts" in the record were false and that the state "had no interest" in the case "at least, in its inception," but had initially brought the case on behalf of the American Colonization Society, to allow Georgia to give the remaining slaves to the Society. At some point that changed, however, and as Johnson explained, it was "notorious" that both "the slaves, as well as the proceeds of those which were sold . . . have, in fact, been delivered up by the state . . . to Bowen." Johnson argued that this proved that the state was "not contending for herself."[59] The Eleventh Amendment claim was legally inapplicable.

Johnson argued that the real owner of the slaves was Madrazo, since they had been stolen from him by Aury and Moore. By using the Eleventh Amendment to deny Madrazo the right to make his claim, Marshall insured that these illegally imported slaves would remain in Georgia, and that Bowen would gain for his violation of the laws banning the importation of slaves. An alternative theory of the case would have recognized the legitimacy of the prize court, with the conclusion that Madrazo lost all rights to the slaves at that point. Under this theory Bowen gained legal possession of the slaves, but he would have lost all rights to them when he illegally imported them into Georgia. This would have meant the slaves were free and should be returned to Africa. No one on the Supreme Court endorsed this analysis and outcome. A few years after this case, in his last decision on slavery, Marshall summarily rejected an attempt by Madrazo to obtain compensation for the slaves taken from him.[60] Thus, the slaves remained in Georgia, in the possession of the state, which was free to keep them, sell them, or return them to Bowen.

An Uncreative Jurisprudence

John Marshall is rightly seen as one of the most innovative jurists in our history. His opinions were often masterpieces of brilliant thinking, penetrating logic, and creative jurisprudence. When Marshall wanted to reach a certain result, he rarely faltered, and usually explained his position with unassailable logic and forceful theory. Marshall rarely left a crack—much less a hole—in his argument for some opponent to penetrate. He could take a mundane issue, like Marbury's commission to be a justice of the peace, and turn it into a major constitutional event, almost always expanding national power in the process.

In *Dartmouth College* v. *Woodward* (1819), Marshall deftly turned a political fight in a small state (New Hampshire) over the fate of a tiny college into a major opinion about contract rights.[61] In adjudicating the fallout from the great Yazoo Land fraud, he found that lands legitimately purchased from the state of Georgia had been legally sold to subsequent purchasers, even though the original land sale was a result of a bribed state legislature. Marshall concluded that subsequent purchasers could establish good title to the land.[62] In this and other cases he helped secure the rights of land purchasers and set the stage for a more orderly settlement of the young nation's western lands. As a major land speculator and the owner of vast acreage throughout Virginia and Kentucky, Marshall doubtless had more than an intellectual interest in this case.

He could find power in the necessary and proper clause of the Constitution to enable Congress to charter a bank, despite the fact that nothing in the Constitution appeared to enable Congress to start a bank or grant a corporate charter.[63] In upholding the constitutionality of the Bank of the United States in *M'Culloch* v. *Maryland,* Marshall again expanded the power of Congress and the supremacy of the Constitution in what is generally considered to be his greatest opinion. These cases illustrate his creative jurisprudence in developing Constitutional law to meet the needs of the new nation.

Sadly, Marshall's slavery jurisprudence, although not aggressively proslavery, always ensured that slaves did not get their freedom, and that whites did not suffer unduly for their illegal slave trading. Chief Justice Marshall dealt with issues of race, slavery, and Indian rights as we might expect from a slaveholding Virginian. As he shaped our Constitution in America's formative years, Marshall never transcended his social class, his cultural assumptions, his oft-stated fears of free blacks, and his huge financial investment in human beings.

Greatness is achieved in many ways, but one measure is the ability to rise above one's origins, surroundings, and social class to look at larger issues. Marshall's opinions on race and slavery, although not as famous—or infamous—as those of his successor, nevertheless helped set the stage for the massive constitutional protection of slavery and the federal support of white supremacy until the Civil War. Similarly, his jurisprudence on Indians that limited the rights of indigenous peoples established precedents that still haunt our culture. Consider his last opinion on this issue, in *Worcester* v. *Georgia*.[64] It is sometimes seen as a failed attempt to gain a measure of justice for the Cherokee and by extension all Indians—but the thrust of that opinion was to protect the rights of the national government to enforce treaties against the states and not to respect the rights of indigenous peoples.

In Marshall's slave trade and freedom suit opinions we see the finest legal mind in the nation—the most creative jurist of his age—using his intellectual strength to protect slave traders and rivet the chains of bondage on blacks who had strong claims to freedom. For Marshall the only issues in most slave cases were the property rights and economic interests of businesses, entrepreneurs, and slave owners. In close cases, where he admits statutes are ambiguous, Marshall supported slavery and rejected freedom. These cases diminish the greatness of the "Great Chief Justice."

One of Marshall's most admiring biographers argues that his slavery cases were "routine cases of statutory construction and application of the rules of evidence."[65] But such an analysis obscures the fact that Marshall always construed statutes and rules of evidence, and resolved all ambiguities, in favor of slavery. If they were routine, why did he consistently reverse lower courts that found slaves to be free? If the cases were routine, why did Marshall consistently support slave traders, protecting them from statutes designed to suppress what most of the civilized world considered the greatest horror of the age? While he was ready to use natural rights to support contracts, land purchases, or oppose bankruptcy laws, he categorically opposed the application of natural law to the greatest human rights violation of the age. During the Virginia Constitutional Convention of 1829 Marshall made it clear he did not believe in the "natural rights of Man."[66] When it came to slaves or free blacks, Marshall saw people who were entitled to almost no rights. Marshall never adopted the harsh language of Chief Justice Taney, who asserted that blacks were "so far inferior, that they had no rights which the white man was bound to respect."[67] But he certainly reflected those sentiments in his jurisprudence, in the Virginia constitutional convention, as a leader of the American Colonization Society, and in his massive acquisition of slaves throughout his life.

One of Marshall's biographers argues that "the interest" in these slave cases "lies principally in showing the chief justice's characteristic determination to stick to the well-trod path of the law, untempted by the seductive call of the emotions."[68] Such an argument does not ring true. His angry dissent in *Ogden* v. *Saunders* suggests that where money and contracts were involved, Marshall could be emotional. Indeed, Marshall followed few well-trod paths. His famous opinions in *Marbury, Fletcher* v. *Peck, M'Culloch, Dartmouth College, Gibbons,* and *Cohens* v. *Virginia* are correctly seen as "great" opinions precisely because they did not follow the "well-trod path." We do not revere Marshall for his ability to follow the same path as all other judges before him, but for his ability to shape the law.

When human liberty was at stake he was less engaged. When claims of liberty challenged property rights, Marshall was coldly analytical, applying his immense intellectual power to explain why people who had legitimate claims to freedom should remain slaves or to explain why people who had notoriously violated the ban on the slave trade should not be punished or even denied the fruits of their illegal activity. When it came to slavery and freedom Marshall in some cases chose to go against the well-trod path of the law—in order to preserve slave property.

When considering the fates of African Americans, slaves, and the people he bought and sold, conveyed to his sons, and used to support his lifestyle, Marshall always supported slavery and consistently opposed liberty. When it came to slaves who had a legitimate claim to freedom under the laws of Virginia or Maryland and when it came to Africans illegally transported to the United States as slaves, Marshall shaped the law in favor of human bondage. In the end, the Great Chief Justice was, sadly, supremely unjust.

4

Joseph Story: New England Icon in the Service of Slavery

$\mathbf{A}$ NATIVE OF Massachusetts, the first state to totally abolish slavery, Joseph Story came to the Court with a New Englander's hostility to slavery. His numerous treatises became fundamental tools in creating a national legal system. His most important work, *Commentaries on the Constitution,* was strongly nationalist and hostile to states' rights. He fiercely supported the supremacy of the Constitution and the national government. His opinion in *Martin* v. *Hunter's Lessee* (1816)—rejecting Virginia's attempts to seize land owned by a British subject in violation of the treaty ending the American Revolution and the Jay Treaty of 1794—is arguably the most powerful statement of judicial nationalism from the Founding to the Civil War.[1] As a Harvard professor he trained many elite, nationalistic lawyers who became leaders of their profession, serving banks, commercial enterprises, and the emerging manufacturing economy. Some of Story's other students, including Wendell Phillips, Richard Henry Dana, and Charles Sumner, were even more famous as abolitionists and political supporters of racial equality.

Although raised in Massachusetts and educated at Harvard, both Federalist bastions, by 1803 Story had become a partisan Jeffersonian. This was the party of slavery, and northern Jeffersonians had to negotiate a compromise with that. Some New England Jeffersonians tried to shift the argument, claiming that they were resisting the "slavery" of Federalist aristocrats who wanted to "launch this country from liberty to slavery, from republican to a monarchical government."[2] Absurd as this rhetoric sounds today, it allowed northern Jeffersonians to deflect the critique that they were supporting the party of slavery.

Story ignored slavery in his enthusiasm for an idealized Jeffersonian Virginia, which he believed was "the most patriotic, disinterested and magnanimous state in the Union." He claimed to be "really at bottom a Virginian" because the "clime" was "more congenial with my nature than the petty prejudices and sullen coolness of New England" which was "Bigoted in opinion," and corrupted by the spirit of the Salem witch trials, though "we have no *witches* amongst us." Oblivious to southern slavery, he asserted that the "republican cause" was "founded on the immutable rights of man" and he was ready to make "any sacrifice for its preservation." Fueling his Jeffersonian zeal was a misplaced belief that Republicans supported a strong national government, and in the wake of the War of 1812, the Party would "extend the national authority over the whole extent of the power given by the Constitution."[3]

Story joined the Court in 1811 and quickly became a loyal ally of Chief Justice John Marshall. When Marshall denied a freedom claim to a slave whose mother had proved that she had never been a slave, Story backed the Chief Justice. When

Marshall denied slaves the opportunity to prove their freedom in *Mima Queen* v. *Hepburn*, Story silently concurred, refusing to join Justice Gabriel Duvall's persuasive and morally powerful dissent, even though Duvall and Story had been put on the Court by James Madison within months of each other.[4] Story never once strayed when the Chief Justice failed to vigorously enforce the federal laws banning the African slave trade.[5] In his early years on the Court, Justice Story said virtually nothing about slavery and never lifted his pen in defense of human liberty. He supported Chief Justice Marshall's proslavery jurisprudence.

Justice Story as a New Englander: The Missouri Crisis and the African Slave Trade

In 1815 Story vigorously attacked the morality of the African slave trade in his circuit court opinion in *Fales* v. *Mayberry*. Then, from 1819 to 1822, Story aggressively attacked the African slave trade and by implication slavery itself in charges to grand juries and in his circuit court opinion in *United States* v. *La Jeune Eugenie* (1822). No longer enamored with Virginia, Story sought "not only to preserve the Union under the Constitution but to make the nation over in the image of New England." Story believed New England virtue would "rescue America from Southern states' rights democracy and the corrupting genius of Thomas Jefferson." Story's contribution to this constitutional revolution can be found in some of his opinions, especially *Martin* v. *Hunter's Lessee*, and in his massive three-volume *Commentaries on the Constitution* (1833).[6] No longer a Jeffersonian, Story had moved into the nationalist wing of the old Republican Party that provided space for John Quincy Adams, Henry Clay, and Daniel Webster. By the 1830s these men would be firmly entrenched in the new Whig Party, while the political descendants of Thomas Jefferson would morph into the Democratic Party of Andrew Jackson, John C. Calhoun, and Roger B. Taney.

Story's brief period of antislavery exuberance stemmed in part from Virginia's growing and aggressive states' rights ideology, the debates in Congress over the Missouri Compromise, and the new federal legislation designed to fully suppress the illegal African slave trade. In the context of these issues Story became a reborn New Englander, forcefully opposing slavery.

The response of Virginia's leaders to Story's opinions in *Fairfax's Devisee* v. *Hunter's Lessee* (1812) and *Martin* v. *Hunter's Lessee* (1816) probably made Story regret his early admiration for Virginia. In *Fairfax's Devisee,* Story ruled that Virginia had violated treaties with England (and thus the Supremacy Clause of the Constitution) when the state confiscated some 300,000 acres of land once belonging to Thomas, Lord Fairfax, the former royal governor of the colony. A defiant Virginia Court of Appeals refused to obey Story's mandate in *Fairfax's Devisee* v. *Hunter's Lessee,* insisting the Supreme Court had no jurisdiction over the issue. Support for the state court decision came from what soon became known as the Richmond Junto, a group of aggressively states' rights, proslavery state political leaders; their spiritual and intellectual godfather was Thomas Jefferson, whom Story now saw as an enemy of constitutionalism and nationalism, and the source of Virginia's growing states' rights obsession.[7]

Virginia's defiance led to Story's remarkably powerful opinion in *Martin* v. *Hunter's Lessee,* which completely rejected Virginia's states' rights arguments while vindicating the authority of the Supreme Court and the supremacy clause of the Constitution. Virginia finally backed off, but *Martin* further infuriated the Richmond states' rights fanatics, including their intellectual leader, Jefferson, sitting on his mountaintop at Monticello. Three years later, Chief Justice Marshall upheld the constitutionality of the Bank of the United States in *M'Culloch* v. *Maryland* (1819) and shortly after that he asserted the power of the Court to hear a criminal appeal from a state court in *Cohens* v. *Virginia* (1822).[8] Story watched the Richmond Junto viciously attack John Marshall after *M'Culloch* and listened to Virginia's hyper-states' rights arguments in *Cohens*. The Virginians objected to the nationalizing effects of Marshall's and Story's opinions, even when, as in *Cohens*, they won the case. None of these cases was even remotely about slavery, but the Virginia crowd had exaggerated fears that these precedents would somehow be used to allow the national government to interfere with slavery.

In 1819 Missouri sought admission to the union as a slave state, with ten thousand slaves who constituted about 15 percent of the population. Northerners argued that Congress should apply the line between slavery and freedom established in the Northwest Ordinance to the territories west of the Mississippi. This would make Missouri a free state, because almost all of Missouri was north of the terminus of the Ohio River. Southerners responded that the Ohio River ended at the Mississippi River and the Northwest Ordinance applied only to the territories directly north of the Ohio River—the old northwest—and not to any new western territories.

The real issue was not the jurisdiction of the Northwest Ordinance or western geography, but whether it was prudent public policy to create a new slave state. Southerners wanted to bring slavery west as they settled the vast territories acquired by Jefferson from France in 1803. Northerners wanted to end the western expansion of slavery.

Unlike today, nineteenth-century Supreme Court justices were often politically active. John Marshall was the president of the Virginia branch of the American Colonization Society and a delegate to the Virginia state constitutional convention in 1829. From 1832 until 1860 John McLean was a potential presidential or vice presidential candidate in almost every election. Levi Woodbury, Story's successor on the Court, was considered a likely vice presidential candidate for 1852, until his untimely death. In 1818 Story accepted a quasi-political position as a member of the Harvard Board of Overseers, and in 1820 he was a delegate to the Massachusetts constitutional convention. In 1819 and 1820 Story publicly spoke his mind on the Missouri question.[9]

In December 1819, at a public meeting in his hometown of Salem, Story "forcefully" opposed admitting Missouri as a slave state, emphatically endorsing a resolution that asserted it was the "duty" of the government "to prevent the extension of so great a political and moral evil as slavery." Story agreed that prohibiting new slave states was both "constitutional and expedient." He argued that the "spirit of the Constitution, the principles of free government, the tenor of the Declaration of Independence, and the dictates of humanity and sound policy were all directly opposed to the extension of slavery." Story later drafted a memorial in Boston against admitting Missouri as a slave state, and Story was openly identified with vigorous opponents of the Compromise. When the Massachusetts congressional delegation supported the compromise admitting Missouri as a slave state, admitting Maine as a free state, and banning slavery in most of the rest of the Louisiana

Territory, Story complained that these representatives were "faint hearted" and he regretted their "weak, vacillating policy."[10]

Story noted that in these debates Virginia representative John Randolph of Roanoke "abused all the Eastern States in a most bitter style," in a "severe philippic" containing "a great many offensive allusions." Story pointed out that Randolph "let out the great secrets of Virginia, and babbled that policy by which she has hitherto bullied us, and led us, and wheedled us, and governed us."[11] No longer "at bottom a Virginian," Story was now truly a New Englander and thoroughly fed up with the pretensions of the Old Dominion's states' rights slaveocracy. He seemed remorseful for his former gushing admiration of Virginia. "We have foolishly suffered ourselves to be wheedled by Southern politicians," he wrote to Edward Everett, "until we have almost forgotten that the honors of the Constitution and the Union are as much our birthright and our protection, as the rest of the United States." Story hoped the Missouri crisis would "arouse the spirit of New England."[12]

While jettisoning his warm feelings for the social and political "clime" of Virginia, Story remained closely allied with his colleague and friend John Marshall and supported his jurisprudence that was hostile to free blacks and unsupportive of attempts to suppress the African slave trade. But, like Story, Marshall was a strong nationalist and fierce supporter of a powerful Constitution, and unlike Randolph and the states' rights Virginians, Marshall kept his views on slavery and race out of the public eye and did not flaunt his continuing investments in human flesh. Instead, he expressed alarm at the Richmond Junto and supported a compromise on Missouri— although, unlike Story, he wanted Missouri to enter the Union as a slave state.

Story opposed the expansion of slavery on moral grounds, but was also offended by the proslavery arrogance of the Virginia crowd. Like almost all lawyers, politicians, and jurists, Story did not believe that Congress or the Court could possibly threaten slavery in the states where it existed. He rejected the fearful fantasies of the proslavery Virginians who believed Congress and the Court were conspiring to end slavery.

As the circuit justice for most of New England, Story heard a smattering of cases involving the illegal African slave trade and he condemned the trade in powerful charges to federal grand juries. Banning the trade was the least controversial issue surrounding slavery. Since 1794, George Washington, John Adams, Thomas Jefferson, and James Monroe had signed laws regulating and then banning the trade. Even states' rights Virginians agreed that the Constitution empowered Congress to ban the trade.

Fales v. *Mayberry* (1815), Story's first slave-trade case, came out of Rhode Island, which had been a center of New England's small slave-trading industry before the Revolution and had emerged as a base for the illegal trade. Fales and others sued Mayberry over money owed them from an illegal slaving voyage in 1799, which brought 150 slaves to the Caribbean. At the time, the slave trade was legal in the British West Indies, but a 1794 law prohibited Americans from participating in the African trade as investors, sailors, owners, or outfitters of ships. Story ruled that the suit "cannot be maintained" because it was based on an illegal enterprise. The plaintiffs claimed they had not been parties to the illegal trading, but had acquired the debt stemming from the voyage in a separate transaction. Story scoffed at this fraudulent deal. "It is not, however, pretended," he observed, that when Fales accepted assignment of the debt he was "without notice of the original transactions." Story denounced the assignment of the debt to a third party who pretended to be innocent of the underlying illegal slave-trading as "the most cheap and facile absolution, that fraud or cunning could devise." Allowing the suit under these circumstances "would be a carte blanche for a general pardon of all offences." Thus, the suit could not be maintained: "A party alleging his own turpitude shall not be heard in a court of justice to sustain an action founded upon it; and, where the parties stand in *pari delicto,* the law leaves them, as it finds them, to reap the fruits of their dishonesty, as well as they may."[13]

Story's legally correct holding was unsurprising, but his comments on slavery were dramatic. He declared that "the traffic in slaves is a most odious and horrible traffic, contrary to the plainest principles of natural justice and humanity." Citing a British jurist, Story concluded that "abstractedly speaking," slavery "cannot have a legal existence."[14] This was the beginning of a short crusade against the trade that made Story the judiciary's most important critic of slavery.

In 1819 and 1820 Story forcefully denounced the illegal slave trade (and indirectly attacked slavery) in his charges to federal grand juries in New England. At the time, grand juries were made up of leading citizens whose task was, under the guidance of the judge, to investigate criminal behavior and indict lawbreakers. Story was justly proud of these charges and his frontal assault on the immorality of slavery. He told Jeremiah Mason, the former Federalist senator from New Hampshire, "I have fought against the slave trade in Rhode Island, *pugnis et calcibus.* My charge was well received there." Story later allowed these charges to be published as pamphlets.[15]

In his charges, Story first noted that "in former times" piracy had "crimsoned the ocean with much innocent blood" but that a new federal law declared that pirates should "suffer death." He then turned "to that most detestable traffic, the *Slave Trade*" which he asserted was a form of piracy. His verbal assault on the slave trade quickly morphed into a full-blown attack on slavery itself:

> The existence of Slavery under any shape is so repugnant to the natural rights of man and the dictates of justice, that it seems difficult to find for it any adequate justification. It undoubtedly had its origin in times of barbarism, and was the ordinary lot of those who were conquered in war. It was supposed that the conqueror had a right to take the life of his captive, and by consequence might well bind him to perpetual servitude. But the position itself on which this supposed right is founded, is not true. No man has a right to kill his enemy except in cases of absolute necessity; and this absolute necessity ceases to exist, even in the estimation of the conqueror himself, when he has spared the life of his prisoner. And even if in such case it were possible to contend for the right of slavery, as to the prisoner himself, it is impossible that it can justly extend to his innocent offspring through the whole line of descent.[16]

Few national officials—and none as highly placed as Story—had ever publicly offered such a devastating critique of the fundamental immorality of slavery.

Even as he published this impressive attack on slavery, Story backed away from calling for abolition: "I forbear however, to touch on this delicate topic, not because it is not worthy of the most deliberate attention of all of us; but it does not properly fall within my province on the present occasion." The Supreme Court had no jurisdiction over slavery in the states, and Story did not challenge this Constitutional understanding. He could only "lament" that slavery existed "in any part of our country." He blamed America's "ancestors" for slavery, telling the grand jury that it was the "design of many of the present owners of slaves" to bring about the "gradual abolition" of slavery.[17]

In these grand jury charges, Story pushed for vigorous suppression of the African slave trade. He hoped that the congressional limitations on the trade would "stay" the slave trade's "polluted march, and wicked men would be overawed by its potent punishments." But, sadly, he told the grand jurors there were "too many melancholy proofs, from unquestioned sources, that it is still carried on with all the implacable ferocity and insatiable rapacity of former times." With unusually blunt language for a grand jury charge, Story expressed his outrage that "American citizens are steeped up to their very mouths (I scarcely use too bold a figure) in this stream of iniquity. They throng to the Coasts of Africa" fraudulently sailing "under the stained flags of Spain and Portugal." Speaking to grand juries in Boston, Providence, and Portland, he lamented: "I wish I could say that New England and New Englandmen were free from this deep pollution. But there is reason to believe, that they who drive a loathsome traffic, 'and buy the muscles and the bones of men,' are to be found here also."[18]

Outraged, Story reminded his fellow New Englanders that Americans "have declared that all men are born free and equal, and have certain unalienable rights, among which are the right of enjoying their lives, liberties and property, and of

seeking and obtaining their own safety and happiness."
Quoting from Josiah Wedgwood's emblem of Great Britain's
antislavery society, Story declared: "May not the miserable African ask 'Am I not a man and a brother?' We boast of our
noble struggle against the encroachments of tyranny, but do
we forget that it assumed the mildest form in which authority
ever assailed the rights of its subjects; and yet that there are
men among us who think it no wrong to condemn the shiv-
ering negro to perpetual slavery?" He reminded the grand jurors "we believed in the Christian religion" which "commands
us . . . to love our neighbours as ourselves, and to do unto all
men as we would they should do unto us. . . . And yet there are
men calling themselves Christians who degrade the negro by
ignorance to a level with the brutes, and deprive him of all the
consolations of religion."[19]

Sounding like a full-blown abolitionist, Story condemned
this *"inhuman* traffic," urging the federal grand jurors in New
England to use their "sympathies" and their "judgments in its
suppression." Reciting a battery of evidence from the "records
of the British Parliament," he described how Africans caught
in the trade were *"kidnapped* people. . . . Husbands are stolen
from their wives, children from their parents, and bosom
friends from each other." Story made "no apology" for de-
tailing the horrors of the trade. Reflecting the shared Protestant faith of almost all New Englanders, he reminded the
grand jurors: "In vain shall we expend our wealth in missions
abroad for the promotion of Christianity; in vain shall we rear
at home magnificent temples to the service of the most High;
if we tolerate this traffic, our charity is but a name, and our
religion little more than a fain, and delusive shadow."[20]

Story urged the grand juries to thoroughly investigate any
evidence or rumors of the illegal trade and to bring the wrath

of the United States of America, if not the wrath of God, on those who participated in this "inhuman" commerce. Story's willingness to publish his charges in two separate pamphlets illustrates his deep hatred of slavery and his desire to suppress the trade. In these charges he railed against the African trade:

> It begins in corruption, and plunder, and kidnapping. It creates and stimulates unholy wars for the purpose of making captives. It desolates whole villages . . . for the purpose of seizing the young, the feeble, the defenceless, and the innocent. . . . It manacles the inoffensive females and the starving infants. It forces the brave to untimely death in defence of their humble homes and firesides, or drives them to despair and self-immolation. It stirs up the worst passions of the human soul, darkening the spirit of revenge, sharpening the greediness of avarice. Brutalizing the selfish, envenoming the cruel, famishing the weak, and crushing to death the broken-hearted.[21]

Significantly, a Supreme Court justice had declared that slavery and the trade were "repugnant to the natural rights of man and the dictates of justice." No other member of the U.S. Supreme Court would so profoundly attack slavery in the time before the Civil War. With these charges, Joseph Story had carved out a niche for himself as the Court's most anti-slavery member. In 1819 and 1820 he was truly a just justice.

Two years after his Portland grand jury charge, Story vigorously denounced slavery and the trade in *United States* v. *La Jeune Eugenie* (1822). In 1821 *The Alligator,* an American naval vessel, seized *La Jeune Eugenie* off the coast of Africa "on the suspicion of her being engaged in the slave trade." The ship flew the French flag and carried papers indicating ownership by French citizens in Guadeloupe. But the papers also showed the ship had been built in the United States and only transferred to her French owners after the passage of the federal act of 1818 that facilitated the prosecution of slave traders.

The captain claimed he planned to purchase palm oil in Africa, but evidence in the case showed the "vessel was equipped in the manner that is usual for the slave trade; she had two guns, a false or moveable deck, and a large quantity of water and provisions, and water casks, quite unusual in ordinary voyages, and indispensable in this particular class of voyages." The ship also had handcuffs and fetters on board— hardly necessary for buying palm oil. Europeans on the African coast testified that the ship was buying slaves. The prosecution argued that *La Jeune Eugenie* was actually an American slaver fraudulently sailing under the French flag. But, even if the ship was not American, the prosecution argued the court should "take notice of the French ordinances against that traffic" and refuse to return it to the French claimants. Such a decision was warranted because the "slave trade was contrary to the law of nations, because it was a violation of the law of nature . . . a barbarous, unauthorized, private, piratical warfare, carried on against Africans to make them slaves." Thus, the U.S. attorney argued that the ship was the lawful prize of the United States and the crew of *The Alligator*.[22]

The putative owners argued the ship was legally French, "entirely, and absolutely" denying it was a slaver. They noted: "This vessel was not found with slaves on board." The French claimants also argued, however, that even if it were a slaver, "an American court, in time of peace" had no authority to "condemn, or withhold restitution of, a vessel of a foreign nation, which is found engaged in the African slave trade."[23]

In an elaborate opinion, reflecting his published grand jury charges, Story concluded the ship was indeed a slaver. The evidence "irresistibly established" that the ship's "sole purpose" was to "traffic in slaves." He also doubted the ship was actually French. Under "ordinary circumstances" the "customary documents of France" would have been sufficient proof of the ship's ownership and nationality. But because the ship, with its false decks and chains, was a slaver, the "ordinary" circumstances no longer applied. Slavers notoriously used "disguises" and false documents "to cloak an illegal enterprise, or conceal a real ownership." Because the slave trade depended on "disguises and frauds" and could "be carried on only under certain flags," a ship's papers could not be accepted as proof of its ownership or registry. It was notorious "how easily" false papers were "procured by fraud and imposition upon public officers, and how eagerly they are sought by those, whose cupidity for wealth is stimulated and schooled by temptations of profit, to all manner of shifts and contrivances." Story thought it "no hardship" to require the claimants "to show the bill of sale, by which they acquired their title; to give the names of the American owners [who sold the ship]; and to establish to a reasonable extent, that the transfer was for a valuable consideration." Story was "not satisfied that the property is owned as claimed" by the Frenchmen, and thus he would not order the ship returned to them.[24] But who would get the ship?

Story asserted that the African slave trade was piracy, condemned by international law. Borrowing language from his earlier grand jury charges, he noted that the slave trade "begins in corruption, and plunder, and kidnapping." It leads to "lawless wars, and rapine, and kidnapping, and end[s] in disease, and death, and slavery." Therefore, he continued, "it is of this traffic, in the aggregate of its accumulated wrongs, that I would ask, if it be consistent with the law of nations? . . . We are not to be told, that war is lawful, and slavery lawful, and plunder lawful, and the taking away of life is lawful, and the selling of human beings is lawful." Never before or after this would a Supreme Court justice so emphatically and boldly condemn slavery. Story conceded that slavery might exist under local laws, but knew such local statutes could not justify the Atlantic trade. He noted that virtually every "maritime nation of Europe" had "in the most significant terms, in the most deliberate and solemn conferences, acts, or treaties" acknowledged "the injustice and inhumanity of this trade; and pledged itself to promote its abolition."[25] France, England, and the United States had all agreed to stop the slave trade.

These conclusions left Story in a quandary, however. If the trade was piracy—and illegal under the laws of the maritime world—then the U.S. surely had jurisdiction over a "pirate" ship of unknown nationality. But Story was unwilling actually to implement his own analysis—that the trade was piracy. The claimants of *La Jeune Eugenie* had not proved their ownership. There were good reasons—but no proof—to believe the ship was actually owned by U.S. citizens. Thus, Story concluded the ship could not be libeled and claimed as a prize by the crew of *The Alligator* (although, if it were a pirate ship or a ship owned by an American, it could have been libeled by *The Alligator*). The French claimants had not proved their ownership and, since the ship was clearly a slaver, the probable American owner of the ship dared not claim it. What then should Story do with the ship? He could turn it over to the U.S. government "as unclaimed property, or forfeited property" or remand it to the "Sovereign of France, if he should choose to interpose a claim, or assert a right to proceed against it in his own courts for the supposed forfeiture." Story chose the latter course because it made the United States "not a principal, but an auxiliary, in enforcing the interdict of France, and subserves the great interests of universal justice."[26] Story was sure "the American courts of judicature are not hungry after jurisdiction in foreign causes, or desirous to plunge into the endless perplexities of foreign jurisprudence." Turning the ship over to the French government would "enforce the policy, common to both nations, of repressing an odious traffic, which is denounced by both."[27]

Story's solution avoided a confrontation with the nation's oldest ally over the ownership of the vessel. But it also undermined the suppression of the trade. Service on the coast of Africa was dangerous and unpleasant. Federal law provided a great incentive to crews by allowing them to share in the proceeds from condemned ships. In denying *The Alligator* its forfeiture rights, Story damaged that incentive.

More significantly, Story abandoned his own legal analysis. Relying on the opinion of Sir William Scott, of the British High Court of Admiralty, Story had asserted that it would "impose no hardship therefore in requiring the claimants in this case to show the bill of sale, by which they acquired their title, to give the names of the American owners; and to establish . . . that the transfer was for a valuable consideration. It is well known, that a bill of sale is the universal instrument, to which courts of admiralty look to establish the legal interests in ships; and this is equally a part of our own law and the law of France."[28] The French claimants could not produce such a document, because as Story knew, the French papers themselves were fraudulent. Under this standard, Story had adequate evidence that this American-built ship had never actually been sold to the French claimant, and that it was still owned by Americans. Applying this standard would have guaranteed that the ship was condemned and sold for the benefit of the United States and the crew of *The Alligator,* and the ship would have been taken out of service as a slaver.

Instead, Story returned the ship to the French government, which was notorious for not enforcing its own laws prohibiting the slave trade. Story had acknowledged this when he pointed out that American slavers often used false French papers and flew French flags precisely because France was so lax in cracking down on the trade. That seemed to be exactly the situation in this case, but Story did not follow the evidence and his own analysis.

Rhetorically, Story's opinion was an antislavery tour de force, roundly condemning the slave trade and slavery itself. But turning the ship over to the French government, which had a poor record of suppressing the trade, was not ideal. Story's opinion provided a powerful, detailed attack on the African trade, but its implementation was problematic.

The Supreme Court did not follow *La Jeune Eugenie,* or Story's strong attack on the trade. In *The Antelope* (1825), Chief Justice Marshall held that the slave trade did not violate international law and was not piracy, in spite of federal statutes to the contrary. He ignored the illegal nature of the trade and the use of fraudulent papers. *The Antelope* was a case about living people, not merely a ship loaded with the accoutrements of the trade. Many of the Africans on the ship were sold into lifetime bondage. Marshall completely rejected Story's brilliant opinion in *La Jeune Eugenie,* essentially dressing down his closest colleague on the Court for arguing that the trade violated international law and natural law.[29]

Marshall rewarded Story's years of loyalty by publicly rebuking him with an opinion that sent scores of Africans into

bondage. Story silently concurred, just as he silently acquiesced in every one of Marshall's decisions denying freedom
claims of slaves who had strong arguments that they were entitled to their liberty. Sadly, after 1822, with the exception of
upholding one slave trade verdict in 1825, Story had little to
say that was remotely hostile to slavery.[30] In 1819 Story had
hoped the debate over Missouri would "arouse the spirit of
New England." After 1822 Story apparently forgot that spirit.
For the next two decades his jurisprudence would be increas-
ingly deferential to slavery and the South.

Slavery and Interstate Commerce

Groves v. *Slaughter* (1841) involved the importation of slaves
into Mississippi. The facts were quite simple. Robert Slaughter
sold slaves to Groves and other Mississippi residents, taking
notes worth over seven thousand dollars. The purchasers refused to honor their notes, claiming the contracts were void
because the Mississippi Constitution of 1832 provided that the
"introduction of slaves into this state, as merchandise, shall
be prohibited from and after the first day of May, 1833." The
Constitution did not prevent residents from buying slaves in
other states and bringing them into Mississippi, or stop migrants to the state from bringing slaves with them. Beyond
the immediate parties, hundreds of thousands of dollars were
at stake, since many other Mississippi planters had purchased
slaves brought into the state after 1833. In a fairly straightforward opinion, Justice Smith Thompson held that the clause
in the state constitution required a statute to implement it.
Thus, Groves had to pay on the notes. Because he ruled that
the Mississippi constitutional provision was not actually in
force, Justice Thompson found it "unnecessary" to consider

the looming constitutional question: whether Mississippi's ban on the importation of slaves, if implemented, violated the commerce clause.[31]

Other justices, however, considered this problem. John McLean of Ohio, the Court's most committed opponent of slavery, emphatically endorsed the right of the states to ban slaves from their borders. He stressed that Ohio not only prohibited slaves as merchandise, but also prohibited bringing any slaves into the state for any other purpose. McLean distinguished the interstate trade in merchandise, including the products of slave labor, from the slaves themselves. He argued that Ohio could not ban southern cotton or sugar, but it was free to ban southern slaves. Similarly, Mississippi could ban the importation of slaves as merchandise if it chose. Taking a states' rights antislavery position, McLean asserted that "power over slavery belongs to the states respectively. It is local in its character" and that each state "has a right to protect itself against the avarice and intrusion of the slave dealer; to guard its citizens against the inconveniences and dangers of a slave population."[32] No southerner could have argued with McLean's articulation of slavery as a creature of state law, but his use of a states' rights analysis to prevent masters from bringing their slaves into the North surely could not have made them comfortable.

Chief Justice Taney felt compelled to respond to McLean, even though he essentially agreed with him. Speaking for the slave South, he reiterated that the "power over [slavery] is exclusively with the several states, and each of them has a right to decide for itself whether it will or will not allow persons of this description to be brought within its limits."[33]

Justice Henry Baldwin of Pennsylvania offered a proslavery nationalist opinion. He argued that for the "internal tranquility of the state, the health, or morals of the people" states were free to prohibit free blacks, immigrants, and "diseased, convicted, or insurgent slaves, or such as may be otherwise dangerous to the peace or welfare of the state." But the states could not ban slaves as merchandise if they allowed their citizens to buy slaves in other states and bring them back. Baldwin considered "slaves as property," as "articles of commerce" that were "recognized" as "property capable of being transferred from hand to hand as chattels." At the same time, he affirmed that "the extent of the right of property in the owner of a slave, depended on the law of each state." If a state recognized slave property, then it was subject to the commerce clause, and at the same time the owners would be "protected from any violations of the rights of property by Congress, under the fifth amendment to the Constitution." Baldwin further argued that a slave owner had a constitutional right to "pass through Pennsylvania, or Ohio" with their slaves and "no law of either state could take away or affect his right of property."[34]

Baldwin's opinion was a frontal attack on Story's arguments in *La Jeune Eugenie* that slavery violated the law of nature and could only be established by positive law. The opinion was also a direct assault on the emerging law of freedom in the North. In 1836 Chief Justice Lemuel Shaw of Massachusetts—Story's colleague and ally—held in *Commonwealth* v. *Aves* that slaves became free if their masters voluntarily brought them into the state. Other New England states were in agreement. These decisions were based on Lord Chief Justice Mansfield's holding in *Somerset* v. *Stewart* (1772) that slavery could only exist if there were positive law—legislation—creating the status, and the default rule was always for freedom.[35]

But Baldwin was now on record declaring that this free-state jurisprudence was unconstitutional. John McLean had already weighed in to support the interest of Ohio on the other side. This would become a more important issue in the 1850s, but it was clearly on the horizon. Where was the justice from Massachusetts in this important debate between McLean and Baldwin, with Chief Justice Taney partially weighing in?

Story was silent. Without writing an opinion, Story agreed that there were no constitutional impediments to Mississippi's ban on slaves as merchandise, but dissented from the holding in favor of the slave merchant Slaughter. Story, with no explanation or opinion, found that the notes were void. Perhaps this was a throwback to his opinion in *Fales,* where he held that a contract based on illegal slave-trading was void. But in *Fales,* Story vigorously attacked slavery, pointing out that no court could enforce certain kinds of contracts. Here was a chance for Story to remind the legal profession that slavery was abhorrent, as he had so eloquently proclaimed two decades earlier. The great issue of the moment was before him, and he had nothing to say.

The *Amistad*

The *Amistad* looms large in our history. Stephen Spielberg's movie brought the horrors of the African slave trade to the big screen. It has been memorialized as an icon of liberty and a great antislavery moment. From the perspective of social and political history this makes sense. Opponents of slavery mounted a massive campaign to gain freedom for the Amistads—as the Africans on the ship became known. But the movie and popular culture mischaracterize the legal issues and Justice Story's narrow opinion in the case. If the

Amistad case is a great antislavery moment, that moment happened in spite of Story's opinion, which neither denounced slavery nor offered any legal or moral support for abolition, even as it liberated a shipload of Africans who had been brought to Cuba in violation of Spanish law.

On June 28, 1839, the *Amistad* left Havana for central Cuba. On board were three mariners, two Cuban slaves, two Cuban sugar planters, and fifty-three Africans who had recently been imported, illegally, into Cuba from Sierra Leone. The planters, José Ruiz and Pedro Montez, had purchased the Africans and were transporting them to their sugar plantations in central Cuba. The bill of sale claimed the Africans were Cuban-born slaves, and the ship's manifest listed each African with a Spanish name. With one minor exception, none of the Africans spoke any Spanish. They were all Mende speakers from West Africa.

A few days into the voyage the Africans revolted, killing the three crewmen and a slave cook who had taken great satisfaction in taunting them. The Amistads spared the two Spanish owners and the slave cabin boy. Through gestures and a few Spanish words, the leader of the Amistads—later known as Joseph Cinque—ordered Ruiz and Montez to steer the ship east, towards Africa. They did sail east during the day, but at night they headed north and west, hoping to reach the southern United States. Instead, in August 1839, the *Amistad* reached Long Island Sound, where the Coast Guard brig *Washington*, under the command of Lieutenant Thomas R. Gedney, towed it to New Haven, Connecticut. By this time, due to shortages of food and water, only thirty-nine of the Africans were still alive.

The arrival of the *Amistad* created vast legal confusion. Lieutenant Gedney sought salvage for the ship and its contents (including the slaves) for himself and his crew. The Spanish government claimed the ship, including the Africans, as did Ruiz and Montez. The U.S. attorney initially insisted that the Africans be turned over to the president of the United States, to be returned to Africa under the antislave trade laws. He also thought, however, that the Africans might be prosecuted for murder and mutiny. Later, under directions from the Van Buren administration, the U.S. attorney asked the Court to return the ship, including the Africans, to Spanish authorities. Meanwhile, abolitionists in Connecticut, engaging counsel to represent the Africans, argued the Amistads should be freed because they had been illegally imported into Cuba, in violation of Spanish law.

These competing claims ended up in the U.S. courts in Connecticut. After numerous proceedings, Justice Smith Thompson, riding circuit, ruled that whatever happened on the high seas on a Spanish ship was not a crime under U.S. law and thus the Amistads could not be charged for killing the crew or taking over the ship. United States District Judge Andrew T. Judson then ruled there could be no salvage claims relating to the Africans, because slaves could not be "merchandise" under Connecticut law. Judson allowed Lieutenant Gedney and his crew to claim salvage for saving the ship and its nonhuman cargo. Following Judson's ruling the Amistads were released from jail and housed in a less coercive setting, where they got better food, medical care, and new clothing, and were soon being educated and evangelized by abolitionists. Meanwhile, some concerned abolitionists, working with a linguistics professor from Yale, found an African-born British seaman, James Covey, who could speak Mende. This meant that the Amistads could tell their own story in court. The British government fully cooperated,

giving Covey extended shore leave for the trial and also providing overwhelming evidence of the illegal slave trade into
Cuba.

The trial revolved around three sets of claims. The Van
Buren administration asserted that under the Pinckney Treaty
of 1795 and the Adams-Onís Treaty of 1819, the ship and its
contents, including the Africans, should be turned over to
Spanish authorities. Lieutenant Gedney demanded salvage
for the ship and the value of the Africans (if they were returned to Cuba as slaves). Abolitionist lawyers argued the
Amistads were illegally brought to Cuba, were never slaves,
and should be returned to Africa by the U.S. government
under laws suppressing the African slave trade.

Judge Judson was a Jacksonian Democrat known to be
hostile to abolitionists. President Van Buren was so certain
of what the outcome of the case would be that he sent a coast
guard vessel to New Haven, to whisk the Amistads to Cuba
before their lawyers could file an appeal. But things did not
play out as the president expected. The evidence was overwhelming that the Amistads were Africans, not Cuban-born
slaves. They spoke no Spanish. They did not know their
Spanish "names" on the ship's manifest, and Covey's transla-
tions of their testimony made it impossible to support the
preposterous claims of the Van Buren administration or the
Spanish government. Judson, to the surprise of abolitionists,
ruled in favor of liberty. Referring to the two leaders of the
Amistads, Judson declared: "Cinquez and Grabeau shall not
sigh for Africa in vain. Bloody as may be their hands, they
shall yet embrace their kindred." Judson ordered that the
Amistads "be delivered to the president of the United States
to be transported to Africa."[36] The slave cabin boy was to be
returned to his owner, as provided for by the relevant trea-

ties. The ship and its nonhuman cargo were to be turned over to the Spanish government, after one-third of its value was paid as salvage to Gedney and his crew.

The Van Buren administration appealed, arguing that the Amistads were legally the property of their Cuban owners, and should be returned under treaties of 1795 and 1819. The government conceded the Amistads' African birth, but argued the courts had no authority to go behind the ship's papers, and thus, under the treaties, the United States was obligated to accept at face value Spain's claim that they were "Cuban born" slaves who should be returned to Spanish authorities.

In February 1841 oral arguments before the Supreme Court lasted eight days. Among the lawyers representing the Amistads was former president John Quincy Adams, whose published arguments ran to 135 pages. Sarcastic and brilliant, he eviscerated the position of the Van Buren administration, particularly castigating the president for planning to send the Amistads to Cuba to prevent an appeal to the Supreme Court. Justice Story wrote to his wife that Adams's argument was extraordinary: "Extraordinary, I say, for its power and its bitter sarcasm, and its dealing with topics far beyond the record and points of discussion."[37] Adams wanted the Court to consider the immorality of slavery and the slave trade. He hoped Justice Story would represent the "spirit of New England" and American liberty as he had two decades earlier in *La Jeune Eugenie.*

Writing for the Court, Story ignored these issues. For Story, the only issue was the application of the various treaties with Spain to the facts of the case. If the Africans were "lawfully held as slaves under the laws of Spain" then Story saw "no reason why they may not justly be deemed within the intent of the treaty, to be included under the denomination of merchandise, and, as such, ought to be restored to the claimants: for, upon that point, the laws of Spain would seem to furnish the proper rule of interpretation."[38] There were no moral issues here. In his opinion, Story fully recognized the legality of slavery in Cuba and the obligation of the United States to enforce the Spanish law of slavery.

This was a shrewd strategy, since Story then concluded that it was "plain beyond controversy . . . that these negroes never were the lawful slaves of Ruiz or Montez, or of any other Spanish subjects." On the contrary, they were "natives of Africa, and were kidnapped there, and were unlawfully transported to Cuba, in violation of the laws and treaties of Spain. . . . By those laws, and treaties, and edicts, the African slave trade is utterly abolished; the dealing in that trade is deemed a heinous crime; and the negroes thereby introduced into the dominions of Spain, are declared to be free." Story noted that Ruiz and Montez had "full knowledge" of these facts when they "made the pretended purchase of these negroes."[39] Only the slave cabin boy could be returned to Cuba.

Story upheld most of the district court's decision. He reversed the part of Judson's decree, however, that commanded that the Amistads be returned to Africa by the president. Instead he ordered "that the said negroes be and are hereby declared to be free, and that they be dismissed from the custody of the Court, and be discharged from the suit and go thereof quit without day."[40] It is hard to know why Story reached this conclusion. Under the slave trade act of 1819 the United States was obligated to provide for the "removal beyond the limits of the United States, of all such negroes, mulattoes, or persons of colour, as may be so delivered and brought within their jurisdiction."[41] The Amistads were clearly the fruit of the illegal African trade, and Ruiz and Montez purposefully steered the ship into U.S. waters. But Story, no friend of the antislavery movement, forced American abolitionists to spend almost a year raising money to send the Africans home. The Amistads finally reached their homeland in January 1842.

For two years the *Amistad* was a major cause célèbre. It brought to the United States living proof of the horrors of the African slave trade. It involved three levels of the federal courts, the president of the United States, the secretary of state, the attorney general, a former president, the governments of Spain and Great Britain (which tried to intervene on behalf of the Africans), and a host of lawyers in a complicated adjudication of treaties, state law, federal law, Spanish law, and international law. Almost buried under the weight of this mountain of legal paper, treaties, and arguments were the lives and futures of thirty-nine innocent victims of kidnapping. Perhaps what is most remarkable about this case is that in the end these people received some measure of justice. But this was an outcome based on a treaty. The cabin boy, who was legally a slave in Cuba, was returned to that island to live out his life in bondage.

Justice Story probably was pleased he had helped a shipload of Africans avoid a lifetime of bondage, although he denied them a quick return to Africa, courtesy of the United States government. His next slavery-related case was surely less satisfactory. His decision in it—the last major slavery decision of his career—produced a menacing outcome for the 170,000 free blacks living in the North.

Prigg v. *Pennsylvania* and the Infamy of the Justice from Massachusetts

In American popular culture and for many academics, the *Amistad* is remembered—or, thanks to the Spielberg film, misunderstood and misremembered—as the most important Supreme Court decision involving slavery before *Dred Scott* (1857). Actually the case had little to do with slavery directly, did not affect slaves in the United States, and had no jurisprudential impact. From the perspectives of supporters and opponents of slavery, U.S. public policy and law, and African Americans, *Prigg* v. *Pennsylvania* (1842) was the Court's most important case before *Dred Scott*.[42] Arguably, for the lives of northern free blacks, fugitive slaves, and southern slave owners, *Prigg*, while less well-known today, was actually more important than *Dred Scott*.

The roots of *Prigg* date from around the War of 1812, when John Ashmore, a farmer in Harford County, Maryland, allowed a slave couple (whose names have been lost to history) and their daughter Margaret to live as free people. In 1824 John Ashmore died, and the inventory of his estate listed only two slaves, both young men. Shortly after this, Margaret married Jerry Morgan, a free black from Pennsylvania. They lived in Harford County, in the same neighborhood as Ashmore's widow, possibly on land owned by her or by her daughter and son-in-law, Susanna and Nathan Beemis. In 1830 the U.S. Census, taken by the Harford County sheriff, recorded Margaret and Jerry Morgan and their two children as "free" blacks. By 1832 the Morgans had moved to Jerry's hometown of York, Pennsylvania, where Margaret had at least one more child, who under Pennsylvania law was a free person at birth. In 1837, Nathan Beemis, the son-in-law of the late John Ashmore, traveled with Edward Prigg and two other Marylanders to York to claim the Morgans as fugitive slaves. The fact that Beemis was easily able to find Margaret suggests that she was in contact with Mrs. Ashmore after she moved to Pennsylvania.[43]

Acting under an 1826 Pennsylvania law designed to prevent kidnapping—known as a personal liberty law—Beemis and his cohorts secured a warrant from Justice of the Peace Thomas Henderson. Accompanied by a local constable, they brought the Morgans to Henderson. After hearing the evidence, Henderson released them. Jerry Morgan was clearly a free man, born in Pennsylvania. The same was true for Margaret's Pennsylvania-born child (or children). Margaret had lived her whole life as a free person and never been claimed as a slave. Beemis, who claimed the Morgans on behalf of his mother-in-law, had no documentary evidence that Margaret or her Maryland-born children were slaves.

Beemis said he would take the Morgans back to their home, but instead seized Margaret and her children (leaving behind the freeborn Jerry) and dragged them to Maryland. Eventually they were sold to slave traders, disappearing from the historical record. The York County grand jury indicted all four men under the 1826 law. Maryland's governor privately conceded they had broken Pennsylvania's law but refused to honor Pennsylvania's extradition requisition. Eventually a compromise sent only Edward Prigg back to Pennsylvania, where authorities agreed that if convicted he would not be incarcerated until all appeals had been exhausted. A jury easily convicted him and the Pennsylvania Supreme Court affirmed the conviction without an opinion. In 1842, Justice Story wrote the majority opinion reversing Prigg's conviction.

In his opinion Story reached five major conclusions: (1) the federal fugitive slave law of 1793 was constitutional; (2) no state could pass any law adding additional requirements to that law which could impede or interfere with the return of fugitive slaves; (3) the Constitution provided a common law right of recaption—a right of self-help—which allowed slave owners to seize fugitive slaves and remove them without complying with the provisions of the federal fugitive slave law, as long as this could be accomplished without a breach of the peace; (4) state officials ought to enforce the federal law of 1793 but could not be required to do so; (5) no one seized as a fugitive slave was entitled to any due process hearing or trial beyond a summary proceeding to determine if the person seized was the person described in the affidavit or other papers provided by the claimant. A claimant did not have to comply with even this minimal procedure, however, if he exercised self-help under a common law right of recaption.

This sweeping opinion endangered all northern blacks, threatened the public peace, and undermined the stability of northern society. By striking down Pennsylvania's personal liberty law, and by extension similar laws in other states, Story left the northern states without any legal authority to prevent kidnapping of free blacks. Story's right of self-help allowed a slave owner "to seize and recapture his slave" anywhere in the nation.[44] This allowed slave catchers to kidnap free blacks without worrying about state intervention. Under Story's opinion, Beemis and Prigg could have dragged the freeborn Jerry Morgan to Maryland, and Pennsylvania officials would have been unable to stop them. The ruling threatened black families and communities throughout the North.

Story claimed that the fugitive slave clause "contemplates the existence of a positive, unqualified right on the part of the owner of the slave" to recapture a runaway slave, and that "no state law or regulation" could "in any way qualify, regulate, control or restrain" that right. He declared:

> we have not the slightest hesitation in holding, that under . . . the Constitution, the owner of a slave is clothed with entire authority, in every state in the Union, to seize and recapture his slave, whenever he can do it, without any breach of the peace or any illegal violence. In this sense and to this extent this clause of the Constitution may properly be said to execute itself, and to require no aid from legislation, state or national.[45]

This extraordinary conclusion meant that anyone could seize any black and remove that person to the South without any state interference or even a hearing before any judge as long as no "breach of the peace" occurred.

The very definition of a "breach of the peace" under Story's opinion was problematic. In dissent, Justice John McLean noted that under the law of slavery it was *never* a breach of the peace for a master to whip, beat, or otherwise physically harm a slave. McLean concluded: "If the master has a right to seize and remove the slave, without claim, he can commit no breach of the peace, by using all the force necessary to accomplish his object."[46] Under Story's logic, it would never be a breach of the peace for a master to take his slave by brutal force; nor could this force be considered "illegal violence" as long as it was directed against a slave. Because of the ability to avoid any judicial superintendence of this process, the same force, leading to removal to the South, could also have been used against free blacks.

Even if the law of southern slavery did not apply in the North, there were practical problems with Story's position. Seizures at night or in isolated areas could be accomplished without anyone's observing a breach of the peace. Once a black was shackled, intimidated, and perhaps beaten into submission, travel to the South could be accomplished without any obvious breach of the peace. If state officials could not investigate a white transporting a black in chains, then kidnapping of free blacks could always be accomplished. A rash of kidnappings of free black children had led to the enactment of Pennsylvania's 1826 personal liberty law. By striking down state personal liberty laws and creating a right of self-help, Story left northern states powerless to prevent such kidnappings.

Story's opinion effectively nationalized southern slave law. In the South, race was a presumption of slave status. By giving slave catchers a common law right of recaption, Story applied this presumption to the entire nation. The fact that slave catchers could now operate in the North without having to prove the seized person's slave status threatened all northern blacks.

In reaching these holdings, Justice Story ignored the language of the fugitive slave clause and the structure of the Constitution, rewrote the history of the Constitution, reshaped or ignored relevant precedents, and ignored the facts of the case to justify his opinion. He created a mythological origin of the fugitive slave clause to legitimize his harsh interpretation of it.

For Story, the greatest danger of this constitutional minefield was its potential for disruption of the Union. As a jurist, scholar, teacher, and politician, Story had always sought to strengthen the national government. In *Prigg* he tried to accomplish this by giving slaveholders the result they wanted and then somehow convincing the North that the Constitution dictated this result. No longer as enraged by slavery as he had been two decades earlier, and unwilling to stand up to southern bluster, Story now supported southern demands for a thoroughly proslavery interpretation of the Constitution.

To persuade the North to accept his opinion, Story fabricated a history that elevated the fugitive slave clause to a central compromise of the Constitutional Convention. Story delivered his account of the Convention with a tone of magisterial authority:

> Historically, it is well known that the object of this clause was to secure to the citizens of the slaveholding states the complete right and title of ownership in their slaves, as property, in every state in the Union into which they might escape from the state where they were held in servitude. The full recognition of this right and title was indispensable to the security of this species of property in all the slaveholding states; and, indeed, was so vital to the preservation of their domestic interests and institutions, that it cannot be doubted that it constituted a fundamental article, without the adoption of which the Union could not have been formed.[47]

To bolster his assertion that the fugitive slave clause was "fundamental" and "indispensable" to the ratification, Story claimed that at the Convention "several" of the states "required as a condition, upon which any constitution should be presented to the states for ratification, a full and perfect security for their slaves as property, when they fled into any of the states of the Union." He equated southern demands for the fugitive slave clause with counting slaves for representation and the protection of the African slave trade, asserting that without these essential clauses "the Convention would have been dissolved, without a constitution being formed." Story offered this history as inconvertible "facts as they were. They cannot be denied. . . . I am satisfied with what was done; and revere the men and their motives for insisting, politically, upon what was done. When the three points relating to slaves had been accomplished, every impediment in the way of forming a constitution was removed."[48] Two decades earlier Story had equated the slave trade with piracy; he now chose to "revere" the men who protected it, and who had provided for the capture of black people who tried to escape the bondage caused by that piracy.

Story's assertion that the fugitive slave clause was "a fundamental article" of constitutional compromise, and that this was well known during the ratification struggle, set the stage for the rest of his opinion. Because the clause was fundamental, it required exclusive federal enforcement. Otherwise the master's "right" to capture a runaway slave "would never, in a practical sense be the same in all the states. It would have no unity of purpose, or uniformity of operation. The duty might be enforced in some states; retarded, or limited in others; and denied, as compulsory in many, if not in all." Story argued that "It is scarcely conceivable that the slaveholding states would have been satisfied with leaving to the legislation of the non-slaveholding states, a power of regulation, in the absence of that of Congress, which would or might practically amount to a power to destroy the rights of the owner." Without exclusive federal enforcement, each state would have the power "to dole out its own remedial justice, or withhold it at its pleasure and according to its own views of policy and expediency."[49] This, Story believed, could not have been the intentions of the framers.

The tale Story told in *Prigg* differed significantly from what he had written a decade earlier in *Commentaries on the Constitution of the United States*. There he had denied that the clause was a key constitutional compromise, asserting that it was effectively a gift from the North "for the benefit of the slaveholding states." He claimed this proved that the South "at all times had its full share of benefits from the Union." Significantly, Story did not claim in *Commentaries* that the clause was part of a bargain, a quid pro quo, for something in the Constitution that the North wanted.[50] Nor did he argue that it was "a fundamental article, without the adoption of which the Union could not have been formed" as he claimed in *Prigg*.[51]

Story's claim that the clause was an essential element of the constitutional bargain of 1787, equivalent to the three-fifths compromise or the slave trade compromise, was a strong argument in favor of his proslavery opinion. But James Madison's *Notes of the Debates of the Federal Convention* told a very different history.

Late in the Constitutional Convention, Pierce Butler and Charles Pinckney of South Carolina proposed that a fugitive slave clause be added to the article requiring the interstate extradition of fugitives from justice. James Wilson of Pennsylvania objected: "This would oblige the Executive of the State to do it, at the public expence." Butler discreetly "withdrew his proposition in order that some particular provision might be made apart from this article." A day later, the Convention, without debate or formal vote, adopted the fugitive slave provision as a separate article of the draft constitution. Eventually the two clauses emerged as succeeding paragraphs in Article IV, Section 2, of the Constitution.[52]

The paucity of debate over the clause is remarkable because, throughout the Convention, slavery had led to acrimonious and morally charged debates that sometimes threatened to derail the whole project. But, unlike the debates over the slave trade, the three-fifths clause, the taxation of exports, and the regulation of commerce, the fugitive slave clause generated no serious discussion. Story argued that this lack of debate and the unanimous adoption of the clause showed its importance.[53] But this unanimity should have alerted Story to the relative unimportance of the clause. Every other slavery-related clause at the Convention led to fierce debates. Some of the longest and most bitter debates at the Convention occurred over the three-fifths clause and the slave trade provision. On the other hand, the Convention barely discussed the fugitive slave clause, because no one saw it as requiring federal enforcement or even state action. It gave southerners a "right" they did not have, but placed it in Article IV, which dealt with interstate relations and comity and did not provide any remedy to masters seeking runaways.

During the ratification struggle, Northerners objected to the three-fifths clause, the domestic insurrection clauses which obligated northerners to suppress slave rebellions, and the slave trade clause. Sometimes their rhetoric made readers flinch. For example, a New York antifederalist thought that Americans might become "a happy and respectable people" if they could only "relinquish every idea of drenching the bowels of Africa in gore, for the sake of enslaving its freeborn innocent inhabitants."[54]

Despite the vigorous attacks on most of the major slavery-related provisions, no antifederalists publicly discussed the fugitive slave provision.[55] They did not see it as obligating either themselves or the federal government to become involved in the dirty business of capturing runaway slaves. If they had, they certainly would have objected to it, as they objected to the three-fifths clause, the slave trade provision, and the domestic insurrections clause. The authors of *The Federalist* discussed the three-fifths provision and the slave trade, but ignored the fugitive slave clause.[56] Contrary to Story's telling, the fugitive slave clause was relatively unimportant in 1787, which is why virtually no one in the North seemed to notice it.

Some southerners praised the clause as a boon to their interests, but not as a major component of the constitutional bargain or as something that would lead to federal enforcement. When the antifederalist George Mason complained that the Constitution might threaten slavery, James Madison detailed the various clauses that protected slavery, noting that the fugitive slave clause "was expressly inserted to enable owners of slaves to reclaim them." This was an improvement over the existing situation where, if a slave escaped to a free state, "he becomes emancipated by their laws. For the laws of the States are uncharitable to one another in this respect." Under the fugitive slave clause, southerners had "a better security than any that now exists," but Madison never suggested the clause guaranteed federal enforcement, even though that would have strengthened his argument for ratification. When Patrick Henry predicted the Constitution would lead to abolition, Edmund Randolph pointed to the fugitive slave clause to prove that this was not so. He said that under the clause "authority is given to owners of slaves to vindicate their property."[57]

The North Carolina delegates reported that "the Southern States" gained "a much better Security for the Return of Slaves who might endeavour to Escape than they have under the original Confederation." Similarly, Charles Cotesworth Pinckney reported to the South Carolina House of Representatives: "We have obtained a right to recover our slaves in whatever part of America they may take refuge, which is a right we had not before."[58] It was a plus for the South, but not a major compromise. None of these returning delegates suggested that the fugitive slave clause was a fundamental part of the bargain or that it would lead to federal enforcement. The structure of the Constitution supported this interpretation. The fugitive slave clause is in Section 2 of Article IV, which entirely focuses on relations between states. Sections 1, 3, and 4 of Article IV give specific enforcement powers to the federal government, but Section 2 is the only part of that article which does not authorize federal implementation, implying that the framers did not intend to grant Congress such power.

Story's history of the fugitive slave clause does not comport with the records of the Constitutional Convention or the discussion during ratification. Significantly, both sources were available to him in 1842 when he wrote *Prigg*. The history he invented supported his goal of nationalizing the law. By reshaping the clause into a fundamental part of the bargain over the Constitution, he could argue for exclusive federal jurisdiction over the return of fugitive slaves.

In the 1830s, southerners felt slavery was under attack. In his *Commentaries on the Constitution of the United States*, published in 1833, Story tried to assuage the South by describing the clause as a gift from the North to the South; then, in *Prigg*, Story elevated the clause to a central part of the constitutional bargain.

In the *Commentaries*, Story claimed that the lack of a fugitive slave provision in the Articles of Confederation "was felt as a grievous inconvenience by the slave-holding states, since in many states no aid whatsoever would be allowed to the masters; and sometimes indeed they met with open resistance."[59] In 1787, however, no state prevented masters from recovering runaways. Pennsylvania, Connecticut, and Rhode Island specifically recognized the right to recover a fugitive slave even while they were dismantling slavery themselves. New York and New Jersey were still slave states. In his *Commentaries*, Story ignored this history because it suited his nationalistic purpose to elevate the clause to an important gift from the North "for the benefit of the slaveholding states," indicating northern goodwill toward the "peculiar interests of the south." Story used the example of the clause "to repress the delusive and mischievous notion that the south has not at all times had its full share of benefits from the Union."[60]

In *Prigg*, Story shifted the argument, asserting that the Constitution obligated the U.S. government to guarantee the interests of the South, prevented the North from interfering with the rendition of fugitive slaves, and even allowed masters to seize and remove alleged fugitives without any due process procedure at all. All this was necessary, Story argued in *Prigg*, because the Constitution required it.

The inconsistency between Story's analysis in his *Commentaries* and his later analysis in *Prigg* reflected his different goals. In the *Commentaries*, Story wanted to provide an interpretation of the Constitution that would strengthen nationalism in the South. Writing just after the emergence of

militant abolitionism in the North and in the wake of the nullification crisis in South Carolina, Story tried to convince the
South that the fugitive slave clause was essentially a gift from
the North, added solely "for the benefit of the slaveholding
states."[61] This analysis was designed to renew southern faith
in the fundamental spirit of the Constitution.

In *Prigg*, Story did not have to appeal to the South. The
opinion was overwhelmingly proslavery. Rather, Story had to
convince the North to accept his proslavery opinion. Thus he
put a new spin on constitutional history, arguing that the
Constitution required both the federal law of 1793 and his
harsh interpretation of it in *Prigg*. Story hoped the North
would accept *Prigg* because it was "required" by the Constitution itself. He no longer argued that the fugitive slave clause
was a gift to the South, but claimed it was an essential part
of the constitutional bargain. Story nationalized slavery as a
vehicle for strengthening the federal government.

In upholding the fugitive slave law of 1793, Story asserted
that all the existing precedents, consisting of just three state
cases, totally supported his position. In doing so, the justice
and legal scholar created another "story" that departed significantly from the evidence. In fact, one of the cases he cited
for authority held the exact opposite of what Story claimed it
held. Furthermore, Story ignored two state cases that did not
support his position.

Although the Fugitive Slave Law had been in force for a
half century, there was very little case law on it in 1842. A few
lower federal courts had enforced the law, but the district
judges offered little guidance or intellectual support for
Story.[62] While riding circuit, Henry Baldwin had delivered
the only existing opinion by a Supreme Court justice on the
law. This was a suit for damages against Pennsylvanians who

helped a slave escape. In a perfunctory opinion with virtually no analysis, Baldwin upheld the 1793 law and found for the slave owner.[63]

More important than any federal cases were the discussions of the 1793 law in the state courts. By the time *Prigg* reached the Supreme Court, there were five state precedents involving the 1793 Law. Three, from Pennsylvania, Massachusetts, and New York, had been officially reported. A case from New Jersey was not officially reported, but the case and the opinion were covered by newspapers and cited by an important Ohio abolitionist lawyer a few years before *Prigg*. The fifth case was the Pennsylvania Supreme Court's decision upholding Prigg's conviction, which had not been reported. But of course Story had the full benefit of the view of that court, since he was reviewing its judgment.[64]

Despite the mixed response of state courts to the 1793 law, Story inaccurately asserted that all state precedents supported his position. Story wrote that the law had been interpreted in "Massachusetts, New York, and Pennsylvania, and on all these occasions its validity has been affirmed."[65] Story used this assertion of support from state cases to bolster his view that the 1793 act was "clearly constitutional in all its leading provisions." Here Story was in part creating a legal straw man. In *Prigg*, neither the trial court nor the Pennsylvania Supreme Court claimed that the 1793 law was unconstitutional. Nor did Pennsylvania deny that it had an obligation to return actual fugitive slaves to their owners. Rather, Pennsylvania's position was that it had a right to protect its *free* black citizens from being illegally removed from the state. Story, however, ignored this issue and never came to terms with the fact that all parties agreed that at least one of Morgan's children was born a free person in

Pennsylvania, and was never a fugitive slave from Maryland. On the other hand, the highest courts in New York and New Jersey had emphatically held that the 1793 law was unconstitutional, but Story never discussed this issue.

Having misstated the legal issues before him, Story argued that if the interpretation of the clause and the 1793 law "were one of doubtful construction, such long acquiescence in it, such contemporaneous expositions of it, and such extensive and uniform recognition of its validity, would in our judgment entitle the question to be considered at rest." Story did not explain what decisions were "contemporaneous" to the law, because in fact there were none. In 1819 and 1823 two state cases upheld the law; in 1832 and 1835 the New York and New Jersey courts found the law unconstitutional; and in 1839 Pennsylvania did not address its constitutionality but emphatically denied that the law prohibited states from protecting their free black populations from kidnapping. Story argued that he needed to follow the state precedents upholding the law because the alternative was that "the interpretation of the Constitution is to be delivered over to interminable doubt."[66] But Story could accomplish this only by misrepresenting one opinion and completely ignoring two others.

Story's use of state cases to bolster his opinion was jurisprudentially dishonest and historically inaccurate. Of the five important state decisions on the fugitive slave law, two supported it, two did not.[67] The fifth case, the Pennsylvania Supreme Court's decision in *Prigg* itself, did not question the constitutionality of the 1793 law. But the Pennsylvania court also upheld its right to protect free blacks from kidnapping and concluded that all or some of the blacks taken to Maryland were free people who had been kidnapped by Prigg.

In 1819, Pennsylvania's chief justice, William Tilghman (who was one of the few slaveholding judges in the North), enforced the federal law, denying that a fugitive slave had the right to a jury trial. He did not otherwise examine the constitutionality of the federal act. In 1823, Chief Justice Isaac Parker of Massachusetts upheld the 1793 law but limited his analysis to "a single point: whether the statute of the United States giving power to seize a slave without a warrant is constitutional." Parker upheld this warrantless seizure because "slaves are not parties to the constitution, and the Fourth Amendment" had "no relation" to the parties. Parker noted that "the constitution does not prescribe the mode of reclaiming a slave, but leaves it to be determined by Congress."[68] The implication of this opinion was that while slaves might be seized without a warrant, free blacks—such as Margaret Morgan and her freeborn child—could not be seized without a warrant.

The opinions of Chancellor Reuben Walworth of New York and Chief Justice Joseph C. Hornblower stand in marked contrast to the meager analysis of Tilghman and Parker. Both judges offered a careful and elaborate analysis of the constitutional issues involved in the 1793 law and fugitive slave clause. Both opinions were relatively recent, reflecting the constitutional dynamics of antebellum federalism. Both judges thought the 1793 law was unconstitutional.

Although Hornblower's opinion was unreported, it was well-known and Story certainly had access to it.[69] It is possible he felt that because it was unreported he could ignore it. But it is just as likely that he ignored it because it did not support his claims in *Prigg*. Hornblower emphatically declared the 1793 law unconstitutional.

In *Jack* v. *Martin* (1835), Chancellor Walworth, speaking for New York's highest court, also found the 1793 law unconstitutional because Congress lacked the power to pass it. Walworth had "looked in vain among the powers delegated to congress by the constitution, for any general authority to that body to legislate on this subject. It is certainly not contained in any express grant of power, and it does not appear to be embraced in the general grant of incidental powers contained in the last clause of the constitution relative to the powers of congress." After careful consideration of the Constitution's text and the state statutes existing in 1787, Walworth concluded that the 1793 law was unconstitutional. He wrote:

> I find it impossible to bring my mind to the conclusion that the framers of the constitution have authorized the congress of the United States to pass a law by which the certificate of a justice of the peace of the state, shall be made conclusive evidence of the right of the claimant, to remove one who may be a free native born citizen of this state, to a distant part of the union as a slave; and thereby to deprive such person of the benefit of the writ of *habeas corpus,* as well as of his common law suit to try his right of citizenship in the state where the claim is made, and where he is residing at the time of such claim.[70]

Walworth's opinion in *Jack* v. *Martin* was not aimed at preventing the rendition of fugitive slaves. Walworth upheld Martin's claim to the slave Jack and firmly supported the obligation of state officials to return fugitive slaves, asserting that every "state officer or private citizen, who owes allegiance to the United States and has taken the usual oath to support the constitution" was obligated to enforce the fugitive slave clause of the Constitution.[71] Nevertheless, he categorically denied the constitutionality of the 1793 law.

Despite Story's reputation as a great legal scholar, he distorted Walworth's opinion. Walworth—speaking for the highest court of the largest state in the Union, with a huge presence in the national legal community—emphatically rejected the constitutionality of the 1793 law. But, citing Walworth's opinion, Story wrote that "on all these occasions" the "validity [of the 1793 law] has been affirmed."[72] This statement is simply wrong. Furthermore, the Pennsylvania Supreme Court, in affirming Prigg's conviction, disagreed with Story's interpretation of the law. Determined to let nothing stand in his way, Story did more than ignore countervailing precedents; he rewrote them to support his own opinion.

The cost of Story's interpretation of the fugitive slave clause and the relevant precedents would be borne by northern blacks. After *Prigg*, a slave catcher could seize any black, whether slave or free, and remove that person to the South. No state court could intervene; no state official could question the actions of the slave catcher. The facts of *Prigg* illustrate the dangers of Story's opinion.

When Prigg and his companions seized Margaret Morgan, she made no claim of "mistaken" identity. Although she was the child of people who were born slaves, Morgan had lived her entire life as a free person. The circumstances of her arrival in Pennsylvania reveal the problems with Story's aggressively proslavery opinion. These facts show that Morgan and her children had viable claims to freedom under Pennsylvania law and under Maryland law. In other words, although once a slave, by 1837 Morgan may have been legally free. And certainly, regarding her Pennsylvania-born child or children, there was no question of freedom from birth and no claim of fugitive slave status; under no reasonable interpretation could a child born in Pennsylvania have been considered subject to the federal law of 1793.[73] Justice Story glossed over these facts in his desire to write a sweeping, nationalistic opinion despite the fact that the circumstances of Morgan's life underscore the necessity of personal liberty laws to protect free blacks wrongly claimed as fugitives under federal law.

In *Prigg*, Justice Story repeated, in the barest details, that the Pennsylvania trial court had convicted Prigg of removing Margaret from the state "with force and violence . . . with a design and intention of selling . . . her as a slave or servant for life," contrary to Pennsylvania's 1826 law. He recounted Prigg's response that Morgan "was a slave for life, and held to labour and service under and according to the laws of Maryland, to a certain Margaret Ashmore, a citizen of Maryland; that the slave escaped and fled from Maryland into Pennsylvania in 1832."[74] Almost as an afterthought, Story added that "one of the children was born in Pennsylvania, more than a year after the said negro woman had fled and escaped from Maryland."[75] Story never commented on how his decision condemned this freeborn citizen of Pennsylvania to a life of bondage.

The facts, as Story presents them, raise three important questions which the Justice never addressed. First: Was Morgan in fact a "slave for life" under Maryland law? Second: Had Morgan in fact "escaped and fled from Maryland into Pennsylvania?" And third: What was the status of the child—and was it only one child—who "was born in Pennsylvania?"

Failing to address these issues allowed Story to create a right of self-help for slave hunters while striking down Pennsylvania's personal liberty law. Story asserted that "the owner of a slave is clothed with entire authority, in every state in the Union, to seize and recapture his slave, whenever he can do it without any breach of the peace, or any illegal violence. In this sense and to this extent this clause of the Constitution may properly be said to execute itself; and to require no aid from legislation, state or national."[76]

Because he did not consider the facts of Margaret Morgan's life, Story did not address how a state would be able to protect the liberty of its freeborn citizens, such as Morgan's child. Only by ignoring the free status of the child and the possible free status of Morgan herself could Story justify the right of self-help while striking down the state protections for free blacks.

Margaret Ashmore claimed Margaret Morgan on the grounds that she had never been legally emancipated. Morgan had a legitimate claim to freedom, however, because Mrs. Ashmore apparently knew she had moved to Pennsylvania and silently acquiesced in this. Because Morgan's status was never brought before any Pennsylvania court, this issue was not raised in Prigg's trial.[77] Nevertheless, Story might have addressed these issues in his opinion, if he had been interested in protecting the liberty of free blacks. These facts might have been enough to send the case back to trial in Pennsylvania, to determine if Morgan had in fact been free all along. After all, if Margaret Morgan was free under Pennsylvania law because she came to the state with the knowledge and implicit permission of Mrs. Ashmore, then she was never a fugitive slave. Morgan did not actually "escape" from Maryland, but calmly and openly moved to Pennsylvania. And in all likelihood, Ashmore knew when she left and where she had gone, and did nothing to stop her. Even if the Supreme Court had decided it could not consider Morgan's claims to freedom because she was not a party to the case, this potential claim to freedom should have alerted Story to the importance of allowing states to protect the liberty of their residents.

Morgan may also have had a claim to freedom under Maryland law. Technically Morgan was a slave because she had never been formally manumitted. Maryland, like all other slave states, did not allow a master to manumit slaves de facto. In 1837, however, a Maryland court implied that a slave might become free because "he appeared at all times openly, and it was notorious to his neighbors" that he resided in Pennsylvania.[78] This was analogous to the concept of adverse possession in real property law. Because Ashmore had allowed Margaret to adversely possess herself by living free in both Maryland and Pennsylvania for her entire life, Margaret might have had a claim to freedom. The finding of the 1830 census that she was free would certainly have bolstered this claim.

If Margaret were free, then her children were also free. And if somehow she only became free by living in Pennsylvania, then her children became free there as well. Even if she was not free, at least there was no disputing the free birth of her Pennsylvania-born child (or children). Under Pennsylvania law, anyone born in the state was born free.[79]

If either Margaret Morgan or any of her children were free under Pennsylvania law, then Prigg had no right to remove them from the state. Similarly, the state had a presumptive right to protect them from kidnapping. Shortly before the legislature adopted the 1826 law, five free black children were kidnapped from Philadelphia and sold as slaves. While three of the young boys were returned to Philadelphia after "they fell into the hands of a humane protector" in Mississippi, the other two died during their illegal captivity.[80]

While the 1826 law might have been used to frustrate the return of some fugitives, its purpose was to prevent kidnapping and avoid conflicts between Pennsylvania and her slaveholding neighbors. At the time of its adoption, "it is unlikely" that many people "understood that the law was subject to interpretations which would virtually deny the recovery of runaways in Pennsylvania." The 1826 act was aimed at kidnappers, not slave catchers, only punishing those who used "force or violence" or "fraud and false pretense" to "take, carry away, or seduce any negro or mulatto . . . with a design and intention of selling and disposing of . . . such negro or mulatto, as a slave."[81] Passed before the emergence of the militant abolitionist movement in the 1830s, the law was not the work of antislavery activism, but a genuine attempt to protect free blacks from kidnapping.

Story might have tried to balance the need to prevent kidnapping with the rights of masters to claim actual fugitives. In dissent, Justice McLean argued for precisely this position. Story, however, showed little interest in protecting the liberty of Pennsylvania's free black population. By striking down the 1826 law, Story left Pennsylvania powerless to prevent the kidnapping of its own citizens. He willingly sacrificed the fate of free blacks for his dream of strengthening federal laws.

After Justice Story's death, his son William Wetmore Story claimed that his father "repeatedly and earnestly spoke" of *Prigg* as a "triumph of freedom."[82] This phrase does not appear in any of Justice Story's letters, and there is no independent evidence to support the claim. It is doubtful that Justice Story thought his opinion was a "triumph of freedom." Rather, the "triumph of freedom" seems to be just one more story, invented by a dutiful son, to defend his father's reputation.

William Wetmore Story claimed the decision favored freedom "because it promised practically to nullify the Act of Congress,—it being generally supposed to be impracticable to reclaim fugitive slaves in the free States, except with the aid of State legislation, and State authority." William Wetmore Story assumed that without the active aid of state judges, sheriffs, and the like, masters would be unable to remove fugitives from the North. This analysis stemmed from Story's assertion in *Prigg* that the 1793 law was "clearly constitutional in all its leading provisions," with the possible exception "of that part which confers authority upon state magistrates" to enforce the law. Story noted that a difference of opinion might exist as to "whether state magistrates are bound to act" under the law but that no doubt was "entertained by this Court that state magistrates may, if they choose, exercise that authority, unless prohibited by state legislation." William Wetmore Story argued that a "triumph of freedom" would occur if state officials refused to enforce the federal law. Some northern judges and legislators would in fact take advantage of this part of Story's opinion to withdraw their support for enforcement of the federal law, partially shaping Story's opinion into a triumph of freedom.[83]

In reality, William Wetmore Story's claims for the antislavery thrust of *Prigg* do not comport with the text of Justice Story's opinion, his Court career, or his actions after the decision. As a lawyer, scholar, and judge, Story was a committed nationalist. His *Commentaries on the Constitution* was "the most influential statement of constitutional nationalism made in the Nineteenth Century."[84] In *Prigg*, Story created a federal common law right to recapture a slave. Rather than limiting the reach of the federal government, this conclusion expanded federal power at the expense of the northern

states. This result is consistent with the rest of Story's jurisprudence, his nationalism, and his lifelong commitment to
creating a federal common law.

In 1812, Story silently opposed the outcome in *United
States* v. *Hudson and Goodwin,* where the Court found that
the national government could not enforce the common law
of crimes. A year later, in *United States* v. *Coolidge* (1813), Story,
while riding circuit, tried to apply federal common law to admiralty cases. Citing *Hudson and Goodwin,* in 1816 the Supreme Court reversed this attempt to create a new form of
federal common law.[85] Unable to convince the Court, Story
urged Congress to pass legislation to "give the Judicial Courts
of the United States power to punish all crimes and offenses
against the Government, as at common law." In 1818, Story
sent a draft of such legislation to Senator David Daggett of
Connecticut. In 1825, Congress amended the federal criminal code, based on a draft that Story provided. In 1842, he
urged Senator John Macpherson Berrien to recodify all federal criminal law and extend the common law to federal
admiralty jurisdiction.[86]

Story's attempts to create a federal common law of crimes
paralleled his successful effort in *Swift* v. *Tyson* (1842) to create
a general federal common law for civil litigation.[87] Significantly, Story wrote the opinion in *Swift* in the same term that
he wrote the opinion in *Prigg.*

By nationalizing slavery in *Prigg,* Story could create a
federal common law right of recaption for slaves, just as he
had persistently tried to expand federal common law in
other areas of jurisprudence. The antislavery sentiments
he once felt were long forgotten. In defending this constitutionally protected common law right of recaption, Story
declared:

the clause contains a positive and unqualified recognition of the right of the owner in the slave, unaffected by any state law or regulation whatsoever, because there is no qualification or restriction of it to be found therein. . . . If this be so, then all the incidents to that right attach also; the owner must, therefore, have the right to seize and re-possess the slave, which the local laws of his own state confer upon him as property; and we all know that this right of seizure and recaption is universally acknowledged in all the slaveholding states.[88]

This analysis nationalized the law of slavery by imposing the law of the slave states on the North. Part of this southern law had to do with race. In the South, all blacks were presumed to be slaves and were treated as such unless they could prove otherwise. Under Story's ruling, this legal presumption now applied in the North. All free blacks were subject to being seized as slaves, and no northern law could protect them. Under Story's ruling, the Constitution fundamentally altered the principle that slavery was a creature of local or "mere municipal regulation." It was now a national institution.[89]

Story's son was correct that *Prigg* allowed for some practical nullification of the fugitive slave law, which could be seen as creating a "triumph of freedom." After *Prigg*, some northern judges refused to hear fugitive slave cases, some local officials refused to help claimants, and some legislatures actually prohibited state support for the federal law.[90] It is important to make a distinction, however, between what state officials did after *Prigg* and what Story intended in his decision.

It would have been completely out of character for Story to have tried to sabotage his own decision. This was not his style.[91] Indeed, it is simply impossible to believe that Story, who had devoted almost his entire life to developing a conservative, formalistic rule of law, would late in his career sabotage one of his most important nationalist opinions in hopes of achieving a secret goal.

Whatever the implications of the opinion were for state policies, Story clearly wanted the states to help return fugitive slaves. Even as he argued for exclusive federal power to regulate fugitive slave rendition, Story did not rule out active, and even legislatively creative, state participation in the capture and incarceration of runaway slaves: "We entertain no doubt whatsoever, that the states, in virtue of their general police power, possess full jurisdiction to arrest and restrain runaway slaves, and remove them from their borders, and otherwise to secure themselves against their depredations and evil example, as they certainly may do in cases of idlers, vagabonds, and paupers."[92] In other words, Story hoped the states would act as slave catchers, arresting and incarcerating fugitives until they could be claimed under the federal law by their owner. His characterization of fugitives as providing "evil example," equivalent to "idlers" and "vagabonds," underscores Story's lack of respect for black people and their human dignity.

Tied to this invitation for state legislative action, Story clearly thought state officers should enforce the federal law. "As to the authority so conferred upon state magistrates, while a difference of opinion has existed . . . none is entertained by this court, that state magistrates may, if they choose, exercise that authority. . . ."[93] This is consistent with his career of favoring a strong national government and hoping that the states would support the federal government. Story was a thoroughgoing judicial nationalist. *Prigg* could be a triumph of freedom only if northern states refused to enforce federal laws and then passed legislation in opposition to the national government, which is certainly something Story did not support. This would have amounted to nullification, which Story hated and feared. Throughout Story's judicial and earlier political career, he had always vigorously opposed states' rights claims and nullification, which in his mind were the ultimate threats to the Union and the constitutional nationalism he held dear. *Prigg* may have pitted Story's personal hostility to slavery against his lifelong commitment to constitutional nationalism. If so, his nationalism easily won.

The "triumph of freedom" analysis also assumes that Story not only disliked slavery, but was somehow a secret abolitionist. Surely Story disliked slavery, as did most northerners. But Story was never an abolitionist; rather, he opposed the abolitionists because he believed they threatened the Union.

Story's goal in *Prigg* was to nationalize fugitive slave rendition. He in fact hoped Congress would follow his decision with a stronger fugitive slave law, and would further enhance the power of the national government. Shortly after the Court decided *Prigg,* Story wrote to Senator John Macpherson Berrien of North Carolina about various legislative matters. After recounting their previous collaboration on federal legislation Story offered a startling proposal to amend existing federal laws so that "in all cases, where by the Laws of the U. States, powers were conferred on State Magistrates, the same powers might be exercised by Commissioners appointed by the Circuit Courts." He elaborated:

> I was induced to make the provision thus general, because State Magistrates now generally refuse to act, & cannot be compelled to act; and the Act of 1793 respecting fugitive

slaves confers the power on State Magistrates to act in delivering up Slaves. You saw in the case of Prigg . . . how the duty was evaded, or declined. In conversing with several of my Brethren on the Supreme Court, we all thought that it would be a great improvement, & would tend much to facilitate the recapture of Slaves, if Commissioners of the Circuit Court were clothed with like powers.[94]

Story offered Berrien the solution to the problem of federal exclusivity and the role of the states in enforcing the Fugitive Slave Law. The federal government would supply the enforcement mechanism, through commissioners in every county. The fundamental problem with this idea was how to enact it in a Congress where northerners held a majority in the House of Representatives. Story, the justice, had the answer for Berrien, the politician:

This might be done without creating the slightest sensation in Congress, if the provision were made general. . . . It would then pass without observation. The Courts would appoint commissioners in every county, & thus meet the practical difficulty now presented by the refusal of State Magistrates. It might be unwise to provoke debate to insert a Special clause in this first section, referring to the fugitive Slave Act of 1793. Suppose you add at the end of the first section: "& shall & may exercise all the powers, that any State judge, Magistrate, or Justice of the Peace may exercise under any other Law or Laws of the United States."[95]

This was not the letter of a man hoping for a triumph of freedom; nor does it sound like the voice of a man who had once opposed the spread of slavery and had condemned the African slave trade as piracy. This was the letter of a justice committed to the aggrandizement of federal power, the return of fugitive slaves, and the removal of their "evil example" from the North.

This letter is doubly damning for William Wetmore Story's claim of the "triumph of freedom." In *Life and Letters,* he reprinted its first part, which dealt with bankruptcy law, but edited out and did not reprint the material quoted above.[96] The son deliberately hid the evidence proving that his father never thought *Prigg* was a "triumph of freedom" and never wanted it to be such. *Prigg* was a triumph of slavery and a disaster for free blacks, and the author of the opinion knew this. He also wanted to insure that his handiwork would be implemented. Story might have written a milder opinion in *Prigg* that balanced the rights of free blacks with claims of masters seeking fugitives. Perhaps he would have lost in the Court on this opinion, and he would have had to join Justice McLean in dissent. But the fact is, *Prigg* dovetails with so much of Story's career that it is impossible to think that he did not endorse all the points he made. His letter to Berrien underscores this.

Justice Story, Judicial Nationalism, and Slavery

When appointed to the Court, Story was enamored with Thomas Jefferson and Virginia. As such, he avoided speaking about slavery. By 1818, Story was openly hostile to slavery. In 1819, Story vigorously opposed the western spread of slavery. In *La Jeune Eugenie* and his grand jury charges on the slave trade, he expressed his revulsion toward the African trade and slavery itself. In the 1830s, he privately opposed Texas annexation and secretly advised public opponents of the annexation, which he thought was "grossly unconstitutional." Although no supporter of the abolitionists, Story privately told Harriet Martineau that the gag rules passed by Congress to prevent the reading of abolitionist petitions were "in effect a denial of the constitutional right of petition."[97] On the other hand, after *La Jeune Eugenie*, Story never again spoke out against slavery from the bench or in any public forum.

Why, then, did this Massachusetts man—who personally found slavery abhorrent—take an unnecessarily proslavery position in *Prigg*? Why did he write an opinion that jeopardized the freedom of more than 170,000 free blacks in the North? Why did he claim that the Constitution *required* that southerners should have an unimpeded right to seize any black in the North, and without even a hearing, be able to remove that person to the South? Why did he propose a law to Senator Berrien for the massive federal intrusion in the North to support slavery? Why did he hold that the Constitution mandated that the northern states have no power to interfere with the kidnapping of their neighbors and fellow citizens?

The answers are rooted in Story's profound constitutional nationalism and his fear of southern nullificationists. In *Prigg*, Story asserted that the right to seize a fugitive slave was a case "arising under the Constitution" obligating Congress to "prescribe the mode and extent in which it shall be applied, and how, and under what circumstances the proceedings shall afford a complete protection and guaranty to the right."[98] In essence, Story claimed that the Constitution required him to protect the right of masters to recover fugitive slaves and to seize *any* northern black—slave or free—at will, with the free states prohibited from interfering. In *Prigg*, Story found that Congress had the exclusive power to regulate the rendition of fugitive slaves. This is one of the earliest examples we have in constitutional law of the preemption doctrine. But, inconsistently, Story asserted a right of self-help that could ignore the exclusive acts of Congress.

Story used *Prigg* to further strengthen the national government. It was an opportunity he could not pass up. The cost was the freedom of some blacks—such as Margaret Morgan and her children. It was a cost Story was willing to make African-Americans pay—as long as he could rationalize it as essential to expanding federal power.

We cannot know if the outcome was a function of his own personal views of blacks, his dislike of abolitionists, his fear of southern extremists, or simply his lifelong desire to enhance the power of the national government and to defeat antislavery states' rights tendencies. But the result is clear. A justice who had once thought slavery was deeply immoral rewrote history, misstated precedents, and made up new constitutional doctrine to nationalize southern slave law and impose it on the entire nation. The decision jeopardized the liberty of every black in the North, whether free or fugitive. The injustice of this opinion was profound.

A year after *Prigg*, Justice Story refused to issue a writ of habeas corpus for George Latimer, a fugitive slave captured in Boston. The case was fairly straightforward. Even without *Prigg*, Story doubtless would have ruled against Latimer. Abolitionists vilified him for this, comparing him to the repressive seventeenth-century English judges Sir William Scroggs and Judge George Jeffreys (the "Hanging Judge"). The abolitionists dubbed Story the "SLAVE-CATCHER-IN-CHIEF FOR THE NEW ENGLAND STATES."[99]

This was surely unfair, since Latimer clearly was a fugitive slave. On the other hand, given Story's support for self-help and the right of recaption, the condemnation was perhaps earned. He had in fact become the slave-catcher-in-chief for the entire nation, nationalizing southern law, allowing any black, anywhere, to be seized by any white without any proof. Under *Prigg* no state could protect free blacks or interfere in the seizure or the rendition.

The great judicial nationalist who had once condemned slavery as a relic of barbarism had nationalized slavery. This was a man who once bristled that Virginia had "bullied us, and led us, and wheedled us, and governed us."[100] Now he was himself bullied by Chief Justice Taney and the South. Story's jurisprudence only encouraged southerners to demand even more protections for slavery. Under Story's creative reading of history, and his expansive and equally suspect interpretation of the language of the Constitution, southern slave law was now the law of the land. Part of the explanation for this is Story's fears about the Union. Certainly the nullification crisis in 1832 to 1833 had frightened him, as had John C. Calhoun's theories of state sovereignty, and the rise of militant antislavery. Story doubtless saw his role as mediating on the Court to keep the South within the Union. But in *Prigg* there was no mediation. The South and slavery won it all.

5

Roger B. Taney:
Slavery's Great Chief Justice

In February 1865 the United States Senate considered what should have been a routine appropriation to fund a bust of the late Chief Justice Roger Brooke Taney, to be placed alongside those of other chief justices in the basement of the Senate, where the Supreme Court met. This honor was almost pro forma.

But no other justice was like Roger Taney. At the time of his death, in October 1864, he was denounced and vilified. He was the author of the Court's opinion in *Dred Scott* v. *Sandford* (1857).[1] That was enough for opponents of slavery to oppose the appropriation. Senator Charles Sumner of Massachusetts argued: "If a man has done evil during his life he must not be complimented in marble." Sumner noted that England had never honored the hated Lord George Jeffreys, notoriously called the hanging judge in the seventeenth century, who was "famous for his talents as for his crimes." For Taney the test was the same. Like Jeffreys, Taney had been "the tool of unjust power," undeserving of honor. Taney had "served . . . none other than the Slave Power" and had "administered justice at last wickedly, and degraded the judiciary of the country, and

172

degraded the age." Sumner reminded the Senate that Taney's opinion in Dred Scott "was more thoroughly abominable than anything of the kind in the history of the court. Judicial baseness reached its lowest point in that occasion." Sumner suggested that there be a "vacant space in our courtroom" to "testify to the justice of our Republic. Let it speak in warning to all who would betray liberty." Rather than be remembered in marble, Taney's career should be left to scholarship to assess. There, Senator Sumner confidently predicted, "the name of Taney is to be hooted down the page of history."[2]

Sumner's prediction was generally correct in the nineteenth century. But Taney's reputation has waxed and waned in the last century. Jurists and scholars have praised his economic jurisprudence, arguing this legacy is far more important than the single decision in *Dred Scott*. In addition to trying to marginalize *Dred Scott*, admirers have claimed that in his early years Taney personally opposed slavery, supported blacks rights, and manumitted all his slaves. They point out that as a young lawyer he defended a Methodist minister, Jacob Gruber, whose antislavery sermon was said to promote slave rebellions. The first two contentions are problematic at best, the third is simply untrue, and Taney's defense of Gruber is widely misunderstood. Most modern scholars accept the assessment of Don E. Fehrenbacher, that by the 1850s Taney had become "a bitter sectionalist" determined to protect slavery and defeat northern hostility to the institution.[3]

Was *Dred Scott* an aberration, a mistake by an aging justice? Or was *Dred Scott* the culmination of a career focused on supporting slavery and persecuting free blacks? Charles Sumner posed his own question about Taney, and also answered it: "What is the office of Chief Justice, if it has been used to betray Human Rights? The crime is great according to the position of the criminal." Does Taney's career merit that condemnation?

Dred Scott in Brief

Before considering Taney's life, career, and relationship to slavery, it is necessary to offer a brief summary of *Dred Scott*— because all discussions of Taney lead to *Dred Scott*. We cannot understand his career without understanding the case.

Dred Scott was born in Southampton Country, Virginia, between 1795 and 1800. His owner, Peter Blow, eventually moved to St. Louis and, in the early 1830s, Scott was purchased by Dr. John Emerson, an Army surgeon. In the 1830s and 1840s Emerson took Scott to Fort Armstrong, in Illinois, and then to Fort Snelling, in present-day Minnesota. Slavery was illegal in Illinois, and any slave taken to the state had a strong legal claim to freedom. Fort Snelling was in the Wisconsin Territory, where the Missouri Compromise of 1820 prohibited slavery. Under existing precedents, including those in Missouri, Scott became free by living in these places. Scott never asserted his freedom while living in either place, perhaps because he did not know he had a legal claim to freedom or perhaps because he saw little value in gaining his freedom in these remote frontier outposts. While at Fort Snelling, Scott married Harriet Robinson, a slave owned by the local Indian agent, and Emerson acquired her as well. They would later have two children, including one who was born on a steamboat north of Missouri, between the free state of Illinois and the Iowa Territory, where slavery was also prohibited. Scott and his family were back in St. Louis when Emerson died in 1843. After Emerson's death the sons of Peter Blow, his original owner, offered to lend Scott the money to buy his freedom. When Emerson's widow, Irene Sanford Emerson, refused this offer, Scott sued for his freedom on the grounds that he had become free through his residence in two jurisdictions where slavery was illegal. This was based on jurisprudence dating from the English case of *Somerset* v. *Stewart* (1772), which held that slavery could exist only by positive law—statutes—and therefore that if slaves were taken to places where there were no laws creating slavery, they became free. In the past Missouri had accepted this precedent, and many slaves in the state had gained freedom through residence in free jurisdictions. Indeed, in 1850, a jury of twelve white men in St. Louis declared Scott and his family to be free. In 1852, however, the Missouri Supreme Court rejected nearly thirty years of precedents, and reversed Scott's victory.

At this point the case might have ended. By 1852, however, Mrs. Emerson had moved to Springfield, Massachusetts, where she married Dr. Calvin Chaffee, who ironically would become an antislavery Republican Congressman later in the decade. Sometime during the courtship and relocation, Mrs. Emerson sold (or possibly gave) Scott and his family to her brother, John F. A. Sanford. By 1854 Sanford was living in New York. This change of residence allowed Scott's new lawyer, Roswell M. Field, to begin a new case in federal court, based on the power of federal courts to hear lawsuits "between Citizens of different States" (known as "diversity" jurisdiction, in reference to the diversity of the litigants' state citizenship).

Scott asserted that he was a free citizen of Missouri, illegally held in slavery by Sanford, a citizen of New York. Sanford challenged this jurisdiction, arguing that even if Scott was free, as an African-American, he could never be a citizen of Missouri. District Judge Robert W. Wells, a slave owner originally from Virginia, rejected this argument, and allowed Scott to sue, but eventually held for Sanford on the grounds that the federal court should follow the ruling of the state supreme court. Scott appealed to the United States Supreme Court arguing that the federal judge (and by implication the state court) had improperly interpreted the Missouri Compromise, and that the state courts were obligated to uphold the federal law.

After nearly eleven years of litigation in state and federal courts, the Supreme Court finally decided the case in 1857. In his sweeping, fifty-five-page "Opinion of the Court," Taney sought to settle all the nation's divisive political questions relating to slavery in favor of the South.

Briefly, Taney held that Scott could not sue in federal court, because free blacks could never be citizens of the United States. In language that was shocking even for the time, Taney asserted that blacks "are not included, and were not intended to be included, under the word 'citizens' in the Constitution, and can therefore claim none of the rights and privileges which that instrument provides for and secures to citizens of the United States." On the contrary, he argued, they were "a subordinate and inferior class of beings who had been subjugated by the dominant race, and, whether emancipated or not, yet remained subject to their authority, and had no rights or privileges but such as those who held the power and the Government might choose to grant them." Taney concluded that blacks were "so far inferior, that they had no rights which the white man was bound to respect."[4] This infamous language went far beyond Sanford's argument that a free black *in Missouri* could not be a citizen of that state.

After determining that Scott could not sue in federal court, Taney should have dismissed the case for lack of jurisdiction. At the end of the case Taney would do just that. But before dismissing the case Taney also held that slaves were a specially protected form of property under the Constitution, that Congress had no power to ban slavery in the territories, that the ban on slavery in the Missouri Compromise was unconstitutional, and that Congress had no power to pass laws to regulate or govern the federal territories. These conclusions were shocking because Congress had passed scores of laws regulating the territories, and Article IV of the Constitution empowered Congress "to dispose of and make all needful rules and regulations respecting the territory or other property belonging to the United States."

This brief summary illuminates why the case is central to understanding Taney's relationship to slavery. Taney's actions and jurisprudence both before and after *Dred Scott,* however, illustrate why he was slavery's greatest ally on the Court.

Taney's Maryland Years

Far more than John Marshall, whom he succeeded in 1836, Roger Brooke Taney was a product of the wealth and privilege of the plantation South. Born in 1777 in Calvert County, Maryland, Taney grew up on his father's tobacco plantation. His family had settled in the area in the 1660s, gradually acquiring significant quantities of land and slaves. By the mid-eighteenth century the Taneys had converted to Catholicism, perhaps to be closer to some of the leading families in the colony—especially the Carrolls. By the eve of the Revolution, Taney's father, Michael Taney, was one of the wealthiest men in the county. But despite his prestige and wealth, Michael Taney was only a first lieutenant in the county militia during the Revolution, and saw no service beyond the county. Michael Taney was a patriot, but unlike John Marshall (or Marshall's father, Thomas) he did not make many sacrifices or take any risks during the war. While Thomas Marshall commanded the county militia as a colonel and John Marshall served with George Washington, Michael Taney was a minor officer who stayed home. After the war, Michael Taney served briefly in the Maryland House of Delegates—a role that was almost pro forma for a wealthy planter—but otherwise tended to his slaves and land, living the life of a country gentleman. By 1810 he had large landholdings and at least twenty-seven slaves.[5]

In 1792 Michael Taney was wealthy enough to send fifteen-year-old Roger to Dickinson College in Lancaster, Pennsylvania. Taney graduated in 1795, having been elected valedictorian of his class, an honor reflecting his intelligence and geniality. Taney's three years at Dickinson were the only time he ever lived in a free state. Taney would spend the rest of his life in the narrow cultural milieu of the slaveholding Chesapeake, living in Maryland and Washington, D.C. After graduating from Dickinson, Taney never again lived with people who were not southerners and slave owners. This made him far more parochial than John Marshall.

After college Taney studied law in Annapolis with Judge Jeremiah Townley Chase of the Maryland General Court. In 1799 the twenty-two-year-old, newly minted lawyer returned to Calvert County, where he was elected as a Federalist to the state legislature. In 1800, however, Taney lost his seat, as Jeffersonian Republicans carried most of the county.

In 1801 Taney moved to Frederick, in western Maryland, where he formed a partnership with Francis Scott Key, whose father was a wealthy planter with significant political connections in the state. Key's uncle, Philip Barton Key, was one of Maryland's most prominent lawyers and politicians. In 1806 Taney solidified these connections by marrying his partner's sister, Anne. For the next two decades Taney was a successful lawyer and politician, winning a five-year term in the state senate in 1816 and becoming the leader of the Federalists in that state.[6]

Roger and Ann grew up on plantations surrounded by slaves who served them in everyday life and produced the tobacco that supported a life of comfort. Slavery created the wealth that sent Taney to college in Pennsylvania and supported him as he began his legal career. From "an early age" Taney "owned slaves."[7] Although his biographers claim he manumitted his own slaves, he freed only some of them. In the course of his life, slaves served his family in households in Frederick, Baltimore, and Washington, D.C. Eventually he would inherit more land and slaves from his father. His household gained slaves, too, when his wife brought some to the marriage in 1806, and inherited more in years to follow.

In 1816 Taney's first law partner and brother-in-law, Francis Scott Key, was one of the founders of the American Colonization Society. The Society was dedicated to transporting free blacks and former slaves to West Africa. Most free blacks saw colonization as a pernicious effort to remove them from their homeland. By the 1830s white opponents of slavery agreed with this analysis. Certainly many white members of the Society supported that goal. Other white members, however, saw the Society as a vehicle for encouraging manumission—and its existence did mean that some slaves gained their freedom.

Taney joined the Society shortly after its founding and across the next several years he manumitted some, but not all, of his slaves. Taney supported legislation to prevent the kidnapping of free blacks and he briefly served as a lawyer for an organization which tried to prevent such kidnappings. There is no record that he actually argued any cases for the organization. In this period he also lent money to a free black who was trying to purchase his wife, who was still a slave. This sort of charitable *noblesse oblige* was consistent with Taney's Federalist politics, and his moderate position as a slaveholder, a colonizationist, and a supporter of the rule of law. At the same time, in the Maryland senate he supported a resolution to prevent Maryland slaves from escaping into Pennsylvania.[8]

Taney's most important action involving slavery in this period did not concern blacks. Rather, it involved the free speech rights of Rev. Jacob Gruber, a white Methodist minister from Pennsylvania. In 1818 Gruber gave a sermon in Hagerstown, Maryland, denouncing the usual litany of sinful behavior, including sexual immorality, profanity, and drinking. In line with traditional Methodist teachings, he also condemned slavery, arguing that it was inconsistent to hold the Declaration of Independence "in one hand, and a bloody whip in the other while a negro stood trembling, with his back cut and bleeding." Among the three thousand people at this open-air revival were about four hundred blacks. Gruber did not urge slaves to revolt or escape, but he did urge his fellow white Christians to consider the immorality of owning slaves.

Taney defended Gruber against a charge of "inciting" slaves to revolt. His biographers claim this proves Taney was personally antislavery. But lawyers often don't agree with their clients, especially in civil liberties cases. Taney doubtless thought Gruber's sermon was innocuous and not incendiary. He might also have been, as a Roman Catholic in an overwhelmingly mainstream Protestant state, particularly solicitous of the rights of a religious minority (which Methodists were at the time). Taney offered a classic free-speech defense: "Any man has a right to publish his opinions on that subject [slavery] whenever he pleases. It is a subject of national concern, and may at all times be freely discussed." In his argument, Taney referred to slave traders as "those reptiles, who live by trading in human flesh." But hostility to the slave trade should not be misunderstood as hostility to slavery. Many southerners found the trade to be particularly abhorrent. Taney also declared that "the evil of slavery" was a "blot on our national character," but this too was a common platitude among upper South leaders, even as they continued to own slaves. He explained that "a hard necessity" compelled Marylanders "to endure the evil of slavery for a time." Consistent with many Chesapeake slave owners in this period, he blamed slavery on the British, explaining it "was imposed upon us by another nation, while we were yet in a state of colonial vassalage."[9] As a matter of history this claim was utter nonsense, but it doubtless sat well with the Maryland jury that acquitted Gruber.

It is impossible to know what Taney's real views of slavery were at this time. In the Maryland senate he opposed a resolution urging Maryland's members of Congress to support the admission of Missouri as a slave state, but his opposition seems to have been based on the belief that the state legislature should not tell federal representatives how to vote. Taney probably opposed the ban on slavery in the west that was part of the Missouri Compromise.[10] We do not know how much

Taney believed his rhetoric in the Gruber trial. Timothy Huebner argues that in the Gruber trial Taney was a "moderately antislavery lawyer," and this may indeed have been his personal view.[11] But if so, this was also the last time Taney ever said anything in public that was even remotely hostile to slavery. Thus, it is not unreasonable to conclude that his arguments in Gruber's case were those of a conscientious advocate, rather than his own views.

In Gruber's case Taney supported the right of *white* people to engage in public debate on important matters. The case had nothing to do with the rights of slaves or free blacks. After Gruber he quickly emerged as a politician who zealously protected slavery and was unalterably opposed to the rights of free blacks.

Taney is most remembered for his opinion in *Dred Scott* v. *Sandford*, which was overwhelmingly racist and proslavery. Throughout the last century Taney's defenders, including Felix Frankfurter, Alpheus T. Mason, G. Edward White, and Henry J. Abraham, have tried to explain away this opinion as a mistake or an aberration. Edward S. Corwin considered the entire performance by the Court in *Dred Scott* a gross abuse of trust, but refused to single out Taney for special condemnation. Charles Evans Hughes, who served two separate terms on the Supreme Court, said that *Dred Scott* was a "well-intentioned mistake." Yale Law Professor Alexander Bickel called it a "ghastly error," but condemned it only as an "error."[12]

More recently, Henry J. Abraham called *Dred Scott* a "monumental aberration" and complained that "the Taney Court has not only been widely misunderstood but even maligned" because of *Dred Scott*. He argues "it is simply too facile a rationalization to use exclusively the tragic *Dred Scott* decision of 1857, which came in the waning years of Taney's chief justiceship, as a basis for that misunderstanding."[13] Similarly, G. Edward White claims that Taney's "intention" in *Dred Scott* "was benign," asserting "he was concerned not with preserving slavery as such but with maintaining peaceful coexistence between competing ideologies in the nation." White fails to explain how striking down the Missouri Compromise—which had in fact helped maintain "peaceful coexistence" for more than three decades—accomplished that goal. Nor does he explain how sectional harmony was maintained by denying any legal rights to the nation's half-million free blacks—many of whom owned property and some of whom, in the North, voted and even held public office.[14] Had Taney been interested in allowing for peaceful discussion of competing views, he would have written or endorsed a narrow opinion, perhaps upholding Sanford's right to Scott, but not including a discussion of free black citizenship, not denying the power of Congress to regulate the territories, and not striking down the ban on slavery in the Missouri Compromise. Taney did not take this route, and White's recent analysis fails to confront the reality of what he did do.

None of the scholars who defend Taney offer any discussion or analysis of *Prigg* v. *Pennsylvania*, the problem of fugitive slaves, freedom suits by blacks, or Taney's consistent hostility to granting any rights to free blacks, which he had first articulated twenty-five years before *Dred Scott*.

Taney's declaration in *Dred Scott* that free blacks "had no rights which the white man was bound to respect" shocked many Americans in 1857 and still does today. But this was hardly his only proslavery opinion. Nor was it the first time he expressed views that free blacks had no political or legal rights under the U.S. Constitution. Before he went on the Court, Taney was deeply committed to slavery and completely

opposed to the idea that free blacks had rights under the Constitution. His language in *Dred Scott* on black rights was not
an invention of the moment. As Attorney General in 1832 he
told President Andrew Jackson that blacks had no political
or legal rights, except those they might "enjoy" at the "sufferance" and "mercy" of whites, and that blacks, "even when free,"
were a "degraded class" whose "privileges" were "accorded to
them as a matter of kindness and benevolence rather than
right."[15] His *Dred Scott* opinion reaffirmed this position. Well
before *Dred Scott*, Taney displayed his opposition to rights for
free blacks and his absolute commitment to protecting slavery.
He never retreated from these positions. During the Civil War
he did all he could to obstruct President Lincoln's attempts
to preserve the Union. He even drafted an opinion striking
down the Emancipation Proclamation, in case he would gain
the opportunity to do so.[16] On slavery, emancipation, or even
holding the Union together, Taney never offered anything that
resembled compromise or mediation.

The changing view of slavery and Chief Justice Taney over
time dovetailed with the general disillusionment following
World War I that led many scholars to claim that the Civil
War was a great mistake caused by a blundering generation.
Blame for the conflict fell more often on abolitionists than
on fire-eating, proslavery Southerners. Some historians
blamed the crisis of the Union on the nation's mediocre political talent. With the deaths of Henry Clay, Daniel Webster,
and John C. Calhoun, Congress seemed bereft of leadership.
The antebellum decade's quartet of easily-forgotten White
House residents—Zachary Taylor, Millard Fillmore, Franklin
Pierce, and James Buchanan—personified this vacuum in
statesmanship. Yet curiously, these scholars never saw Taney
as blundering in *Dred Scott*. Instead, compared to these

Lilliputian presidents, Chief Justice Taney seemed to be a giant. On the eve of the Great Depression, Taney's stock among historians was rising faster than the shares on Wall Street.

Another reason for Taney's rising stock in the first four decades of the twentieth century was that his economic jurisprudence aligned with progressive notions of constitutional and economic policy. Taney generally supported state economic regulation without federal interference or supervision. Although many of his economic decisions had a proslavery subtext, Progressives and early New Dealers seeking a usable past and judicial precedent to support government regulation of the economy reimagined Taney as an early progressive. In an era when the Court persistently struck down progressive state legislation, the Taney Court offered a model for allowing state experimentation in economic regulation. Taney's support for federalism, particularly in the economic context, pleased progressives, who saw the states as engines for reform. In 1962, a historian argued that "on economic matters" Taney "faced the future" by supporting state laws which challenged entrenched economic interests.[17] Because this was also the goal of most progressive reformers, Taney "became the darling of political liberals."[18]

No one was more responsible for Taney's rehabilitation than Harvard Law School's Felix Frankfurter. In the middle of the New Deal, Frankfurter argued that Taney should be judged by his commercial decisions and not by his decisions on slavery, which Frankfurter downplayed or mischaracterized. His analysis reflected a prevailing opinion about the Civil War's causes—and myopia about the need to protect minorities from oppressive majorities.[19]

Frankfurter praised Taney for being "tolerant of legislative freedom for the states in the absence of Congressional legislation, the more so because implied restrictions upon the states were necessarily the creatures of judicial discretion." Having seen the Supreme Court regularly strike down progressive state legislation on precisely such grounds—and having watched the Court eviscerate the early New Deal legislation—Frankfurter admired Taney's support of state laws and his judicial restraint on economic issues. Frankfurter thought judges should emulate Taney's "conception of the judicial function, [specifically] his unwillingness to open the door to judicial policy-making wider than the Constitution obviously required."[20]

Frankfurter was able to offer this analysis only because he ignored *Dred Scott* and Taney's other slavery cases, including his striking down of northern state legislation to protect free blacks from kidnapping. But Frankfurter was so enamored of Taney that he reached this astounding conclusion: "Least of all was he a 'pro-slavery' man in any invidious sense; he was merely concerned lest the Union be broken by extreme action, and the South become the economic vassal of Northern capitalism."[21] Obsessed with the power of modern corporations, Frankfurter dismissed Taney's decisions on slavery as less important: "Certainly not slavery, but Taney's fear of the growing power of finance was most clearly reflected in his opinions" and thus he was "alert against an application of the Constitution which would foster an economic development regarded by him as mischievous."[22]

Taney's economic jurisprudence did not, however, stem from any jurisprudential theory; it emanated from his own political views, which were hostile to the North. Taney was a good Jacksonian. Consequently, most of his economic decisions simply supported his policy goals. Taney's slavery and race jurisprudence was results-oriented, just like his economic jurisprudence. That economic jurisprudence dovetailed with the demands of the southern slaveocracy, and may have been motivated by these goals. To offer a simple example, in *Mayor of New York* v. *Miln* (1837), the Taney Court carved out an exception to the commerce clause that allowed states to regulate who could enter their boundaries.[23] This decision allowed southern states to arbitrarily arrest free black sailors whose ships entered their ports.

Today, only the most dyed-in-the-wool, lost-cause partisans doubt that the root cause of the Civil War was slavery, or more precisely, the South's implacable demand that slavery be allowed to exist forever. In 1861, the Confederate vice president Alexander Stephens declared that slavery and racism formed "the cornerstone" of the putative Southern nation. Lincoln made the point in his second inaugural address. "All knew," he said, that slavery "was somehow the cause of the war."

With slavery once again central to our understanding of the crisis of the Union, *Dred Scott* looms larger. Taney's overwhelmingly proslavery jurisprudence in other cases and his blatant hostility to the Union during the Civil War further undermine his reputation. Harold Hyman and William Wiecek conclude this: "Deeply conscious of his Maryland roots, Taney was to the core a Southerner, fiercely defensive of his region against the 'aggressions' of the Northern states."[24] Don E. Fehrenbacher, whose book on *Dred Scott* won a Pulitzer Prize, agrees: "Taney's opinion, carefully read, proves to be a work of unmitigated partisanship, polemical in spirit though judicial in its language, and more like an ultimatum than a formula for sectional accommodation." By the 1850s Taney had abandoned all pretense of neutrality in sectional issues. "Behind his mask of judicial propriety" Taney was "seething with anger at 'Northern insult and Northern aggression.'"[25]

Taney's Economic Jurisprudence and Slavery

Before joining the Court, Taney had been a Maryland legis-
lator, state attorney general, United States attorney general,
ad interim secretary of the treasury, and briefly, secretary of
war. As attorney general he drafted Jackson's famous mes-
sage vetoing the rechartering of the Second Bank of the
United States. As *ad interim* secretary of the treasury, Taney
began removing federal deposits from the bank. In 1836 he
became chief justice. From 1836 to 1864 Chief Justice Taney
was a powerful and often dominant (until the Civil War
began) figure on the Court. He wrote more than 270 majority opinions but only a dozen dissents. This record suggests Taney was almost always able to sway the Court to
his views. He could be tactful and genial at times and, unlike Marshall, he willingly assigned important decisions to
other members of the Court. But it is clear that in general
he played a major role in shaping the results. Some of his colleagues found him charming. Justice Samuel F. Miller, a
Lincoln appointee, later wrote of his own earliest encounter
with Taney:

> I had never looked upon the face of Judge Taney, but I
> knew of him. I remembered that he had attempted to
> throttle the Bank of the United States, and I hated him
> for it. . . . He had been the chief Spokesman of the Court
> in the *Dred Scott* case, and I hated him for that. But from
> my first acquaintance with him, I realized that these feel-
> ings toward him were but the suggestions of the worst
> elements of our nature; for before the first term of my
> service in the Court had passed, I more than liked him; I
> loved him.[26]

On the other hand, Taney could be dogmatic and intolerant of dissent. Justice Benjamin Robbins Curtis resigned from the Court because of Taney's nastiness toward him after he had shown the temerity to dissent in *Dred Scott,* eviscerating many of Taney's arguments.

Taney helped shape the booming American economy. In the *Charles River Bridge* (1837) case, he allowed the states to promote economic and industrial development in an age of rapid technological change. He concluded that "any ambiguity" in a corporate charter "must operate against the adventurers [stockholders] and in favor of the public."[27] This strengthened state governments by giving them more latitude in economic regulation. This contrasts with his slavery case opinions denying Northern states the right to regulate the status of people and protect free blacks from kidnapping.

In *Mayor of New York* v. *Miln* (1837) the Taney Court upheld New York City's law regulating immigrants arriving by ship. While giving states some control over immigration, this case also protected the right of the slave states to prohibit free blacks from entering their jurisdictions. Justice Philip Barbour, a slave owner from Virginia, claimed it was "as necessary for a state to provide precautionary measures against the moral pestilence of paupers, vagabonds, and possibly convicts, as it is to guard against the physical pestilence, which may arise from unsound and infectious articles imported." If New York could not regulate immigrants, then South Carolina could not arrest free blacks who entered the state. Thus, the demands of slavery affected the development of constitutional law. Implicit in these cases was the Supreme Court's recognition that the South had a special interest in protecting its slaves from the "corruption" of northern free blacks.[28] In *The License Cases* (1847) the Taney Court upheld the right of states to ban the importation of liquor, while in *Cooley* v. *Board of Port Wardens of Philadelphia* (1852) it upheld a law requiring any ship entering Philadelphia harbor to take on a local pilot. Both decisions reflected Taney's general deference to the states, and empowered the slave states to interfere with interstate commerce to protect slavery.[29] In *The Passenger Cases* (1849), the Court struck down, on commerce clause grounds, state laws taxing immigrants. This decision strengthened the federal government, and potentially weakened the power of southern states to regulate blacks entering their jurisdiction. Significantly, this provoked one of Taney's rare dissents.[30]

Despite his general deference to state economic regulation, Taney encouraged interstate economic development. In *Bank of Augusta* v. *Earle* (1839), Taney held that a bank chartered in one state might do business in another, unless specifically prohibited from doing so. This ruling left the states in the position of having to specifically ban out-of-state corporations from doing business within their jurisdictions.[31] Taney expanded federal jurisdiction in *Propeller Genesee Chief* v. *Fitzhugh* (1852) with a sophisticated, nondoctrinaire approach to economic development. Here he reversed the Marshall Court's doctrine in *The Thomas Jefferson* (1825), which had allowed the states to regulate traffic on inland waters. Taney asserted that the national government could regulate water traffic inside the United States because the Great Lakes "are in truth inland seas. Different States border on them on one side, and a foreign nation on the other. A great and growing commerce is carried on upon them."[32] On an economic decision of truly national concern, such as the regulation of inland waterways in *Genesee Chief,* Taney pragmatically deferred to the national government.

Had Taney's reputation rested on these economic decisions, the Congress in 1864 would not have hesitated to
authorize a bust for the late chief justice. The record is impressive, even if one disagrees with the policy choices the Court
made. For Frankfurter and other scholars who agreed with
Taney's policy choices and his apparent deference to state legislatures, the chief justice's record was the stuff of greatness.

Slavery, Race, and Chief Justice Taney

But Taney's decisions on race, slavery, and the Civil War offer
a different story. Here we see a justice who aggressively protected slavery, made war on free blacks, and never sought to
offer compromises for both sections.

Taney biographers and other scholars have portrayed him
as a moderate on the issue of slavery and race by highlighting
his early ambivalence about slavery and his defense of the
Reverend Jacob Gruber. But the latter appears to be his last
act that could be construed as opposing slavery. As attorney
general and chief justice, Taney protected slavery and undermined the rights of free African-Americans at every turn.
Equally important, during the Civil War, Taney hindered
Lincoln's policy of upholding the Constitution and keeping
the Union intact.

In 1831, as President Andrew Jackson's attorney general,
Taney argued (as he would in *Dred Scott*) that African-
Americans had no legal rights, but could only "enjoy" privileges
accorded by the "mercy" of whites. As he would do again in
Dred Scott, Taney ignored the fact that blacks voted in a
number of states at the time of the ratification of the Constitution, as well as in the 1830s.[33] Instead, Taney asserted:

The African race in the United States even when free, are every where a degraded class, and exercise no political influence. The privileges they are allowed to enjoy, are accorded to them as a matter of kindness and benevolence rather than of right. They are the only class of persons who can be held as mere property, as slaves. And where they are nominally admitted by law to the privileges of citizenship, they have no effectual power to defend them, and are permitted to be citizens by the sufferance of the white population and hold whatever rights they enjoy at their mercy. They were never regarded as a constituent portion of the sovereignty of any state, but as a separate and degraded people to whom the sovereignty of each state might accord or withhold such privileges as they deemed proper. They are not looked upon as citizens by the contracting parties who formed the Constitution. They were evidently not supposed to be included by the term citizens.

Taney further concluded that the Declaration of Independence did not apply to blacks, who were not entitled to the natural rights of "life, liberty, and pursuit of happiness."[34] While this position probably correctly interpreted the views of the primary author of the Declaration—Thomas Jefferson— it overlooked the facts that blacks had served in the Revolutionary army, that free blacks held property in every state, that a number of states had taken steps to end slavery, and that some states gave blacks the rights to testify against whites, to vote, and to hold public office. As attorney general, Taney chose not to acknowledge that free blacks had voted in at least six states at the time of the adoption of the Constitution. Indeed, evidence exists that in Taney's own home state of Maryland at least some free blacks voted at this time.[35]

Attorney General Taney's opinion on the rights of free African-Americans demonstrates that the anti-black, pro-slavery views he later expressed in *Dred Scott* were not aberrations or mere reflections of the changing politics of the 1850s. Rather, he had held these views for at least a quarter of a century before *Dred Scott*. His opinion as attorney general affected internal policy choices by the Jackson administration, bolstering Jackson's hands-off policy toward southern regulations of free blacks from the British Empire and the North.

Taney's first slavery case, *United States* v. *Garonne* (1837), illustrates his callous hostility to blacks and black freedom. The case involved slaves who had been taken to France by their owners and then taken back to Louisiana. The U.S. attorney determined that bringing slaves back to the United States violated the bans on the African slave trade—and after losing in district court, appealed to the Supreme Court.[36]

One of the black passengers was a young girl named Priscilla, who had been taken to Paris and then been sent back on the *Garonne* to New Orleans by her owner. Under the law of France, Priscilla became free when her owner brought her to that country. But Chief Justice Taney cavalierly dismissed this: "For even assuming that by the French law she was entitled to freedom, the Court is of opinion that there is nothing in the act of congress . . . to prevent her mistress from bringing, or sending her back to her place of residence; and continuing to hold her as before, in her service."[37] But if Priscilla was free the moment she landed in France, then once free she would always be free, because there was no federal or Louisiana law making her a slave. And if she was free in France, then it was an obvious violation of the ban on the slave trade to bring this free person into the United States in order to enslave her. Taney ignored this well-settled rule, and held that it was permissible for Priscilla's owner to take her out of the United States—whereupon she became free—only to return her to the United States as a slave.

In the *Garonne* case, Taney argued that the ban on the slave trade was not meant to prohibit masters from traveling with their slaves out of the country and back. This was certainly a reasonable reading of the law, and might very well have applied to situations where the travel was to slave jurisdictions such as Cuba, Brazil, or the new Republic of Texas. But Priscilla's situation was different, because she had become free under French law. Taney refused to consider that development. She remained a slave in Louisiana.

The outcome here foreshadowed Taney's position in *Dred Scott*. Priscilla had been taken to a foreign country where slavery was illegal yet did not gain her freedom, even though federal law, international law, common law, and precedent supported that outcome. In *Dred Scott*, a slave taken to a free state and a territory where slavery was illegal was also refused his freedom, even though federal law, common law, and precedent supported that outcome.

In 1841 the Court heard two major slave cases, *United States* v. *The Amistad* and *Groves* v. *Slaughter*.[38] *Amistad* was a cause célèbre when it reached the Court, but the case had little impact on the jurisprudence relating to slavery. *Groves*, on the other hand, was a rather mundane case which involved the interstate sale of slaves and raised no great political issues—but it was fraught with important constitutional questions affecting slavery and the economy.

Amistad involved a Spanish schooner by that name filled with Africans who had recently, and illegally, been imported to Cuba as slaves. After a revolt on board, the ship eventually ended up in Long Island Sound, where a Coast Guard vessel interdicted it. Various suits arose over the status of the vessel and the Africans on it. Ultimately the Supreme Court, in an opinion by Justice Joseph Story, ruled that the Amistads had been illegally taken from Africa and could not be held as slaves under Spanish or American law.[39]

Taney silently concurred in Story's opinion, but this hardly made Taney an opponent of slavery. Many openly proslavery leaders considered the African trade to be an immoral business that violated both natural law and good public policy. Moreover, slave owners in the upper South stood to benefit from a clampdown on the illegal African trade, because vigorous suppression of it raised the market value of the hundreds of thousands of slaves from the east coast who were sold further south and west in the domestic slave trade. Taney's acquiescence in the *Amistad* cannot be seen as antislavery. Indeed, little or nothing about the *Amistad* case can be interpreted as antislavery.

On its face, *Groves* v. *Slaughter* also did not raise pro- or antislavery issues. It was essentially a commercial case between slave sellers and slave buyers. Mississippi's 1832 constitution prohibited the importation of slaves for sale. This was not an antislavery provision, but an attempt to reduce the flow of capital out of the state. Slaughter, a professional slave dealer, sold slaves in Mississippi and received notes signed by Groves and others. Groves and his codefendants later defaulted on the notes, arguing that sales of slaves in Mississippi were void. Speaking for the Court, Justice Smith Thompson of New York determined that Mississippi's constitutional prohibition on the importation of slaves was not self-executing and that, absent implementing legislation, the prohibition in the Mississippi constitution was inoperative.

Thus he held that the notes were valid. This was a reasonable result based on commercial rules, and was consistent with the outcome in *Bank of Augusta* v. *Earle* (1839), where Taney had ruled that out-of-state banks could operate in any state in the absence of an explicit act of the legislature prohibiting out-of-state corporations from doing business in that state.

Indicative of his highly partisan approach to slavery, Taney wrote a separate opinion, insisting that the federal government had no power over slavery. This was one of only fourteen separate opinions that Taney wrote in his twenty-eight years on the bench. Taney's opinion dealt with an issue that was not directly before the Court and was unnecessary for the outcome of the case. Taney did not want to leave any implication that, under the commerce clause, Congress might regulate slavery: "the power of this subject [slavery] is exclusively with the several States; and each of them has a right to decide for itself, whether it will or will not allow persons of this description to be brought within its limits from another State, either for sale, or for any other purpose." He emphatically asserted that Congress had no power to regulate the interstate sale of slaves, "either by virtue of its power to regulate commerce, or by virtue of any other power conferred by the Constitution of the United States."[40]

Taney's separate opinion is consistent with his other decisions that allowed the states to regulate economic development—the decisions that Frankfurter and other progressives admired so much. *Groves* reveals, however, that behind Taney's commercial jurisprudence was a hidden goal: to protect slavery and to protect the right of the slave states to regulate this aspect of their economy. In that sense, Taney's opinion in *Groves* lines up perfectly with his opinion as attorney general on the rights of free blacks. He wrote that opinion in response to statutes adopted by most southern coastal states prohibiting free blacks from entering their jurisdictions. Taney in effect had argued that because blacks had no rights and could be reduced to slavery at the whim of white society, the southern states were free to exclude free blacks from their jurisdictions.

Some of Taney's most important decisions, giving states greater control over their economies, are sandwiched between his opinion as attorney general and *Groves*. This suggests that slavery lurked in the background of Taney's economic decision-making, and that his desire to protect slavery influenced his commercial jurisprudence.

Prigg v. *Pennsylvania* (1842) reveals Taney's jurisprudential inconsistency and his proslavery consistency. In *Prigg* Taney rejected his jurisprudence of the previous year in *Groves* v. *Slaughter*, where he had asserted that the states could decide the status of people in their jurisdictions. In *Prigg* he denied that Pennsylvania had the right to protect the liberty of free blacks who were born in the Keystone State. Edward Prigg and his cohort removed Margaret Morgan and her children from Pennsylvania to Maryland without first obtaining a certificate of removal as required by Pennsylvania's 1826 personal liberty law. In a sweeping victory for slavery, Justice Story struck down the Pennsylvania law, upheld the federal fugitive slave law of 1793, and further declared that slave owners had a constitutional right to seize their slaves anywhere they found them, without resort to any legal process, as long as the seizure could be done without a breach of the peace. In reaching these conclusions Story swept aside the fact that at least one of the people Prigg seized had been born in Pennsylvania and was therefore free under that state's laws.[41]

In his opinion, Justice Story had noted in passing that the federal government could not require state officials to enforce the fugitive slave law of 1793 because, not being paid by the federal government, state officials could not be forced to work for it. Story was emphatic, however, that the states *should* enforce the federal law as a matter of patriotism, moral obligation, and (unenforceable) constitutional duty.[42] This part of Story's decision was consistent with well-accepted notions of federalism and states' rights that in other contexts Chief Justice Taney had consistently supported.

But here Taney abandoned his usual support for state autonomy. In another of his rare separate opinions, Taney argued that the states had an affirmative obligation to pass laws to enforce the fugitive slave clause because the Constitution "impose[s] it as a duty upon the people of the several states to pass laws to carry into execution, in good faith, the compact into which they thus solemnly entered with each other."[43] Taney dissented "from that part of the opinion of the Court which denies the obligation and the right of the state authorities to protect the master, when he is endeavouring to seize a fugitive from his service, in pursuance of the right given to him by the Constitution of the United States; provided the state law is not in conflict with the remedy provided by Congress."[44]

Taney not only supported state power for the southern states to protect slavery, but inconsistently rejected the right of the free states to protect the rights of free African-Americans. Instead, in an extraordinary demand for national power, Taney insisted that the free states be forced to act as slave catchers for the South. While often seen as the protector of states' rights and federalism, Taney abandoned all such pretensions in *Prigg* in order to protect slavery and at the same time undermine the rights and security of northern free blacks.

Taney's separate opinion underscores the inconsistency—or hypocrisy—of his arguing in *Groves* that the states should be able to determine the status of people in their jurisdiction. Prigg initially seized Margaret's husband, Jerry Morgan, who was a free black born in Pennsylvania. If there had been no law in Pennsylvania requiring Prigg to get a warrant from a state judge, he would have simply removed Jerry to Maryland along with his family—including at least one Pennsylvania-born child. No one involved in the case thought Jerry was a fugitive, given that he had been born a free man in Pennsylvania. But under Taney's opinion (as well as Story's), Pennsylvania would not have had the power to protect Jerry from kidnapping.

One other aspect of Taney's separate opinion in *Prigg* illustrates his thinking. In explaining that masters had a right to recover their slaves anywhere in the nation, he added "I do not speak of slaves whom their masters voluntarily take into a non-slaveholding state." This might have implied that masters did not have a constitutional right to take their slaves into the free states. But if he meant that, he could have been more explicit. Instead, he followed that statement with: "That case is not before us."[45] The implication is clear (especially in light of his later jurisprudence) that when "that case" would come before the Court, Taney was prepared to find such a right, not in the fugitive slave clause, but somewhere else in the Constitution.

A few paragraphs after this, Taney used the privileges and immunities clause of the Constitution to bolster his argument that the northern states had to proactively enforce the fugitive slave clause. He wrote: "The Constitution of the United

States declares that the citizens of each state shall be entitled to all the privileges and immunities of citizens in the several states. And although these privileges and immunities, for greater safety, are placed under the guardianship of the general government; still the states may by their laws and in their tribunals protect and enforce them. They have not only the power, but it is a duty enjoined upon them by this provision in the Constitution."[46] Plausibly, this analysis could have been used to imply that the southern states had an obligation to grant privileges and immunities to free black citizens from the North, but given Taney's opinion to President Jackson on free black citizenship, later reiterated in *Dred Scott*, we know that is not the case. Rather, Taney was signaling that the southern slave owners would have a claim under the privileges and immunities clause to carry their slaves into the North. The case was not before Taney at that time, but he anticipated such a case coming before the Court and was laying the groundwork for a decision along these lines.

In *Strader* v. *Graham* (1851) Taney took another step in this direction.[47] Strader's steamboat had transported Graham's three slaves to Ohio, where they disappeared. Kentucky law held a steamboat operator liable for the value of any slaves who escaped by boarding the boat without written permission of the owner. Strader proved that Graham had previously allowed his three slaves to travel on their own in Indiana and Ohio where they earned money as musicians. Strader argued that by being allowed to work in the North, the slaves had become free. This was consistent with jurisprudence in many slave states, including Kentucky. The Kentucky Supreme Court rejected Strader's argument, however, because that court refused to consider the status of slaves unless they were actually parties to a case. In ruling against Strader, Taney simply accepted the conclusions of the Kentucky court. He also rejected arguments by Strader that the slaves were free under the Northwest Ordinance of 1787, asserting that the Ordinance ceased to have any legal effect once the territories in question became states.

In *Strader* Taney seemed to support the right of a state to decide the status of African-Americans within its jurisdiction. Thus Kentucky did not have to respect the laws of Indiana and Ohio, under which the three slaves were free. Presumably, had Graham's slaves asserted their liberty in Indiana or Ohio, those states would have freed them, and Taney would have held that these non-slave states had the right to do this. But Taney hedged on this issue, declaring: "Every State has an undoubted right to determine the *status* or domestic and social condition, of the persons domiciled within its territory" except as "restrained" by the Constitution.[48] In addition to applying to fugitive slaves, this wording also held open the possibility that slave owners had other federal rights to carry their slaves into the North or the federal territories, as Taney had hinted in *Prigg*. Part of this implication became explicit in *Dred Scott v. Sandford*.

The Dred Scott Case

As an army surgeon, Dr. John Emerson traveled to Fort Armstrong (in Illinois) and to Fort Snelling (in what was then the Wisconsin Territory and is now Minnesota) taking his slave Dred Scott with him. Illinois prohibited slavery in its constitution and Congress had prohibited slavery in the Wisconsin Territory in the Missouri Compromise of 1820 and other territorial laws. After Emerson's death, Scott sued for his freedom based on his residence in these two free jurisdictions.

Scott won his case before a jury of twelve white men in St. Louis in 1850, but in 1852 the Missouri Supreme Court reversed, holding that Scott was still a slave. In 1857 the Supreme Court finally decided the case. Taney's sweeping fifty-five-page "Opinion of the Court" is the apex of proslavery constitutionalism.

Taney might have dealt with Dred Scott's claim to freedom in a very simple way. Scott had lived in free jurisdictions, and the Court might have upheld his freedom. Scott's case differed from the precedent in *Strader* v. *Graham* in two important ways. First, Scott was present and part of the litigation—in fact he had brought the case—unlike the missing slaves in *Strader*. Second, Taney's assertion in *Strader* that the Northwest Ordinance was no longer in force could have been interpreted to mean that, since the federal laws banning slavery in the Wisconsin Territory *were* in force, Missouri was obligated to enforce them. Given Taney's long hostility to free blacks it is not surprising that he did not take this route. But it is important to understand that such a route existed and was legally and jurisprudentially plausible.

Alternatively, Taney might have relied on *Strader* to affirm the decision of the Missouri Supreme Court that Scott was still a slave. Taney could simply have declared that when Scott moved back to Missouri he lost whatever claim to freedom he might have made under the Missouri Compromise. Initially the Court planned to follow this route, with Justice Samuel Nelson of New York writing a narrow opinion denying Scott's freedom. This position would have had seven votes on the Court, and the opinion would have been written by a northerner. Had the Court done this, it is unlikely anyone would remember the case today.

In February 1857, however, Taney's four southern colleagues on the Court asked him to write a comprehensive opinion. Taney agreed, as he wanted to finally resolve the festering issue of slavery in the territories, as did some politicians. Representative Alexander Stephens, who would become the Confederate vice president, urged Justice James Wayne, a fellow Georgian, to take such a position. Similarly, President-elect James Buchanan pressured Justice Robert Grier to settle the territorial question in favor of the South. This would relieve Buchanan of the political difficulties presented by turmoil in the territories. The change of votes by the other southerners allowed Taney to write "the opinion that he had wanted to write all along."[49]

Dred Scott had brought his case to the federal courts under diversity jurisdiction. In 1854, claiming to be a free citizen of Missouri, he sued Sanford in federal court. At the time, Sanford was a citizen of New York.[50] Sanford responded that Scott was "a negro of African descent; his ancestors were of pure African blood" and as such he could not be a citizen of Missouri and so could not sue in federal court. United States District Judge Robert Wells rejected this plea, concluding that *if* Scott was free, he was a citizen of the state in which he lived for purposes of federal diversity jurisdiction.[51] When the case reached the Supreme Court, Taney reexamined this plea and the response of Judge Wells.

Taney might have accepted Sanford's argument that in Missouri free blacks were not citizens. He would have noted that Missouri barred free blacks from moving into the state, and those who lived there could not vote, testify against whites, own certain kinds of property, enter certain professions, or exercise many other rights normally associated with citizenship. In *Strader* Taney had made himself clear: "Every State has an undoubted right to determine the *status* or domestic and social condition, of the persons domiciled within its territory."[52] Taney could have noted that Missouri had exercised this right to deny citizenship to free blacks. This result would have surprised no one, and would have allowed Taney to dismiss the case for want of jurisdiction without ever getting to the issue of slavery in the territories.[53]

But this was Taney's chance to permanently decide the issue of slavery in the territories in favor of the South, to lash out at the North, and to settle once and for all the status of blacks in American society. Taney, the furious sectionalist, hoped to place blacks beyond the pale of legal protection in the United States. This would head off the growing concern for black rights in the Republican Party and much of the North. After *Dred Scott,* Taney could be certain that blacks would not appear before his court—or any other federal court—as plaintiffs, defendants, or attorneys.[54]

Taney asserted that free blacks—even those allowed to vote in the states where they lived—could never be considered citizens of the United States and could never have standing to sue in federal courts as citizens of their own states. Taney offered a slanted history which ignored the fact that free blacks had voted in a number of states at the time of the ratification of the Constitution and continued to vote for members of Congress, presidential electors, and members of their state legislatures (which chose U.S. senators). Although Taney was aware of black voters in 1787, he nevertheless argued that at the adoption of the Constitution all blacks were either slaves or, if free, were without any political or legal rights. He declared that blacks:

are not included, and were not intended to be included, under the word "citizens" in the Constitution, and can therefore claim none of the rights and privileges which that instrument provides for and secures to citizens of the United States. On the contrary, they were at that time [1787] considered as a subordinate and inferior class of beings who had been subjugated by the dominant race, and, whether emancipated or not, yet remained subject to their authority, and had no rights or privileges but such as those who held the power and the Government might choose to grant them.

Taney concluded blacks were "so far inferior, that they had no rights which the white man was bound to respect."[55]

Taney dealt with black citizenship at the very beginning of his opinion. He had been waiting a quarter century to make public what he had told President Jackson in the unpublished opinion he wrote as attorney general. But, by putting this analysis at the very front of the opinion, Taney severely undermined the credibility of the rest of his conclusions. By ruling that Scott, even if free, could not sue in federal court, Taney was forced to dismiss the case for lack of jurisdiction. Critics of the decision, like Lincoln, asserted that once Taney ruled Scott could not sue, he had no case before him, and everything else he said on the regulation of slavery in the territories was *dicta* with no legal or precedential value.

Taney might have turned to the issue of black citizenship last, after making all his other points. This would have been reminiscent of John Marshall's opinion in *Marbury* v. *Madison* (1803), where he set out all the reasons why Marbury should have won the case—as a way of attacking the Jefferson administration—before concluding that the Court lacked jurisdiction. But Taney was too impatient for such a measured opinion. Moreover, such an approach would not have allowed him to settle all the nation's festering constitutional issue over slavery in favor of the South. Taney was equally determined to end northern attacks on slavery and to destroy the new Republican Party, which had been organized to stop the spread of slavery in the territories. Taney's opinion was in part directed at making the new party's main political goal effectively "unconstitutional."

After dealing with black citizenship, Taney turned to permanently securing the rights of masters to own slaves under the U.S. Constitution. He held that a ban on slavery in the territories violated the Fifth Amendment: "the Constitution recognizes the right of property of the master in a slave, and makes no distinction between that description of property and other property owned by a citizen," and thus "no tribunal, acting under the authority of the United States, whether it be legislative, executive, or judicial, has a right to draw such a distinction, or deny to it the benefit of the provisions and guarantees which have been provided for the protection of private property against the encroachments of the Government."[56] Slavery was a specially protected species of property, immune from congressional regulation.

Under this interpretation neither Congress nor a territorial legislature could prohibit slavery. This flew in the face of the Northwest Ordinance, the Missouri Compromise, and many other acts of Congress banning slavery from federal territories. The use of the Fifth Amendment was particularly cynical since that amendment asserted that no person could be "deprived of life, liberty or property, without due process of law." Taney protected "property" in slaves, but ignored the obvious hypocrisy that slavery denied people liberty without due process.

In a tortured interpretation of the Constitution's territories clause, Taney ruled that Congress had no power to pass laws for the federal territories. Article IV of the Constitution empowered Congress "to dispose of and make all needful rules and regulations respecting the territory or other property belonging to the United States." In an unpersuasive analysis, Taney declared that the territories clause of Article IV "was a special provision for a known and particular territory" and did not apply to any new territories.[57] Taney's argument was strained and unconvincing: "The language used in the clause, the arrangement and combination of the powers, and the somewhat unusual phraseology . . . all indicate the design and meaning of the clause" was to be limited to the territories the government owned in 1787. He argued that the clause:

> does not speak of *any* territory, nor of *Territories*, but uses language which, according to its legitimate meaning, points to a particular thing. The power is given in relation only to *the* territory of the United States—that is, to a territory then in existence, and then known or claimed as the territory of the United States. . . . And whatever construction may now be given to these words, every one, we think, must admit that they are not the words usually employed by statesmen in giving supreme power of legislation. They are certainly very unlike the words used in the power granted to legislate over territory which the new Government might afterwards itself obtain by cession from a State.[58]

Even if this linguistic analysis were plausible or persuasive, it did not apply to the Missouri Compromise, because the territory regulated by that law had not been "obtain[ed] by cession from a State," but had been acquired by purchase from France. But Taney was not interested in plausible construction of the Constitution or any realistic understanding of United States history. Thus Taney struck down the Missouri Compromise, a major piece of congressional legislation that had been the keystone of sectional compromise for more than a generation.

Taney had hoped *Dred Scott* would end all debate over slavery in the territories and the place of blacks in the United States. He wanted to give the South a sweeping victory by thoroughly vanquishing black rights, racial equality, and antislavery politics. Taney delivered his *Dred Scott* opinion only a few months after the Republican Party had nearly won the presidential election on a platform that endorsed the "self-evident" principles in the Declaration of Independence that all people "are created equal," and have the "unalienable Rights" of "Life, Liberty, and the pursuit of Happiness." His assertion was that the Republican platform was historically and constitutionally wrong.

> In the opinion of the Court, the legislation and histories of the times, and the language used in the Declaration of Independence, show, that neither the class of persons who had been imported as slaves, nor their descendants, whether they had become free or not, were then acknowledged as a part of the people, nor intended to be included in the general words used in that memorable instrument.[59]

On one level Taney may have been right. Many of the framers—and certainly the vast majority of the Southern framers—did not intend to provide for racial equality through the Declaration of Independence. He continued:

> But it is too clear for dispute, that the enslaved African race were not intended to be included, and formed no part of the people who framed and adopted this declaration; for if the language, as understood in that day, would embrace them, the conduct of the distinguished men who framed the Declaration of Independence would have been utterly and flagrantly inconsistent with the principles they asserted; and instead of the sympathy of mankind, to which they so confidently appealed, they would have deserved and received universal rebuke and reprobation.[60]

His understanding of the intentions of the southern framers at the Constitutional Convention seems plausible:

> It is impossible, it would seem, to believe that the great men of the slaveholding States, who took so large a share in framing the Constitution of the United States, and exercised so much influence in procuring its adoption, could have been so forgetful or regardless of their own safety and the safety of those who trusted and confided in them.[61]

His proslavery analysis of the Declaration and the Constitution comports with what we know happened in Philadelphia, where the southern delegates won a number of victories.[62]

In the end, Taney sought to prove too much. His historical, intentionalist arguments were narrow and partisan. They focused entirely on slaves. He talks about the "enslaved African race" without any consideration of the status of free blacks. He ignored the black soldiers who fought for the patriot cause. He refused to consider that African Americans voted in a number of states in the 1780s. He was oblivious to the connections among the Revolution, the Declaration of Independence, and the ending of slavery in the North. His opinion was not designed to persuade opponents of slavery that he was right; rather it was written to bludgeon them. As things turned out, he severely miscalculated. Rather than acknowledge the complexity of slavery and race relations in a nation that was half slave and half free, Taney simply tried to sweep away opponents of slavery. But he failed. Northern anger over the opinion fueled the Republican Party and helped put Lincoln in the White House.

The Fugitive Slave Law, Secession, and Civil War: The Aftermath of Dred Scott

After *Dred Scott*, Taney continued to push a proslavery constitutional agenda in his opinions in *Ableman* v. *Booth* (1859) and *Kentucky* v. *Dennison* (1861).[63] These cases underscore the proslavery cynicism of Taney's jurisprudence.

In *Ableman*, Taney rejected Wisconsin's attempts to remove from federal custody the abolitionist Sherman Booth, who had helped a fugitive slave escape. In 1854 the federal marshal Stephen Ableman had arrested Booth after he helped to rescue a fugitive slave from the marshal's custody. The Wisconsin Supreme Court issued a writ of habeas corpus on Booth's behalf, asserting that the Fugitive Slave Law of 1850 was unconstitutional because, among other things, it denied alleged fugitive slaves a jury trial and prohibited alleged fugitives from testifying on their own behalf. The 1850 law also abrogated the writ of habeas corpus for alleged fugitives. This was in direct violation of the U.S. Constitution, which stated: "The Privilege of the Writ of Habeas Corpus shall not be suspended, unless when in Cases of Rebellion or Invasion the public Safety may require it." Categorically denying the writ to every alleged fugitive slave obviously violated the Constitution.

Taney refused to even consider the constitutionality of the new Fugitive Slave Law of 1850, even though it was substantially different from the 1793 law upheld in *Prigg*. As in *Dred Scott*, Taney made no attempt to persuade those who disagreed with him. Instead, he asserted without argument that the law was valid. Taney also dismissed Wisconsin's states' rights arguments as though he had never heard of the idea of states' rights. His opinion was a sweeping endorsement of federal power and the supremacy of the Constitution and the Supreme Court's interpretation of it. Chief Justice Marshall could not have written a more thorough assertion of the authority of the Supreme Court. Taney wrote this ultranationalist opinion to protect slavery from the antislavery states' rights ideas of the North.

In *Kentucky* v. *Dennison*, however, Taney pirouetted once again. This was a suit to force Governor William Dennison of Ohio to extradite a free black named Willis Lago who had helped a slave woman escape from Kentucky. The obvious proslavery result would have been to side with Kentucky. This would have been consistent with Taney's opinions in *Prigg*, *Dred Scott*, and *Ableman*, where he rejected states' rights in favor of federal protection of slavery. But, by spring 1861, when the Court decided the case, seven slave states had already left the Union and Abraham Lincoln was about to become president. Sympathetic to the Southern cause, Taney avoided an opinion giving the federal government the power to force state governors to act. Thus, Taney castigated Governor Dennison, but refused to order him to act.

The contrast between *Dennison* and Taney's separate opinion in *Prigg* is significant. In *Prigg* Taney wanted to require state officials to enforce the fugitive slave clause of Article IV, Section 2, of the Constitution. If he had prevailed, presumably state officials could have been charged by the federal government for failure to enforce the law. This outcome suited Taney's proslavery position in 1842. But in 1861 he suddenly denied that the federal government could compel a state official to enforce the fugitives from justice clause in Article IV, Section 2, of the Constitution. There is no way to rationalize these conflicting positions, except to note that what protected slavery in 1842 would not protect it in 1861.

Taken together, the line of cases from the *Garonne* to *Groves* to *Dennison* shows that *Dred Scott* was neither uncharacteristic nor an aberration. *Dred Scott* was part of Taney's larger jurisprudential goal of protecting slavery and the South whenever he could. In all these cases Taney lacked any sort of theoretical mooring for his opinions. He could flit back and forth from states' rights to federal supremacy. When it benefited slavery—as it did in *Garonne, Groves, Strader,* and *Dennison*—Taney was happy to support states' rights and allow states to determine the status of people within their jurisdictions. But in *Prigg, Dred Scott,* and *Ableman,* Taney denied that states could determine questions of citizenship or racial status, because to do otherwise would have allowed free blacks in places like Massachusetts, Rhode Island, and New York to sue in federal court. At the same time, he deferred to

Missouri on Dred Scott's status, rather than supporting either Illinois or the federal law. In these cases, Taney was uninterested in constitutional principles; only in proslavery results that protected the South. When the Civil War began, he applied this constitutional jurisprudence to protecting opponents of the Union.

Taney remained on the Court until his death in 1864. During his last few years as chief justice he did everything in his power to thwart Abraham Lincoln's policies.[64] In *Ex parte Merryman* (1861), Taney, in his capacity as a circuit court justice, denounced Lincoln for the military arrest of a Marylander who was organizing Confederate troops and making war in other ways against the United States. The irony here is that Lincoln suspended habeas corpus under the circumstances set out in the Constitution—"in Cases of Rebellion or Invasion" when "the public Safety may require it." Furthermore, the suspension applied only to a narrow region of the country where the "public safety" made it necessary; unlike the Fugitive Slave Law of 1850, it did not apply to the entire United States. But Taney found Lincoln's suspension unconstitutional and ordered the release of an active terrorist, John Merryman, who had been trying to destroy railroad tracks and bridges and organizing an armed rebellion against the nation. Lincoln ignored Taney's fulminations, and Merryman remained locked up in Fort McHenry.[65]

Meanwhile, Taney privately compared enlistment in the Confederate army to enlistment in the patriot army during the Revolutionary War. He "wrote out gratuitous opinions that were never called into use, holding several acts of the federal government unconstitutional" including draft opinions declaring conscription and emancipation unconstitutional. Refusing to recognize the nature of the Civil War, Taney dissented in the *Prize Cases*. He was, in some ways, the Confederacy's greatest ally in Washington.[66]

By the time he died, Taney was a minority justice, ignored by the president and Congress, held in contempt by the vast majority of his countrymen, and respected most in those places that proclaimed themselves no longer in the Union. Taney's obvious tilt toward the Confederacy showed that he had traveled far from the days when he had advised Andrew Jackson on how to suppress nullificationists. Indeed, he had become one himself.

In the Court of History

At his death, few had anything good to say about Chief Justice Taney. Today it is clear that his impact on the law was great. For the first twenty years of his tenure he successfully guided the Court and helped develop important constitutional doctrines, especially in economic matters. Yet he is most remembered for *Dred Scott*, the most infamous decision in American constitutional history.

Dred Scott should not be examined in isolation, but must be seen in the context of Taney's career. Taney's defenders have claimed that his economic decisions trump *Dred Scott* and that *Dred Scott* was an aberration. But they reach this conclusion by doing exactly what they say should not be done: they look at *Dred Scott* in isolation, ignoring Taney's other decisions on slavery, race, and the Civil War. When Taney's whole career is examined, *Dred Scott* becomes part of more than three decades of efforts to strengthen slavery, protect the South, make war on free blacks, and, after 1861, undermine the Union cause. While Taney was creative in finding legal solutions to questions about banking, commerce, and transportation, he ultimately failed in creating a jurisprudence that could defend fundamental liberty and human rights. That failure will always overshadow his successes.

How do we reconcile Taney's apparently progressive economic jurisprudence with the characterization of him as a seething secessionist and proslavery ideologue? Felix Frankfurter was enchanted by Taney's commercial jurisprudence, which seemed relevant to the teaching and practice of law in the 1930s. Frankfurter, like many scholars in law and political science today, was far more concerned with influencing public policy than with interpreting the past. For this group, "history" is instrumental—law-office history used to argue for a particular set of outcomes. The big issue for Frankfurter was the Great Depression; his goal was to see a Supreme Court that would allow for state and federal legislative innovation and reform. In Taney, Frankfurter thought he found a model that the Supreme Court of the 1930s could emulate. In the eighty years since, other scholars in law and political science have followed Frankfurter's lead.

The Supreme Court had used "substantive due process" to overturn Progressive and New Deal legislation regulating wages, hours, child labor, and working conditions. The Court had held that such laws violated the due-process liberty of individuals to make contracts. Frankfurter and his followers doubtless hoped that the model of Taney—the conservative judge of the nineteenth century—would be useful in convincing twentieth-century judges that this jurisprudence was wrong. But there is a huge irony in Frankfurter's praise of Taney, because *Dred Scott* was the Court's first use of "substantive due process." There Taney wrote:

> These powers, and others, in relation to rights of person, which it is not necessary here to enumerate, are, in express and positive terms, denied to the General Government;

and the rights of private property have been guarded with equal care. Thus the rights of property are united with the rights of person, and placed on the same ground by the fifth amendment to the Constitution, which provides that no person shall be deprived of life, liberty, and property, without due process of law. And an act of Congress which deprives a citizen of the United States of his liberty or property, merely because he came himself or brought his property into a particular Territory of the United States, and who had committed no offence against the laws, could hardly be dignified with the name of due process of law.[67]

How then, do we evaluate Taney's career? His court profoundly affected the American economy. But was Taney necessary for that impact? It seems safe to assume that, had President Jackson promoted John McLean to the chief justiceship, many of the same kinds of economic decisions would have been written. On economic issues, a McLean Court would have looked much like the Taney Court. But on slavery and race, McLean would have been a very different chief justice.[68]

What matters most is Taney's jurisprudence on slavery, race, and secession. In these realms, the chief justice failed to provide meaningful leadership for the Court or the nation. Taney's reading of the territories clause was incredibly strained. By limiting the clause to the territories owned by the United States in 1787, Taney struck down the Missouri Compromise, the Compromise of 1850, and the Kansas-Nebraska Act. This part of Taney's opinion was not supported by any reasonable reading of the clause in Article IV or any historical argument based on the intentions of the framers of the Constitution. His analysis of the territories clause was unpersuasive and contrary to the plain language of the text.

Taney's historical analysis was cramped and constricted. He examined the intentions of only the southern framers, and ignored the intentions of, for example, Benjamin Franklin—a delegate to the Convention in 1787, a delegate to Pennsylvania's ratification convention, and the president of the Pennsylvania Abolition Society. Similarly, Taney ignored the free black voters in six states. In many ways, *Dred Scott* also shows the danger and difficulty of intentionalist jurisprudence.

Taney's opinion illustrates the folly of using an intentionalist analysis when the intentions of the framers were clearly mixed, uncertain, and contradictory. Taney offered an unsophisticated historical claim that was a thinly disguised political argument designed to destroy the Republican Party and any opposition to the spread of slavery into the territories.

Taney rejected the "higher law" arguments of Republicans including Sumner and William H. Seward, and instead offered what could be described as a "lower law" doctrine as he attempted to constitutionalize the most racist and proslavery aspects of southern legal and constitutional theory. This was not restraint, but rather the worst sort of judicial activism, because it was directed at a single section of the nation, a single political party, and a single race. In the end, the opinion was also a political disaster.

Taney will always be remembered more for *Dred Scott* and his slavery jurisprudence than for his opinions relating to the economy. *Dred Scott,* indeed, has come to stand for all that can go wrong in a Supreme Court decision, and all that did go wrong under the proslavery Constitution. It remains the most infamous decision in American constitutional history, and its author suffers accordingly. His blunt language in *Dred*

Scott as well as his other slavery opinions made Senator Sumner and many others hate Taney. But it was his cynical, proslavery jurisprudence, and his aggressive attacks on freedom in the North, that made Sumner's prediction that the "name of Taney is to be hooted down the page of history" come true. To whatever extent we might admire Taney's personal grace, his clever opinions on commercial issues, and his sometimes brilliant analysis of constitutional issues, it will be his racism, proslavery dogmatism, and secessionist sentiments that remain his legacy. When the name Taney comes up, there will always be echoes of hooting.

Coda

FROM THE NATION'S beginning, slavery lurked in the background of the political and legal system. It bedeviled delegates in 1787 and complicated politics from the 1790s to the 1860s. Slavery led to secession and Civil War, caused some 630,000 deaths during that conflict, inflicted unbelievable human suffering, and brought about vast destruction of property. In many ways, the nation is still recovering from its devastation.

In the political sphere, the Electoral College continues to hand presidencies to candidates who win fewer votes than their opponents—a legacy of Madison's contention in the 1787 Convention that a popular vote for president would deny the South its share of power (given its large but nonvoting slave population). Madison's design of the deeply undemocratic Electoral College folded the three-fifths clause into the allotment of electors, and helped slaveholders and their northern doughface allies dominate the executive branch until 1860.[1] Many constitutional doctrines, such as the "police powers" of the states in commerce cases and the notion of unfunded mandates, were created at least in part because of slavery and the jurisprudence created to protect it. Beyond government, the nation's continuing struggle against racism and injustice testifies to slavery's impact on our democratic society.

From 1801 to 1864 the Marshall and Taney Courts dealt with many cases involving slavery. More important than their numbers were their implications for American politics, law, and the larger society. Many involved individual blacks who sought liberty and had strong legal claims to be free. Cases like *Amistad* had little jurisprudential value, but powerfully exposed the evils of the slave trade. *The Antelope* continues to educate Americans about its horrors. *Prigg* v. *Pennsylvania* was a monumental victory for slavery that threatened the liberty of every free black in the nation. *Dred Scott* v. *Sandford* did not cause the Civil War, but it thwarted any political solution to the slavery question. It, along with *Prigg* and *Ableman* v. *Booth,* emboldened the South to believe it could win every legal and political battle over slavery. At the same time, *Dred Scott* caused such outrage that a new, impassioned Republican Party was able to capture the White House and, after Lincoln's victory, the North won the war.

Marshall, Story, and Taney profoundly altered the politics of slavery and the course of national history. As jurists, they faced constraints on how they could affect society. Judges cannot initiate cases; they can only decide the cases that come before them. But within these constraints they have great flexibility. These justices might have made different choices that would have changed the course of history. Chief Justice Marshall never supported a freedom suit even when precedent, logic, and the facts of the case suggested he should have. He always found a way to come down on the side of slavery. This reflected his conservative views on property, his fear of free blacks, and his huge personal investment in slavery. Chief Justice Taney always supported slavery and slave owners—sometimes, as in *Dred Scott,* with a vengeance. Justice Story initially was hostile to slavery, but at the end of his career wrote one of the most proslavery decisions in United States history.

They did not have to reach these results. There was great space in the Constitution for different decisions and different outcomes. The freedom suits brought before the Marshall Court rarely had constitutional implications. The Court could easily have sided with liberty instead of slavery. Emblematic of this jurisprudence was Marshall's statement in one case that the law he was applying was "certainly ambiguous, and the one construction or the other may be admitted, without great violence to the words which are employed."[2] That Marshall chose to side with slavery in this case—as he did in *every* freedom suit where he wrote an opinion—tells us more about the Chief Justice than it does about the statutes and common law of the time. Similarly, in *Prigg* v. *Pennsylvania*, Justice Story could have upheld the federal law of 1793 and still allowed the states to protect their free citizens from being kidnapped. Justice Story did not take that route, and instead wrote an overwhelmingly proslavery decision that threatened the liberty of every free black in the United States. In *Dred Scott*, Chief Justice Taney went out of his way to protect slavery even when he might have supported the same outcome—that Dred Scott was still a slave—with a narrower, less aggressive opinion.

The reasons for this jurisprudence vary with the justices. Marshall, a wealthy landowner, quietly bought and sold slaves all his life. His slavery decisions were conservative and narrow, but always on the side of slavery and property and always against black freedom. In *Mima Queen* he refused to even allow slaves to present the only evidence they had to prove their freedom, arguing that if the evidence were allowed, "no man could feel safe in any property."[3] Property, in the form of human beings, was far more important to him than liberty. His proslavery jurisprudence dovetailed with his lifelong, ambitious accumulation of slaves; his hostility to freedom cases reflected his lifelong fear and loathing of free blacks.

For a few years, Justice Story was openly hostile to slavery. In *La Jeune Eugenie* he offered a powerful indictment of the illegal African slave trade and slavery itself. But that decision, in 1822, was his last antislavery act on the Court. What happened? Story's best biographer, Kent Newmyer, argues that Story's nationalism, his fear of sectionalism, and the rise of southern proslavery disunionism led him to compromise on slavery in favor of the Union. But this explanation does not go very far in explaining his persistent refusal to speak out in favor of liberty in his early years on the Court. Story's silence in *The Antelope*—where Chief Justice Marshall eviscerated Story's antislavery jurisprudence—occurred years before the Nat Turner rebellion, the emergence of militant abolitionism, and the nullification crisis. So too did his silent acceptance for Marshall's refusal to support freedom suits. Story's highly nationalist *Commentaries on the Constitution*, published at the time of the nullification crisis, did not cede everything to slavery and the South as his *Prigg* decision would. But even if Story's motivations were purely nationalistic and patriotic, they are deeply troubling. His silence in case after case, followed by his overwhelmingly proslavery decision in *Prigg*, came at huge cost and threatened the liberty of hundreds of thousands of free blacks. Story might have written a different opinion in *Prigg*, protecting free blacks as well as the property of slave owners. Instead, he nationalized slavery and made war on both free blacks and his neighbors in the North. Whatever his motivations were, his jurisprudence after 1822 made him the loyal servant of slavery.

Chief Justice Taney was raised in the plantation South and always supported slavery. His decisions reflected his background and on one level need little explanation. He had always opposed any rights for free blacks, had always supported slavery, and had always (albeit not to the extent of a large investor in human flesh like Marshall) owned some slaves. Over the years he became more aggressively proslavery, bitter, and angry at opponents of the institution. In the end, he tried to settle all of the nation's political issues over slavery in favor of the South and human bondage. He hoped that he could shut down all opposition to slavery and turn all free blacks into constitutional untouchables. His failure and the Court's was monumental, and his jurisprudence, like Marshall's and Story's, was unjust.

From 1801 until the Civil War, the Supreme Court almost always supported slave owners and the institution of slavery. In a few cases, the Court—but never Marshall, Story, or Taney—upheld freedom claims. Occasionally a few foreign slave traders lost, and in the case of *The Amistad* inspired abolitionists were able to raise public awareness of the horrors of the African trade. But the slave trade cases had no effect on southern slavery, American masters, or African-American slaves. By the 1840s, southerners had come to expect the Court would always protect their interests, and so it did.

A different jurisprudence might have altered the trajectory of American history by providing jurisprudential balance in the political and legal debates over slavery. The Court might have upheld freedom claims, especially when lower courts had done so. The Court might have protected the rights of free blacks in fugitive slave cases while also preserving the legal claims of slave owners. The Court might even have tilted toward due process for fugitive slaves, instead of denying them any rights. Chief Justice Taney's conclusion in *Dred Scott* that blacks "had no rights" accurately reflected the jurisprudence of the Court under Marshall and Taney, but such a harsh and racist conclusion was not the only one available to the Court. Finally, the Court might have showed restraint in interpreting the power of Congress to regulate slavery in the territories. This would have provided Congress with a Constitutional basis for a political solution to the problem of human bondage in the West. Whether Congress could have come up with a solution is unclear, but *Dred Scott* precluded any solution except to give the South a complete victory on this issue.

Curiously, while the South won virtually everything from the Court, it was never enough to satisfy the demands of the slaveocracy. With the election of Lincoln, the Deep South left the Union and the mid-South soon followed. The secessionists were not leaving because of the Court's decisions, but because they feared Lincoln would push the nation in a new direction. Having won so often—having *always* won—southern white leaders could not tolerate losing. The United States Supreme Court was certainly not responsible for secession or the War. But it was responsible for helping to create and nurture a culture of hostility toward liberty and justice for all, and for constantly supporting slavery. Through their jurisprudence, these justices encouraged southerners to attempt to create their own nation, based on the proposition that all men are *not* created equal, and that all people are *not* entitled to life, liberty, and the pursuit of happiness.

NOTES

ACKNOWLEDGMENTS

INDEX OF CASES CITED

INDEX

NOTES

INTRODUCTION

1. Harold M. Hyman and William M. Wiecek, *Equal Justice Under Law: Constitutional Development, 1835–1875* (New York: Harper & Row, 1982), title of chap. 4. See also William M. Wiecek, "Slavery and Abolition Before the United States Supreme Court, 1820–1860," *Journal of American History* 65 (1978): 34–59, 34, 36.

2. These two quotations are from the preambles of the Declaration of Independence and the Constitution, respectively.

3. *Harry* v. *Decker and Hopkins,* 1 Miss. (1 Walker) 36 (1818). In this case the Mississippi Court upheld a freedom claim based on residence in the Northwest Territory.

4. U.S. Constitution, Amendments XIII, XIV, and XV.

5. *Prigg* v. *Pennsylvania,* 41 US (16 Pet.) 539 (1842).

6. In *Johnson and Graham's Lessee* v. *M'Intosh,* 21 U.S. (8 Wheat.) 543 (1823), Marshall offered racist caricatures of Indians as he argued that Indians were uncivilized and had no right to self-determination or to control their lands. In *Cherokee Nation* v. *Georgia,* 30 U.S. (5 Pet.) 1 (1831), Marshall held that the Indian tribes had no right to litigate in the federal courts to defend their sovereignty and their rights; in *Worcester* v. *Georgia,* 31 U.S. (6 Pet.) 515 (1832), Marshall defended the treaty power of the United States and the civil liberties of a white missionary living among the Cherokee, but he did little to protect Indian rights.

7. Paul Finkelman, *Slavery and the Founders: Race and Liberty in the Age of Jefferson,* 3rd ed. (New York: Routledge, 2014), 3–45.

8. *An Article on the Latimer Case* (Boston: Bradbury, Soden, and Co., 1843), 6 (capitalization in the original).

9. Timothy Huebner, "Roger B. Taney and the Slavery Issue: Looking Beyond—and Before—*Dred Scott*," *Journal of American History* 97, no. 1 (2010): 17–38, 18; David Martin, *Trial of the Rev. Jacob Gruber, Minister in the Methodist Episcopal Church, At the March Term, 1819, in the Frederick County Court, For a Misdemeanor* (Fredericktown, Md.: David Martin, 1819); Paul Finkelman, *Slavery in the Courtroom: An Annotated Bibliography of American Cases* (Washington, D.C.: Library of Congress, for sale by GPO, 1985), 158–161.

10. *Dred Scott* v. *Sandford*, 60 U.S. (19 How.) 393, 404–5 (1857); "Unpublished opinion of Attorney General Taney," quoted in Carl Brent Swisher, *Roger B. Taney* (New York: Macmillan, 1935), 154.

11. David J. Danelski and Artimus Ward, eds., *The Chief Justice: Appointment and Influence* (Ann Arbor: University of Michigan Press, 2016).

12. G. Edward White, *The American Judicial Tradition: Profiles of Leading American Judges*, 3rd ed. (New York: Oxford University Press, 2007), 16.

13. George Lee Haskins and Herbert A. Johnson, *History of the Supreme Court of the United States*, vol. 2: *Foundations of Power: John Marshall, 1801–1815* (New York: Macmillan, 1981). Herbert Johnson, *The Chief Justiceship of John Marshall, 1801–1835* (Columbia: University of South Carolina Press, 1997), 95.

1 · THE ANTEBELLUM CONSTITUTION AND SLAVERY

1. William Lloyd Garrison to Rev. Samuel J. May, July 17, 1845, in *The Letters of William Lloyd Garrison*, ed. Walter M. Merrill (Cambridge, Mass.: Harvard University Press, 1973), 3:303. *The Liberator*, May 6, 1842. See also William M. Wiecek, *The Sources of Antislavery Constitutionalism in America, 1760–1848* (Ithaca, N.Y.: Cornell University Press, 1977), chap. 10; and James Brewer Stewart, *Holy Warriors: The Abolitionists and American Slavery* (New York: Hill and Wang, 1976), 98–99, 158–159; Paul Finkelman, *Slavery and the Founders: Race and Liberty in the Age of Jefferson*, 3rd ed. (New York: Routledge, 2014), 3–45.

2. Until of course after the Civil War, when the Thirteenth, Fourteenth, and Fifteenth Amendments used slavery, race, color, and servitude.

3. Connecticut's Roger Sherman, for example, objected to using the word slave, stating he "liked a description better" than explicit language, which was "not pleasing to some people." Max Farrand, ed., *The Records of the Federal Convention of 1787*, rev. ed., 4 vols. (New Haven, Conn.: Yale University Press, 1966), 2:415. In the North Carolina ratifying convention, James Iredell, who had been a delegate in Philadelphia, explained: "The word *slave* is not mentioned" because "the northern delegates, owing to their particular scruples on the subject of slavery, did not choose the word *slave* to be mentioned." Jonathan Elliot, ed., *The Debates in the Several State Conventions on the Adoption of the Federal Constitution*, 5 vols. (1888; repr. New York: Burt Franklin, 1987), 4:176.

4. U.S. Constitution, Art. I, Sec. 2, Par. 3.

5. Farrand, ed., *The Records of the Federal Convention of 1787*, 2: 220–23.

6. U.S. Constitution, Art. I, Sec. 9.

7. On the reopening of the trade see Finkelman, *Slavery and the Founders*, 150–152; and Jed H. Shugerman, "The Louisiana Purchase and South Carolina's Reopening of the Slave Trade in 1803," *Journal of the Early Republic* 22 (2002): 263–290.

8. An Act to Prohibit the Importation of Slaves, ch. 22, 2 Stat. 426 (1807). This law was passed in 1807 and went into effect on January 1, 1808.

9. Farrand, ed., *The Records of the Federal Convention of 1787*, 2:220–223. U.S. Constitution Art. I, Sec. 8, Par. 3 gave Congress power to regulate international and interstate commerce.

10. Letters from a Countryman from Dutchess County (letter of Jan. 22, 1788), in *The Complete Anti-Federalist*, ed. Herbert J. Storing (Chicago: University of Chicago Press, 1981), 6:62; Essays by Republicus (essay of March 12, 1788), in *Complete Anti-Federalist*, ed. Storing, 5:169.

11. U.S. Constitution, Art. I, Sec. 9, Par. 4.

12. Farrand, ed., *The Records of the Federal Convention of 1787*, 2:56–57. This debate is discussed in Paul Finkelman, "The Proslavery Origins of the Electoral College," *Cardozo Law Review* 23 (2002): 1145–1157. The clause is found at U.S. Constitution, Art. II, Sec. 1, Par. 3. Madison also noted that the "right of suffrage was

much more diffusive in the Northern than the Southern States," implying that more northerners than southerners could vote. But this argument was not very persuasive, since the southern states would have been free to expand suffrage in presidential elections.

13. U.S. Constitution, Art. IV, Sec. 2, Par. 3.

14. *Somerset* v. *Stewart*, 98 Eng. Rep. 499, Lofft 1 (1772), quoted at 19.

15. Elliot, ed., *Debates*, 4:286.

16. U.S. Constitution, Art. V. The clause also prohibited any amendment of the capitation tax clause before 1808.

17. U.S. Constitution, Art. I, Sec. 8, Par. 16, and Art. IV, Sec. 4. Wendell Phillips, *The Constitution a Pro-Slavery Compact; or, Selections from the Madison Papers*, 2nd ed. (New York: American Anti-Slavery Society, 1845), v–vi.

18. Farrand, ed., *The Records of the Federal Convention of 1787*, 2:220–223; Consider Arms, Malichi Maynard, and Samuel Field, "Reasons for Dissent," in *Complete Anti-Federalist*, ed. Storing 4:262–263.

19. U.S. Constitution, Art. I, Sec. 9, Par. 5 and Art. I, Sec. 10, Par. 2.

20. U.S. Constitution, Art. V.

21. Pinckney quoted in Elliot, ed., *Debates*, 4:286.

22. Abraham Lincoln, "First Inaugural Address—Final Text (Mar. 4, 1861)," Roy P. Basler, ed., *The Collected Works of Abraham Lincoln* (New Brunswick, N.J.: Rutgers University Press, 1953), 4:262, 263.

23. Wendell Phillips, *Can Abolitionists Vote or Take Office Under the United States Constitution* (New York: American Anti-Slavery Society, 1845), 3.

24. See Matthew Karp, *This Vast Southern Empire: Slaveholders at the Helm of American Foreign Policy* (Cambridge, Mass.: Harvard University Press, 2016), 199–225. The officer corps of the Navy was overwhelmingly northern.

25. "An Act to Establish the Territorial Government of Oregon," Act of August 14, 1848. 9 Stat. 323.

26. Paul Finkelman, "Regulating the African Slave Trade," *Civil War History* 54 (2008): 379–405.

27. The repassage of the Northwest Ordinance is discussed in Finkelman, *Slavery and the Founders*, 46–74; U.S. Constitution, Art. IV, Sec. 3. Par. 2, and Art. I, Sec. 8, Par. 17.

28. Pinckney, quoted in Elliot, ed., *Debates*, 4:286.

29. U.S. Constitution, Art. IV, Sec. 2, Par. 1.

30. The six states were New Hampshire, Massachusetts, New York, New Jersey, Pennsylvania, and North Carolina. There is some evidence of free blacks voting in Maryland and Rhode Island as well.

31. *Harry and Others* v. *Decker and Hopkins*, 1 Miss. (1 Walker) 36 (1818). In this case the Mississippi Court upheld a freedom claim based on residence in the Northwest Territory.

32. The Constitution provided that federal courts could hear private suits between citizens of different states. This was known as "diversity jurisdiction" because of the parties' diversity of state citizenship. See U.S. Constitution, Art. III, Sec. 2, Par. 1.

2 · JOHN MARSHALL: SLAVE OWNER AND JURIST

1. The bronze outside of the Court was done by William Wetmore Story, the son of Marshall's closest colleague on the Court, Joseph Story. The only other justice who has appeared on our coins or currency is Chief Justice Salmon P. Chase, who was on the $10,000 Federal Reserve note (in 1928 and 1934) for his service as a Secretary of the Treasury during the Civil War. Justice James Wilson was on the $10,000 series EE U.S. Savings Bond. The four law schools are John Marshall Law School in Chicago; Marshall-Wythe Law School at the College of William and Mary; Cleveland-Marshall Law School at Cleveland State University; and John Marshall Law School in Atlanta.

2. Frank B. Cross and James F. Spriggs, II, "The Most Important (and Best) Supreme Court Opinions and Justices," *Emory Law Journal*, 60 (2010): 432 (Table I). They are 1. *M'Culloch* v. *Maryland* (1819); 2. *Gibbons* v. *Ogden* (1824); 4. *Marbury* v. *Madison* (1803); 5. *Osborn* v. *Bank of the United States* (1824); and 10. *Cohens* v. *Virginia* (1821). Another Marshall opinion, *Brown* v. *Maryland* (1827), comes in at number 16.

3. Jean Edward Smith, *John Marshall: Definer of Nation* (New York: Henry Holt, 1996); George Lee Haskins and Herbert A. Johnson, *History of the Supreme Court of the United States*, vol. 2: *Foundations of Power: John Marshall, 1801–1815* (New York: Macmillan, 1981); G. Edward White, *The American Judicial Tradition: Profiles of Leading American Judges*, 3rd ed. (New York: Oxford University Press, 2007), 16; G. Edward White, *History of the Supreme Court of the United States*, vols. 3–4: *The Marshall Court and Cultural Change, 1815–1835* (New York: Macmillan, 1988), 689. One exception to this is Donald M. Roper, "In Quest of Judicial Objectivity: The Marshall Court and the Legitimation of Slavery," *Stanford Law Review* 21 (1969): 532–539.

4. R. Kent Newmyer, *John Marshall and the Heroic Age of the Supreme Court* (Baton Rouge: Louisiana State University Press, 2001). *The Papers of John Marshall*, ed. Charles F. Hobson (Chapel Hill: University of North Carolina Press, 2000), 10:156. The Marshall papers were published between 1974 and 2006, with Herbert Johnson, Charles T. Cullen, and Charles F. Hobson serving as the editors of the *Papers*. Hereinafter they will be cited as *Papers of Marshall* with an appropriate volume number.

5. R. Kent Newmyer, "John Marshall, *McCulloch* v. *Maryland*, and the Southern States' Rights Tradition," *John Marshall Law Review* 33 (2000), 875–934.

6. *Papers of Marshall*, 10:156; Charles Hobson, *The Great Chief Justice: John Marshall and the Rule of Law* (Lawrence: University of Kansas Press, 1996), 164.

7. Newmyer, *John Marshall and the Heroic Age*, 434. There are two possible exceptions to this statement. *The Brig Wilson* v. *United States*, 30 F. Cas. 239 (1820) involved the African slave trade but dovetailed with a Virginia law prohibiting free blacks from entering the state. Because Virginia was not a party to the case, Marshall did not have to rule on the Virginia law, thus no federalism issue actually arose. The second case, *Francis Lagrange, alias Isidore, A Man of Colour, Plaintiff in Error* v. *Pierre Chouteau*, 29 U.S. (4 Pet.) 287 (1830), involved whether Missouri had to enforce the Northwest Ordinance, but Marshall ducked the entire matter with a thoroughly weird and disingenuous conclusion that, despite the Northwest Ordinance, there was no federal statute at issue.

8. Hobson, *Great Chief Justice*, 164. When Marshall married at age twenty-seven, his father gave him a slave as a wedding present. Marshall would later inherit a few more slaves from various relatives. Leonard Baker, *John Marshall: A Life in Law* (New York: Macmillan, 1974), 11, 714–715. Frances Howell Rudko, "Pause at the Rubicon, John Marshall and Emancipation: Reparations in the Early National Period?" *John Marshall Law Review* 35 (2001): 75–89, 77. Newmyer, *John Marshall and the Heroic Age*, 415.

9. These included more than twelve slaves in Richmond; sixty-two slaves at Chickahominy in Henrico County; thirty-one at Mont Blanc and twenty-one held for Marshall by his overseer Thomas Hillery in Fauquier County. There is also a record of twenty-two slaves listed at John Marshall (quarters) in Henrico. The Fauquier numbers may undercount Marshall's slaves, since at that time many of his slaves were on land that he owned that was occupied by his sons, and the slaves may have been counted as belonging to the sons. In addition to slaves that the census specifically denotes as belonging to the chief justice, there are over 250 other slaves listed in the census connected to Marshall's children and his other relatives. Many of these had been owned by Marshall but gifted to his children. Some may still have been his. U. S. Census, 1830 Fauquier County, Virginia, database with images, *FamilySearch,* https://familysearch.org/pal:/MM9.3.1/TH-1951–25122–37198–85?cc =1803958, Virginia > Fauquier > Not Stated > image 141 of 162; citing NARA microfilm publication M19 (Washington D.C.: National Archives and Records Administration, n.d.). Overseer, Thomas Hillery for Marshall, 21 slaves, and John Marshall, 31 slaves. U. S. Census, 1830, Fauquier County, Virginia, database with images, *FamilySearch,* https://familysearch.org/pal:/MM9.3.1/TH-1951 -25122-37509-62?cc=1803958, Virginia > Fauquier > Not Stated > image 135 of 162; citing NARA microfilm publication M19 (Washington D.C.: National Archives and Records Administration, n.d.). John Marshall, (quarters), 22 slaves. U.S. Census, 1830, Henrico, Virginia, 326, line 13, citing NARA microfilm publication M19 (Washington D.C.: National Archives and Records Administration, n.d.). John Marshall, 62 slaves.

10. Albert J. Beverage, *The Life of John Marshall,* 4 vols. (Boston: Houghton Mifflin, 1916), 1: 37, 50–68, 69, 95–96, 167.

11. Newmyer, *John Marshall and the Heroic Age*, 2–11.

12. Hobson, *Great Chief Justice*, 3; Smith, *John Marshall*, 164–168; Beverage, *Life of Marshall*, 1:167.

13. In 1790 Richmond was the nation's eighteenth-largest city, with a population under 3,800 people. http://www.census.gov /population/www/documentation/twps0027/tab02.txt.

14. Herbert Johnson, *The Chief Justiceship of John Marshall, 1801–1835* (Columbia: University of South Carolina Press, 1997), 87, 88–89, 90; Albert P. Blaustein and Roy M. Mersky, *The First Hundred Justices: Statistical Studies on the Supreme Court* (Hamden, Conn.: Archon Books, 1978), 142. See also Newmyer, *John Marshall and the Heroic Age,* 399, describing his dominance on the Court. Edward White reports that Marshall wrote 519 signed decisions. G. Edward White, *The American Judicial Tradition: Profiles of Leading American Judges* (Oxford University Press, 2007), 14.

15. *Fletcher* v. *Peck,* 10 U.S. (6 Cr.) 87 (1810); *M'Culloch* v. *Maryland,* 17 U.S. (4 Wheat.) 316 (1819); *Cohens* v. *Virginia,* 19 U.S. (6 Wheat.) 264 (1821); Paul Finkelman and Melvin I. Urofsky, *Landmark Decisions of the Supreme Court,* 2nd ed. (Washington, D.C.: CQ Press, 2008), 34–35.

16. Similarly, see Marshall's opinion in the related case *Ex parte Bollman, Ex parte Swartwout,* 8 U.S. (4 Cr.) 75 (1807), and R. Kent Newmyer, *The Treason Trial of Aaron Burr: Law, Politics, and the Character Wars of the New Nation* (New York: Cambridge University Press, 2012).

17. On Jefferson and slavery see generally, Paul Finkelman, *Slavery and the Founders: Race and Liberty in the Age of Jefferson,* 3rd ed. (New York: Routledge, 2014), 193–280. *The Antelope,* 23 U.S. (10 Wheat.) 66, at 120 (1825).

18. "Revoked Will and Codicils, 12 April 1827–August 1830," *Papers of Marshall,* 11: 6, 7, 8. "Additional codicil to my will, Aug. 17th. 1830," *Papers of Marshall,* 11: 9; *Papers of Marshall,* 1: 317n31, 363, 386–387, notes 27–29.

19. Hobson, *Great Chief Justice,* 164; Newmyer, *John Marshall and the Heroic Age,* 415.

20. Beverage, *Life of Marshall,* 1: 167, 181; *Papers of Marshall,* 1: 296, 297, 305, 308, 317, 317n31, 319n38.

21. *Papers of Marshall*, 1:123; and Beverage, *Life of Marshall*, 1:187–188.

22. *Papers of Marshall*, 1: 363, 377, 377n89, 383, 385, 386–387, notes 27–29, 389, 408.

23. *Papers of Marshall*, 2:346, 349, 351, 375, 406.

24. *Papers of Marshall*, 2:356, 382, 396.

25. *Papers of Marshall*, 2:338n23 (1788), 367n52 (1789), 375 (1789), 408 (death of Sam), 415n49 (1791), 444n94 (1792), 474n18 (1794), 484n77.

26. He also lists the mothers of two of his slaves. It is not clear if this was for identification purposes or if those slaves were also alive at the time. "Revoked Will and Codicils, 12 April 1827–August 1830," *Papers of Marshall*, 11:5.

27. "Revoked Will and Codicils, 12 April 1827–August 1830," *Papers of Marshall*, 11: 6, 7, 8. "Additional codicil to my will, Aug. 17th. 1830," *Papers of Marshall*, 11: 9. U.S. Census, 1830, Fauquier County, Virginia, database with images, *FamilySearch*, https://familysearch.org/pal:/MM9.3.1/TH-1942-25122-42114-33?cc=1803958, Virginia>Fauquier>Not Stated>image 77 of 162); citing NARA microfilm publication M19 (Washington, D.C.: National Archives and Records Administration, n.d.). Edward C. Marshall, 27 slaves. On age of Edward Marshall see https://www.findagrave.com/cgi-bin/fg.cgi?page=gr&GRid=11847253.

28. "Revoked Will and Codicils, 12 April 1827–August 1830," *Papers of Marshall*, 11: 6, 7, 8. "Additional codicil to my will, Aug. 17th. 1830," *Papers of Marshall*, 11: 9. U.S. Census, 1830, database with images, *FamilySearch*, https://familysearch.org/pal:/MM9.3.1/TH-1942-25142-41124-83?cc=1803958, Virginia>Henrico>Not Stated>image 90 of 109; citing NARA microfilm publication M19 (Washington, D.C.: National Archives and Records Administration, n.d.). John Marshall, 62 slaves.

29. "Revoked will and Codicils, 24 September 1831–5 January 1832," *Papers of Marshall*, 12:100.

30. U.S. Census, 1830, Fauquier County, Virginia, database with images, *FamilySearch*, https://familysearch.org/pal:/MM9.3.1/TH-1942-25122-42114-33?cc=1803958, Virginia>Fauquier>Not Stated>image 77 of 162; citing NARA microfilm publication M19

(Washington, D.C.: National Archives and Records Administration, n.d.). Thomas Marshall, 66 slaves.

31. "Revoked will and Codicils, 24 September 1831–5 January 1832," *Papers of Marshall*, 12:102. Thomas Ambler had forty-seven slaves on his plantation in Fauquier County in 1830; it is not clear if any of these also belonged to Marshall or had been gifted to Ambler along with the land Marshall had already given him. U.S. 1830 Census, database with images, *FamilySearch*, https://familysearch.org/pal:/MM9.3.1/TH-1951-25122-38363-74?cc=1803958, Virginia > Fauquier > Not Stated > image 79 of 162; citing NARA microfilm publication M19 (Washington, D.C.: National Archives and Records Administration, n.d.). Thomas M. Ambler, 47 slaves.

32. "Will of John Marshall, 9 April, 1832," *Papers of Marshall*, 12:193–198.

33. "Codicil to the Forgoing will of John Marshall, 13 August 1832," *Papers of Marshall*, 12:193–198. His full name was Robin Spurlock but, even when contemplating freeing him, Marshall did not dignify him with a last name.

34. A picture of Spurlock's daughter, Agnes Spurlock Hilton, exists and has been on display at the John Marshall House in Richmond. http://www.charlescity.org/saf/It is unclear if Spurlock's wife was still alive at the time Marshall wrote this codicil. Sally Hemings was the child of John Wayles, who was also the father of Jefferson's wife, Martha. Thus, Sally and her siblings were Jefferson's half-in-laws, while Sally's children were also his own children, as well as also being his half-nieces and nephews. Finkelman, *Slavery and the Founders*, 216–221, 243.

35. "An Act Reducing into One, the Several Acts Concerning Slaves, Free Negroes, and Mulattoes," *The Revised Code of Virginia, 1819*, Chap. 111.

36. A decade before he died, Marshall had signed a petition to the state legislature requesting that a recently emancipated slave be allowed to remain in Richmond. "Certificate for Jasper Graham, 5 December 1822," *Papers of Marshall*, 9:377–378.

37. Baker, *A Life in Law*, 562–563.

38. John Marshall to James K. Marshall, April 12, 1834, and May 19, 1834, in *Papers of Marshall*, 12: 403, 411.

39. On Washington and slaveholding, see Finkelman, *Slavery and the Founders*, 200.

40. Newmyer, *John Marshall and the Heroic Age*, 416. U.S. Census, 1820, database with images, *FamilySearch*, https://familysearch .org/pal:/MM9.3.1/TH-1942-25144-43992-83?cc=1803955 Virginia > Fauquier > Not Stated > image 39 of 82; citing NARA microfilm publication M33 (Washington, D.C.: National Archives and Records Administration, n.d.); U.S. Census, 1830, Fauquier, Virginia, 467, line 8, Doc J Marshall; National Archives, microfilm publication M19. Newmyer, *John Marshall and the Heroic Age*, 327.

41. Newmyer, *John Marshall and the Heroic Age*, 12:415–416; John Marshall to James K. Marshall, May 19, 1834, *Papers of Marshall*, 12:411; 1830 U.S. Census, Fauquier, Virginia, 473, line 13, John Marshall; National Archives, microfilm publication M19 (57 slaves under James and 38 slaves under John); 1830 U.S. Census, Richmond (independent city), Virginia, 389, line 26, John Marshall; National Archives, M19. (7 slaves); 1830 U.S. Census, Richmond (independent city), Virginia, 447, line 15, John Marshall; National Archives, M19 (1 slave); 1830, U.S. Census, Henrico, Virginia, 326, line 13, John Marshall; National Archives, microfilm publication M19 (62 slaves).

42. "Revoked will and Codicils, 24 September 1831–5 January 1832," *Papers of Marshall*, 12:100.

43. Newmyer, *John Marshall and the Heroic Age*, 414; Jean Edward Smith, *John Marshall: Defender of a Nation* (New York: Henry Holt, 1996), 162, 164–168. Baker, *A Life in Law*, 715.

44. Newmyer, *John Marshall and the Heroic Age*, 414, 418.

45. On Coles, see Finkelman, *Slavery and the Founders*, chaps. 7 and 8; on Carter see Jason Levy, *The First Emancipator: Slavery, Religion, and the Quiet Revolution of Robert Carter* (New York: Random House, 2005).

46. On Washington and slaveholding, see Finkelman, *Slavery and the Founders*, 200.

47. Marshall's years on the court also coincided with a relentless push to remove Indians from the eastern part of the United States. Thomas Jefferson developed the idea of Indian removal. Under James Madison and James Monroe, the nation's policy of war and removal devastated the southeastern Indians. President Andrew

Jackson continued these policies. Marshall's decisions in *Johnson and Graham's Lessee* v. *M'Intosh* 21 U.S. 543 (1823), *Cherokee Nation* v. *Georgia* 20 U.S. 1 (1831), and *Worcester* v. *Georgia* 31 U.S. 515 (1832) provided the legal basis for taking all land from Indians. A full analysis of these major cases is beyond the scope of this book.

48. Because most northern states adopted gradual abolition acts, a small number of people remained in bondage into the nineteenth century, even though slavery as a system was ending. In 1840, New Jersey, the last northern state to adopt a gradual emancipation act, had 674 slaves; and Illinois, the last northern state to enter the Union with a preexisting territorial slave population, had 331 slaves. The best study of the end of slavery in the North during this period remains Arthur Zilversmit, *The First Emancipation* (Chicago: University of Chicago Press, 1967). See also Paul Finkelman, *An Imperfect Union: Slavery, Federalism, and Comity* (Chapel Hill: University of North Carolina Press, 1981). Campbell Gibson and Kay Jung, "Historical Census Statistics on Population Totals by Race, 1790 to 1990, and by Hispanic Origin, 1970 to 1990, For the United States, Regions, Divisions and States," Working Paper no. 56, U.S. Census Bureau, Population Division, 2002.

49. Marshall to Ralph R. Gurley [Secretary of the ACS], Dec. 14, [1831], *Papers of Marshall*, 12:131–132.

50. J[ohn] Marshall, Chairman, "Memorial: To the General Assembly of Virginia," December 13, 1831, *Papers of Marshall*, 12:127, quoted at 128 and 130.

51. J[ohn] Marshall, Chairman, "Memorial: To the General Assembly of Virginia," December 13, 1831, *Papers of Marshall*, 12:127, quoted at 128 and 130. On Jefferson and free blacks, see Finkelman, *Slavery and the Founders*, 270.

52. Marshall to the Marquis de Lafayette, May 2, 1827, *Papers of Marshall*, 11:11–12.

53. This is based on searches of all Supreme Court decisions during Marshall's time on the court in HeinOnline, using "slave*" or "negro*" or "Africa*" as the search term. *Gibbons* v. *Ogden*, 22 U.S. (9 Wheat.) 1 (1824).

54. For extensive discussion of his use of natural law, see Johnson, *Chief Justiceship of Marshall*, 95, and White, *Marshall Court and Cultural Change*, 674.

55. *The Antelope*, at 120.

56. *Sanders* v. *Hamilton*, 21 F. Cas. 320 (C.C.D.N.C.) (1802) (determining the measure of damages in litigation over the ownership of a slave); *Hamilton* v. *Russell*, 5 U.S. (1 Cr.) 309 (1803) (dispute involving the sale of a slave); *Ronald* v. *Barkley*, 20 F. Cas. 1148 (C.C.D.Va.) (1818) (involving slaves who were part of the property in a suit between Barley and the infant heirs of Ronald); United States v. Marshall of the District of North Carolina, 26 F. Cas. 1173 (C.C.D.N.C.) (1833) (determining whether slaves should be conveyed to the United States as part of debt settlement); *Hopkirk* v. *Randolph*, 12 F. Cas. 513 at 517 (C.C.E.D.Va.) (1824) (using and citing a case involving the gift of slaves as an analogy to the gift of real estate by a man who later became insolvent). *Ramsay* v. *Lee*, 8 U.S. (4 Cr.) 401 (1807) (action of detinue for a slave involving an adverse possession of a slave. Marshall finds "five years' adverse possession, with or without right, gives a good title."); *Spiers* v. *Willison*, 8 U.S. (4 Cr.) 398 (1807) (action of detinue for certain slaves); *Mandeville and Jamesson* v. *Wilson*, 9 U.S. (5 Cr.) 15 (1809) (action for assumpsit involving the hire of a slave); *Brent* v. *Chapman*, 9 U.S. (5 Cr.) 358 (1809) (case involving the seizure of a slave by the sheriff and the adverse possession of the slave by another party); *Beverly* v. *Brook*, 15 U.S. (2 Wheat.) 100 (1817) (holding that a ship captain was not liable for the loss of three slaves rented to work on a ship who escaped during a voyage); *Byrd* v. *Byrd*, 4 Fed. Cas. 943 (C.C.D.Va.) (1824) (settling a complicated will); *Garnett* v. *Macon*, 10 F. Cas. (C.C.E.D. Va.) (1825) (slaves mortgaged); *Brooks* v. *Marbry*, 24 U.S. (11 Wheat.) 78 (1826) (slaves part of the property at issue in a debt case); *Boyce* v. *Anderson*, 27 U.S. (2 Pet.) 150 (1829) (holding that a steamship owner was not responsible for the loss of four slaves who drowned while being transported for the master because "the doctrine of common carriers does not apply to the case of carrying intelligent beings, such as negroes.") *United States* v. *Marshall of the District of North Carolina*, 26 F. Cas. 1173 (C.C.D.N.C.) (1833) (slaves sold to satisfy debt to the United States); *Estho et al.* v. *Lear, Administrator of the Thaddeus Kosciuszko*, 32 U.S. (7 Pet.) 130 (1833) (remanding a suit over the will of Thaddeus Kosciuszko, who wanted his estate to be used to free slaves); *Auguste Chouteau's Heirs* v. *U.S.*, 34 U.S. (9 Pet.) 147 (1835) (discussing slaves that were part of Chouteau's estate); *The Life and Fire Insurance Company of New York* v. *Adams*, 34 U.S. (9 Pet.) 573 at 593 (1835) (slaves mortgaged).

57. *Scott* v. *Negro Ben,* 10 U.S. (6 Cr.) 3 (1810) at 6.

58. "An act to prohibit the carrying on the slave trade from the United States to any foreign place or country," Act of March 22, 1794, ch.11, 1 Stat. 347 (1794); "An act in addition to the act entitled 'An act to prohibit the carrying on the slave trade from the United States to any foreign place or country,'" Act of May 10, 1800, ch. 51, 2 Stat. 70 (1800); "An act to prevent the importation of certain persons into certain States, where, by the laws thereof, their admission is prohibited," Act of Feb. 28, 1803, ch. 10, 2 Stat. 205 (1803). "An act to prohibit the importation of slaves into any port or place within the jurisdiction of the United States, from and after the first day of January, in the year of our Lord one thousand eight hundred and eight," Act of March 2, 1807, ch. 22, 2 Stat. 426 (1807).

59. "An Act in addition to 'An act to prohibit the introduction (importation) of slaves into any port or place within the jurisdiction of the United States, from and after the first day of January, in the year of our Lord one thousand eight hundred and eight,' and to repeal certain parts of the same," Act of Apr. 20, 1818, ch. 91, 3 Stat. 450 (1818); "An Act in addition to the Acts prohibiting the slave trade," Act of March 3, 1819, ch. 101, 3 Stat. 532 (1819); "An Act to continue in force 'An act to protect the commerce of the United States, and punish the crime of piracy,' and also to make further provisions for punishing the crime of piracy," Act of May 15, 1820, ch. 113, 3 Stat. 600 (1820); "An Act in addition to 'An act to continue in force 'An act to protect the commerce of the United States, and punish the crime of piracy," and, also, to make further provision for punishing the crime of piracy." Act of January 30, 1823, ch. 7, 3 Stat. 721 (1823).

60. For example, in 1792 Virginia appropriated money to buy "a certain Negro named Saul" from his master and then free him because of his "many very essential services rendered to this Commonwealth, during the late war." "An Act for the Manumission of a Negro named Saul," Act of November 113, 1792, Chap. XCIII, *Hening's Statutes at Large,* 13:619.

61. Finkelman, *Slavery and the Founders,* chaps. 7 and 8.

62. These cases are discussed in Finkelman, *An Imperfect Union,* chap. 7.

63. "An Act concerning Slaves," Chap. LXXVII, *Laws of Virginia, 1785,* 60; and "An Act to amend the Act preventing the farther

importation of slaves," Act of December 17, 1789, Chap. XLV, *Virginia Laws, 1789,* 26–27.

64. *Gobu* v. *Gobu,* 1 N.C. 188 (1802); *Hudgins* v. *Wrights,* 11 Va. (1 Hen. & M.) 134 (1806).

65. In this count I have excluded the two cases surrounding the will of Thaddeus Kosciuszko, who wanted his estate to be used to free slaves and educate them. Kosciuszko appointed Thomas Jefferson the executor of his estate for this purpose, but Jefferson refused to accept this role. This case was about black freedom in the sense that Kosciuszko wanted to use his estate to buy and free slaves, but the Court was never able to get beyond technical issues involving the probate of the will itself. Litigation by residual heirs brought the will to the Supreme Court in *Armstrong* v. *Lear Administrator (with the will annexed) of Kosciuszko,* 25 U.S. (12 Wheat.) 169 (1827), and *Estho et al.* v. *Lear, Administrator of the Thaddeus Kosciuszko,* 32 U.S. (7 Pet.) 130 (1833). Justice Story decided the first case, sending it back to probate court, and Chief Justice Marshall decided the second case, remanding it to the Virginia courts.

66. *Scott* v. *Negro London,* 7 U.S. (3 Cr.) 324 (1806).

67. This law is "An Act to reduce to one, the several Acts concerning Slaves, Free Negroes, and Mulattoes," passed December 17, 1792, found in *Certain Acts of the General Assembly of the Commonwealth of Virginia* (Richmond: Augustine Davis, M.DCC.XCIV [1794]), 70. The relevant section of this law was based on the 1785 act: "An Act concerning Slaves," Chap. LXXVII, *Laws of Virginia, 1785,* 60; and "An Act to amend the Act preventing the farther importation of slaves," Act of December 17, 1789, Chap. XLV, *Virginia Laws, 1789,* 26–27.

68. *Respublica* v. *Blackmore,* 2 Yeates (Pa.) 234 (1797). See also Paul Finkelman, "Human Liberty, Property in Human Beings, and the Pennsylvania Supreme Court," *Duquesne Law Review* 53 (2015): 453–482. *Pleasants* v. *Pleasants,* 6 Va. (2 Call) 319 (1799); *Harry* v. *Decker and Hopkins,* 1 Miss. (1 Walker) 36 (1818). In this case the Mississippi Court upheld a freedom claim based on residence in the Northwest Territory.

69. *Wilson* v. *Belinda,* 3 Serg. & Rawle (Pa.) 396 (1817).

70. *Wilson* v. *Belinda,* at 398–399. On Tilghman and similar cases, see Finkelman, "Human Liberty, Property in Human Beings, and

the Pennsylvania Supreme Court." See also Shel Silverstein, "A Boy Named Sue," recorded by Johnny Cash (1969).

71. *Scott* v. *Negro London*, at 331.

72. Marbury v. Madison, 5 U.S. (1 Cr.) 137 (1803).

73. Ex Parte Bollman and Ex Parte Swartwout, 8 U.S. (4 Cr.) 75 (1807). For a short history of the Burr Trial, see Newmyer, *John Marshall and the Heroic Age*, 175–209.

74. *Scott* v. *Negro Ben*, 10 U.S. (6 Cr.) 3, 4, 6 (1810).

75. *Scott* v. *Ben*, at 7.

76. *Scott* v. *Ben, at* 7.

77. *Hezekiah Wood* v. *John Davis and Others*, 11 U.S. (7 Cr.) 271 (1812).

78. *Wood*, at 272.

79. *Wood*, at 271.

80. John Noonan, *The Antelope: The Ordeal of the Recaptured Africans in the Administration of James Monroe and John Quincy Adams* (Berkeley: University of California Press, 1977), 108.

81. *Wood*, at 271.

82. *Mima Queen and Child* v. *Hepburn*, 11 U.S. (7 Cr.) 290 (1813). In Haskins and Johnson, *Foundations of Power*, this case is given part of a single sentence, only to point out that Justice Duvall dissented from Marshall's opinion and to praise Duvall's knowledge of Maryland law. The authors ignore Marshall's opinion and do not indicate that Marshall found against the slave's liberty. Johnson does, however, discuss the case in *The Chief Justiceship of Marshall*, 345–347.

83. *Wood*, at 291–92.

84. *Papers of Marshall*, 7:385–386n2.

85. *Mima Queen*, at 293, 296.

86. *Mima Queen*, at 293, 296.

87. *Hudgins* v. *Wrights*, 11 Va. (1 Hen. & M.) 134 (1806). See St. George Tucker, *Tucker's Blackstone* (1803; reprint, with an introduction by Paul Finkelman and David Cobin, Union, N.J.: Lawbook Exchange, 1996).

88. Haskins and Johnson, *Foundations of Power*, 392. This seems to be the only time the word slave appears in this volume.

89. Ibid., at 298, 299.

90. *Telfair* v. *Steed's Executor*, 6 U.S. (2 Cr.) 407 at 418 (1805).

91. *Negro John Davis et al.* v. *Wood*, 14 U.S. (1 Wheat.) 6 (1816); *Negress Sally Henry* v. *Ball*, 14 U.S. (1 Wheat.) 1 (1816). This case is reported immediately before *Negro John Davis* v. *Wood*.

92. *Mason* v. *Matilda*, 25 U.S. (12 Wheat.) 590 (1827). As far as I can tell, no scholars of the Marshall Court have ever examined this case.

93. *Mason v. Matilda*, at 592.

94. *Le Grand* v. *Darnall*, 27 U.S. (2 Pet.) 664 at 669 and 664 (1829).

95. *Lagrange, alias Isidore* [sic.], *A Man of Colour* v. *Chouteau*, 29 U.S. (4 Pet.) 287 (1830).

96. *François LaGrange (alias Isadore)* v. *Pierre Chouteau*, 2 Mo. 20 at 22–23 (1828). On the history of the application of *Somerset* to American law, see Finkelman, *An Imperfect Union*. By this time, courts in Louisiana, Kentucky, Missouri, and Mississippi had freed slaves who had lived in the old Northwest. For a history of the slavery provision of the Northwest Ordinance, see Finkelman, *Slavery and the Founders,* chaps. 2 and 3.

97. *LaGrange* v. *Chouteau,* 2 Mo. 20 at 22–23.

98. This case was an appeal from the state supreme court (under Section 25 of the Judiciary Act of 1789) based entirely on meaning of the a federal law—the Northwest Ordinance—and was not filed as a diversity suit. Thus, the question of black citizenship did not arise, as it had in Darnall's case and would arise again in Dred Scott.

99. *LaGrange* v. *Chouteau,* 29 U.S. (4 Pet.) at 290.

100. *Menard* v. *Aspasia,* 30 U.S. (5 Pet.) 505 (1831).

101. *Menard,* at 511.

102. On McLean's pre-Court career, see Paul Finkelman, "John McLean: Moderate Abolitionist and Supreme Court Politician," *Vanderbilt Law Review* 62 (2009): 519–565.

103. *Lee* v. *Lee,* 33 U.S. (8 Pet.) 44 (1834); *M'Cutchin* v. *Marshall,* 33 U.S. (8 Pet.) 220 (1834); *Fenwick* v. *Chapman,* 34 U.S. (9 Pet.) 461 (1835); *Wallingsford* v. *Allen,* 35 U.S. (10 Pet.) 583 (1836).

3 · JOHN MARSHALL AND THE AFRICAN
SLAVE TRADE

1. Paul Finkelman, "The American Suppression of the African Slave Trade," *Akron Law Review* 42 (2009): 431–467, 438–439.

2. "An act to prohibit the carrying on the slave trade from the United States to any foreign place or country," Act of March 22, 1794, ch.11, 1 Stat. 347 (1794); "An act in addition to the act entitled 'An act to prohibit the carrying on the slave trade from the United States to any foreign place or country,'" Act of May 10, 1800, ch. 51, 2 Stat. 70 (1800); "An act to prevent the importation of certain persons into certain States, where, by the laws thereof, their admission is prohibited," Act of Feb. 28, 1803, ch. 10, 2 Stat. 205 (1803).

3. "An act to prohibit the importation of slaves into any port or place within the jurisdiction of the United States, from and after the first day of January, in the year of our Lord one thousand eight hundred and eight," Act of March 2, 1807, ch. 22, 2 Stat. 426 (1807); "An Act in addition to 'An act to prohibit the introduction (importation) of slaves into any port or place within the jurisdiction of the United States, from and after the first day of January, in the year of our Lord one thousand eight hundred and eight,' and to repeal certain parts of the same," Act of Apr. 20, 1818, ch. 91, 3 Stat. 450 (1818); "An Act in addition to the Acts prohibiting the slave trade," Act of March 3, 1819, ch. 101, 3 Stat. 532 (1819); "An Act to continue in force 'An act to protect the commerce of the United States, and punish the crime of piracy,' and also to make further provisions for punishing the crime of piracy," Act of May 15, 1820, ch. 113, 3 Stat. 600 (1820); "An Act in addition to 'An act to continue in force 'An act to protect the commerce of the United States, and punish the crime of piracy,'' and, also, to make further provision for punishing the crime of piracy." Act of January 30, 1823, ch. 7, 3 Stat. 721 (1823). These acts are discussed in Finkelman, "The American Suppression of the African Slave Trade."

4. Act of March 3, 1819, ch. 101, 3 Stat. 532–533 (1819).

5. Act of May 15, 1820, ch.113, 3 Stat. 600 (1820). The statute provided that this penalty was to be in force for only two years, but on January 3, 1823, Congress made it a permanent statute. Act of Jan. 30, 1823, ch.7, 3 Stat. 721 (1823).

6. Marshall to the Marquis de Lafayette, May 2, 1827, *The Papers of John Marshall*, ed. Charles F. Hobson (Chapel Hill: University of North Carolina Press, 2000), 11:12. The Marshall papers were published between 1974 and 2006, with Herbert Johnson, Charles T. Cullen, and Charles F. Hobson serving as the editors of the *Papers*.

7. *Adams* v. *Woods*, 6 U.S. (2 Cr.) 336 (1805). Unfortunately, the editors of the Marshall papers did not include this case or Marshall's opinion in the *Papers*. Leonard Baker mentions the case when discussing Marshall's "common-sense attitude toward law" in the context of his support for the statute of limitations issue in this case, but Baker does not mention that this was a slave trade case or delve into the complexity of it. Had he done so, Baker might not have been able to write such an admiring biography. Leonard Baker, *John Marshall: A Life in Law* (New York: Macmillan, 1974), 518. The comprehensive Holmes' Devise volume ignores this case as well.

8. *Adams* v. *Woods*, at 338, quoting Sec. 32 of the Act of Congress of April 30, 1790.

9. *Adams* v. *Woods*, at 338–339.

10. *Adams* v. *Woods*, at 338, quoting *Atcheson* v. *Everitt*, 98 Eng. Rep. 1142 (KB 1775).

11. *Adams* v. *Woods*, at 342; George Lee Haskins and Herbert A. Johnson, *History of the Supreme Court of the United States*, vol. 2: *Foundations of Power: John Marshall, 1801–1815* (New York: Macmillan, 1981), 437–438.

12. *The Brigantine Amiable Lucy* v. *The United States*, 10 U.S. 6 Cr. 330 (1810). *Adams* v. *Woods*, at 336.

13. U.S. Constitution, Art. I, Sec. 9.

14. The opinion in this case has a strange history. The official report of the case *Brig Caroline, William Broadfoot, Claimant* v. *United States*, 11 U.S. (7 Cr.) 496 (1813) indicates that there was a single, unsigned, one-paragraph opinion reversing the lower court. The editors of the *Papers of John Marshall*, however, found a full opinion by Marshall not published in Cranch's Reports. That opinion is found in *Marshall Papers* 8:404–407. Thus we know that the opinion was Marshall's. This Marshall opinion was also published in William Brockenbrough's reports of Marshall's circuit

court cases, as *The Caroline,* 1 Brockenbrough 384, and incorrectly dated as November 1819.

15. *The Caroline,* at 496–499.

16. *The Caroline,* at 496–499.

17. *The Caroline,* at 500.

18. *The Samuel,* 14 U.S. (1 Wheat.) 9 (1816). See also Thomas C. Shevory, *John Marshall's Law: Interpretation, Ideology, and Interest* (Westport, Conn.: Greenwood Press, 1994).

19. *The Emily and the Caroline (Broadfoot, Claimant),* 22 U.S. (9 Wheat.) 381 (1824).

20. *The Alerta* v. *Moran,* 13 U.S. (9 Cr.) 359 (1815). See also David Head, "Slave Smuggling by Foreign Privateers: The Illegal Slave Trade and the Geopolitics of the Early Republic," *Journal of the Early Republic* 33 no. 3 (2013): 433–462, at 447.

21. *The Alerta,* at 367.

22. *The Josefa Segunda (Carricabura et al., Claimants),* 18 U.S. (5 Wheat.) 338 (1820). This case would come back to the Court as *The Josefa Segunda (Roberts and Others, Claimants),* 23 U.S. (10 Wheat.) 312 (1825) to determine who received payments for the value of the condemned slaves. *The Josefa Segunda* was seized under the 1807 act banning the slave trade. This law provided for the sale of illegally imported Africans for the benefit of the U.S. government and of those who captured the slaver. After the passage of a new slave trade act, illegally imported Africans would be repatriated to Liberia. Act of March 3, 1819, ch.101, 3 Stat. 532 (1819).

23. John Noonan, *The Antelope: The Ordeal of the Recaptured Africans in the Administration of James Monroe and John Quincy Adams* (Berkeley: University of California Press, 1977), 58–59.

24. *The Josefa Segunda,* at 355–357. On the smuggling of slaves into Louisiana, see Head, "Slave Smuggling," 433–450.

25. *The Mary Ann,* 21 U.S. (8 Wheat.) 380 (1823) at 389–391.

26. *The Mary Ann,* at 390.

27. *The Merino (with additional claimants The Constitution, The Louisa, Barrias, and Others),* 22 U.S. (9 Wheat.) 391 (1824).

28. *The Merino,* 22 U.S. at 401.

29. *The Merino,* 22 U.S. at 406–408.

30. *The St. Jago de Cuba, Vinente and others Claimants,* 22 U.S. (9 Wheat.) 409 (1824).

31. Bryant, *Dark Places,* 25–29.

32. Noonan, *The Antelope,* 45–50.

33. Ibid., 53.

34. Ibid., 60.

35. *The Josefa Segunda,* at 358–359.

36. *The Antelope,* 23 U.S. at 114.

37. *The Antelope,* 23 U.S. at 122. Paul Finkelman, "Foreign Law and American Constitutional Interpretation: A Long and Venerable Tradition," *N.Y.U. Annual Survey of American Law* 63 (2007): 29–62.

38. *Ogden* v. *Saunders,* 25 U.S. (12 Wheat.) 213 (1827). See Herbert Johnson, *The Chief Justiceship of John Marshall, 1801–1835* (Columbia: University of South Carolina Press, 1997), 187.

39. *Ogden* v. *Saunders,* at 345.

40. *Ogden* v. *Saunders,* at 347.

41. *Ogden* v. *Saunders,* at 114–115, 116.

42. *Ogden* v. *Saunders,* at 116–120.

43. *The Antelope,* 23 U.S. at 118, quoting *Le Louis,* 165 Eng. Rep. 1464, 1476 (High Ct. of Adm.) (1817); Finkelman, "Foreign Law and American Constitutional Interpretation."

44. See Act of March 3, 1819, ch. 101, 2 Stat. 532. Act of May 15, 1820, ch. 113, §§ 4–5, 2 Stat. *The Antelope,* 23 U.S. at 122.

45. R. Kent Newmyer, *John Marshall and the Heroic Age of the Supreme Court* (Baton Rouge: Louisiana State University Press, 2001), 482.

46. The case involved a libel action against the ship and its contents, and not a criminal prosecution of the traders.

47. Newmyer, *John Marshall and the Heroic Age,* 1.

48. *The Antelope*, 24 U.S. (11 Wheat.) 413 (1826).

49. *The Antelope*, 25 U.S. (12 Wheat.) 546 (1827).

50. *The Plattsburgh* (*Marino, Claimant*), 23 U.S. (10 Wheat.) 133 (1825).

51. *United States* v. *Preston* (*Attorney General of Louisiana*), 28 U.S. (3 Pet.) 57 (1830). Plausibly the Court might have applied the "lottery" process initially used in *The Antelope,* and required that the money be used to randomly purchase slaves in Louisiana to be sent to Liberia. Not surprisingly, no one seems to have thought of this solution.

52. *Governor of Georgia* v. *Madrazo*, 26 U.S. (1 Pet). 110 (1828).

53. *Madrazo*, at 110.

54. Harris Gaylord Warren, "Aury, Louis Michel," *Handbook of Texas Online,* accessed August 1, 2016 at http://www.tshaonline.org /handbook/online/articles/fau04. Head, "Slave Smuggling," 451.

55. *Madrazo*, at 111.

56. *Madrazo*, at 120.

57. *Madrazo*, at 121.

58. *Madrazo*, at 128.

59. *Madrazo*, at 125.

60. *Ex parte Madrazzo*, 32 U.S. (7 Pet.) 627 (1833).

61. *Trustees of Dartmouth College* v. *Woodward*, 17 U.S. (4 Wheat.) 518 (1819).

62. *Fletcher* v. *Peck*, 10 U.S. (6 Cr.) 87 (1810).

63. *M'Culloch* v. *Maryland*, 17 U.S. (4 Wheat.) 316 (1819); see Paul Finkelman, "The Constitution and the Intentions of the Framers: The Limits of Historical Analysis," *University of Pittsburgh Law Review* 50 (1989): 349–398.

64. *Worcester* v. *Georgia*, 31 U.S. (6 Pet.) 515 (1832).

65. Charles Hobson, *The Great Chief Justice: John Marshall and the Rule of Law* (Lawrence: University of Kansas Press, 1996), 165.

66. Newmyer, *John Marshall and the Heroic Age*, 390 (quoting Marshall).

67. *Dred Scott* v. *Sandford,* 60 U.S. (19 How.) 393, 404–405 (1857).

68. Hobson, *Great Chief Justice,* 169.

4 · JOSEPH STORY: NEW ENGLAND ICON IN THE SERVICE OF SLAVERY

1. Joseph Story, *Commentaries on the Constitution of the United States,* 3 vols. (Boston: Hilliard, Gray & Co., 1833); *Martin* v. *Hunter's Lessee,* 14 U.S. (1 Wheat.) 304 (1816).

2. Padraig Riley, *Slavery and the Democratic Conscience: Political Life in Jeffersonian America* (Philadelphia: University of Pennsylvania Press, 2016), 32 (quoting Abraham Bishop of Connecticut).

3. Riley, *Slavery,* 220–221 (quoting Story to Jacob Crowninshield in letters in 1805 and 1806). Story to Nathaniel Williams, June 6, 1805 and February 22, 1815, in *The Life and Letters of Joseph Story,* ed. William Wetmore Story, 2 vols. (Boston: C. C. Little and J. Brown, 1851), 1: 104–105, 253–254. See also Riley, *Slavery,* 204–205.

4. *Hezekiah Wood* v. *John Davis and Others,* 11 U.S. (7 Cr.) 271 (1812); *Mima Queen and Child* v. *Hepburn,* 11 U.S. (7 Cr.) 290 (1813). See Chapter 2 of this book for a discussion of these cases.

5. *The Caroline* v. *United States (Brig Caroline, William Broadfoot, Claimant),* 11 U.S. (7 Cr.) 496 (1813); *The Alerta* v. *Moran,* 13 U.S. (9 Cr.) 359 (1815).

6. *Fales* v. *Mayberry,* 8 F. Cas. 970 (1815). *United States* v. *La Jeune Eugenie,* 26 F. Cas. 832, 833, 840, 834 (C.C.D. Mass. 1822); R. Kent Newmyer, *Supreme Court Justice Joseph Story: Statesman of the Old Republic* (Chapel Hill: University of North Carolina Press, 1985), 156; *Martin* v. *Hunter's Lessee,* 14 U.S. (1 Wheat.) 304 (1816).

7. *Fairfax's Devisee* v. *Hunter's Lessee,* 11 U.S. (7 Cr.) 603 (1812); Newmyer, *Joseph Story,* 106–114, 117.

8. *M'Culloch* v. *Maryland,* 17 U.S. (4 Wheat.) 316 (1819); *Cohens* v. *Virginia,* 19 U.S. (6 Wheat.) 264 (1821).

9. Newmyer, *Joseph Story,* 165, 167; Paul Finkelman, "John McLean: Moderate Abolitionist and Supreme Court Politician," *Vanderbilt Law Review* 62 (2009): 519–565.

10. Excerpts from the Salem speech from the *Salem Gazette* are found in Story, ed., *Life and Letters*, 1:359–361. Story to Stephen White, February 27, 1820, and Story to Jeremiah Mason, June 25, 1820, in Story, ed., *Life and Letters*, 1:361–363, 365. On Story's prominent opposition to the Compromise and the Boston memorial, see Gerald T. Dunne, "Joseph Story: The Middle Years," *Harvard Law Review* 80 (1967): 1687–1689.

11. Story to Stephen White, February 27, 1820, in Story, ed., *Life and Letters*, 1:361–362.

12. Story to Edward Everett, March 7, 1820, in Story, ed., *Life and Letters*, 1:366–367.

13. *Fales* v. *Mayberry*, 8 F. Cas., at 970, 971, 972. See Slave Trade Act of 1794, ch. 11, 1 Stat. 347 (1794).

14. *Fales*, at 971.

15. Joseph Story to Jeremiah Mason, November 26, 1819, in Story, ed., *Life and Letters of Story*, 1:366. Joseph Story, *A Charge Delivered to the Grand Juries of the Circuit Court at October Term, 1819, in Boston and at November Term, 1819 in Providence, and published at their unanimous request* [Boston, 1819]; Joseph Story, *A Charge Delivered to the Grand Jury of the Circuit Court of the United States at its First Session in Portland, for the Judicial District of Maine, May 8, 1820 and Published at the Unanimous Request of the Grand Jury and of the Bar* (Portland, Me.: A. Shirley, 1820).

16. Story, *A Charge Delivered . . . in Portland*, 13–14.

17. Ibid., 14.

18. Ibid., 14–16.

19. Ibid., 16–17.

20. Ibid., 17, 18–21.

21. *La Jeune Eugenie*, at 845.

22. *La Jeune Eugenie*, at 833, 840, 834. See also William P. Mason, *A Report of the Case of the Jeune Eugenie, Determined in the Circuit Court of the United States, for the First Circuit, at Boston, December, 1821. With an appendix.* (Boston: Wells and Lilly, 1822), 3, 50, 7.

23. Mason, *Report of the Case of the Jeune Eugenie*, 2.

24. *La Jeune Eugenie*, at 840–841; Mason, *Report of the Case of the Jeune Eugenie*, 50, 51, 53–54. This report of the case contains the original early nineteenth-century spelling, which was modernized when the Federal Cases were compiled.

25. *La Jeune Eugenie*, at 845, 846.

26. *La Jeune Eugenie*, at 850.

27. *La Jeune Eugenie*, at 851, 850.

28. *La Jeune Eugenie*, at 841.

29. For a history of the *Antelope* case see Jonathan M. Bryant, *Dark Places of the Earth: The Voyage of the Slave Ship the Antelope* (New York: W. W. Norton, 2015).

30. The *Plattsburgh* was an American-built ship used to transport slaves from Africa to Cuba. This ship had cleared the Baltimore harbor in 1819 under the command of an American captain. The evidence showed that the Americans then fraudulently "sold" the ship to a Cuban named Marino, and that the original American captain was still in command. Thus the ship was condemned, with Justice Story denouncing the notorious nature of fraudulent transactions in Cuba by Americans who persisted in trying to import slaves from Africa. *The Plattsburgh (Marino, Claimant)*, 23 U.S. (10 Wheat.) 133 (1825).

31. *Groves* v. *Slaughter*, 40 U.S. (15 Pet.) 449, 496, 497, 503 (1841).

32. *Groves*, at 508.

33. *Groves*, at 508.

34. *Groves*, at 511–512, 513, 514–515, 516.

35. See, generally, Paul Finkelman, *An Imperfect Union: Slavery, Comity, and Federalism* (Chapel Hill: University of North Carolina Press, 1981).

36. *Gedney* v. *L'Amistad*, 10 F. Cas. 141, 151 (D. Conn. 1840).

37. Story to Sarah Story, 28 February 1841, in Story, ed., *Life and Letters*, 2:338–340.

38. *United States* v. *The Amistad*, 40 U.S. 15 Pet. 518, 593 (1841).

39. *Amistad*, at 593.

40. *Amistad*, at 598

41. "An Act in addition to the Acts prohibiting the slave trade," 3 Stat. 532, 533 (1819), Sec. 2.

42. *Prigg* v. *Pennsylvania,* 41 US (16 Pet.) 539 (1842).

43. For the background of *Prigg,* see Paul Finkelman, "Story Telling on the Supreme Court: *Prigg* v. *Pennsylvania* and Justice Joseph Story's Judicial Nationalism," *Supreme Court Review* 1994: 247–294; and H. Robert Baker, *Prigg* v. *Pennsylvania: Slavery, the Supreme Court, and the Ambivalent Constitution* (Lawrence: University of Kansas Press, 2012). See also *Prigg,* at 608–610. U.S. Manuscript Census, 1820, Harford County, Maryland, p 380 (also noted as p 76). Ashmore's birthdate, January 22, 1760, is found in Bill Reamy and Martha Reamy, *St. George's Parish Registers, 1689–1793* (Silver Spring, Md.: Family Line Publications), 85. Deed of Conveyance from John Ashmore to Susanna Bemis, May 11, 1821, in Harford County Historical Society manuscripts. Edward Prigg was one of the two witnesses to this deed. John Ashmore Inventory, Sept 28, 1824, Harford County, Register of Willis, # 1672. U.S. Manuscript Census, 1830, Harford County, Maryland, 387.

44. *Prigg,* at 613.

45. *Prigg,* at 612–613.

46. *Prigg,* at 668 (McLean dissenting).

47. *Prigg,* at 611.

48. *Prigg,* at 638–639.

49. *Prigg,* at 624.

50. Story, *Commentaries on the Constitution,* at § 952.

51. *Prigg,* at 611.

52. The only other response to Butler's proposal was Roger Sherman's sarcastic observation that he "saw no more propriety in the public seizing and surrendering a slave or servant, than a horse." Max Farrand, ed., *The Records of the Federal Convention of 1787,* rev. ed., 4 vols. (New Haven: Yale University Press, 1966), 2:443, quotations, at 2:453–454. The history of this clause is discussed in Paul Finkelman, *Slavery and the Founders: Race and Liberty in the Age of Jefferson,* 3rd ed. (New York: Routledge, 2014), 102–32. See also William M. Wiecek, "The Witch at the Christening: Slavery and

the Constitution's Origins," in *The Framing and Ratification of the Constitution*, ed. Leonard W. Levy and Dennis J. Mahoney, 167–184 (New York: Macmillan, 1987). The clause reads: "No person held to Service or Labour in one State, under the Laws thereof, escaping into another, shall, in Consequence of any Law or Regulation therein, be discharged from such Service or Labour, but shall be delivered up on Claim of the Party to whom such Service or Labour may be due."

53. Finkelman, *Slavery and the Founders; Prigg*, at 638–639.

54. "Letters from a Countryman from Dutchess County" (letter of Jan 22, 1788), in *The Complete Anti-Federalist*, ed. Herbert Storing (Chicago: University of Chicago Press, 1981), 6:62.

55. Privately, the Rhode Island merchant and Quaker abolitionist Moses Brown expressed concern that the Fugitive Slave Clause was "designd to Distroy the Present Assylum of the Massachusetts from being as a City of Refuge for the poor Blacks": Moses Brown to James Pemberton, Oct. 17, 1787, reprinted in *The Documentary History of the Ratification of the Constitution by the States*, vol. 14: *Commentaries on the Constitution, Public and Private*, vol. 2, ed. John P. Kaminski and Gaspare J. Saladino (Madison: State Historical Society of Wisconsin, 1983), 506–507.

56. Federalist 42 and Federalist 54.

57. James Madison, in the Virginia Ratifying Convention, June 17, 1788, in *The Documentary History of the Ratification of the Constitution by the States*, vol. 10: *Virginia*, vol. 3, ed. John P. Kaminski and Gaspare J. Saladino (Madison: State Historical Society of Wisconsin, 1993), 1339; Edmund Randolph in the Virginia Ratifying Convention, June 24, 1788, in *Documentary History*, ed. Kaminski and Saladino, vol. 10, 1484.

58. "North Carolina Delegates [William Blount, Richard D. Spaight, Hugh Williamson] to Governor Caswell," September 18, 1787, reprinted in Farrand, ed., *The Records of the Federal Convention of 1787*, 3:84; Charles Cotesworth Pinckney, Speech in South Carolina House of Representatives, January 17, 1788, reprinted in Farrand, ed., *The Records of the Federal Convention of 1787*, 3:254.

59. Story, *Commentaries on the Constitution*, at § 952.

60. Ibid.

61. Ibid.

62. *In re Susan*, 23 F. Cas. 444 (USDC Ind., 1818), for example, refers to the fugitive slave Susan returned to slavery with no existing opinion of the court; *Case of Williams*, 29 F. Cas. 1334 (USDC Pa., 1839) has the court discharging a black (Williams) who had been seized by a professional slave catcher because the court determines that Williams is not a fugitive slave; *In re Martin*, 16 F. Cas. 881 (USDC N.Y., 1827–1840) is a case of unknown date in which the federal district judge in New York declared the act of 1793 to be constitutional and a New York official then issued a certificate of removal under the law.

63. *Johnson* v. *Tompkins et al.*, 13 F.Cas 840 (USCC Pa., 1833). Baldwin was an extremely weak justice whom many observers believed to be insane. Carl B. Swisher, *History of the Supreme Court of the United States: The Taney Period, 1836–64* (New York: Macmillan, 1974), 51. Baldwin's opinion in *Prigg* suggests the truth of both observations.

64. *Wright* v. *Deacon*, 5 Sergeant and Rawle 62 (Pa. 1819); *Commonwealth* v. *Griffith*, 19 Mass. (2 Pick.) 11 (1823); *Jack* v. *Martin*, 14 Wend. 507 (N.Y. 1835); *State* v. *Sheriff of Burlington*, No. 36286 (NJ 1836, unreported) (also known as *Nathan, Alias Alex. Helmsley* v. *State; Prigg* v. *Pennsylvania* (Pa., 1841, unreported). For a discussion of Chief Justice Joseph Hornblower's unreported opinion in *State* v. *Sheriff of Burlington*, see Paul Finkelman, "State Constitutional Protections of Liberty and the Antebellum New Jersey Supreme Court: Chief Justice Hornblower and the Fugitive Slave Law of 1793," *Rutgers Law Journal* 23 (1992): 753–787. Salmon P. Chase cited this case in an 1837 Ohio case, and a pamphlet report of that case was widely circulated. Salmon P. Chase, *Speech of Salmon P. Chase in the Case of the Colored Woman, Matilda* 18–19 (Cincinnati: Pugh and Dodd, 1837).

65. *Prigg*, at 621.

66. *Prigg*, at 622 and 621.

67. *Wright* v. *Deacon*, and *Commonwealth* v. *Griffith*, upheld the federal law, while *Jack* v. *Martin*, and *State* v. *Sheriff of Burlington*, found the federal law unconstitutional.

68. *Wright*, at 62; *Griffith*, at 11, 18, 19.

69. Ohio attorney Salmon P. Chase had cited it while arguing a case in 1837. Chase, *Speech of Salmon P. Chase,* 18.

70. *Jack,* at 526 and 528.

71. *Jack,* at 526 and 528.

72. *Prigg,* at 621.

73. Thomas C. Hambly, *Argument of Mr. Hambly, of York, (Pa.) in the Case of Edward Prigg* (Baltimore: Lucas & Deaver, 1842), 8.

74. *Prigg,* at 608–609.

75. *Prigg,* at 608–609.

76. *Prigg,* at 613.

77. In May of 1837, Margaret Morgan sued for her freedom in a Harford County court. On August 28, 1837, a jury was sworn, which two days later decided that she was still a slave. More than a dozen witnesses appeared on behalf of the defendant, Margaret Ashmore. Margaret Morgan, on the other hand, does not seem to have been represented by counsel. Docket Book, Harford County Civil and Criminal Court, 1837, in Harford County Historical Society. Margaret and her children were subsequently sold south. Hambly, *Argument of Hambly,* 10.

78. *Pocock v. Hendricks,* 8 Gill and Johnson 421 (Md., 1837). Later in the month of (June 1837), however, the same court also held that a slave was not free, even though he "went at large and acted as a free man" and had been allowed to travel to New York and work there. *Bland* and Woolfolk v. *Negro Beverly Dowling,* 9 Gill and Johnson 19 (Md., 1837). Here, however, the loss of freedom was based on the fact that Dowling voluntarily returned to Maryland, which was not the case with Margaret. *Pocock* involved a suit between two whites, while in *Bland* the slave unsuccessfully claimed his freedom on the grounds that he had purchased it from his owner, Sophia Bland. Other Maryland cases suggested that courts might "presume" a legal manumission when the alleged slave was allowed to live for a long time as a free person and the putative owner made no attempt to claim the slave. In *Burke* v. *Negro Joe,* 6 Gill & Johnson 136 (Md., 1834), Maryland's highest court upheld the freedom of the child of a slave who had been allowed to act as a free person, even though there was no need of manumission. The court

held that there was a presumption of legal manumission "founded upon acts inconsistent with a state of slavery, known to the owner, and which can only be rationally accounted for, upon a supposition that he had intended to free his slave." *Burke,* 6 Gill & Johnson, at 142. This language could easily have been applied to the circumstances of Margaret and her parents. For further discussion of these issues see Baker, *Prigg v. Pennsylvania,* 105–108.

79. "An Act for the Gradual Abolition of Slavery," Act of March 1, 1780, Pennsylvania Laws, 1780, § III, states that: "All persons as well Negroes and Mulattoes, as others, who shall be born within this State from and after the passing of this act, shall not be deemed and considered as servants for life, or slaves; and that all servitude for life, or slavery of children in consequence of the slavery of their mothers, in the case of all children born within this State from and after the passing of this act, as aforesaid, shall be, and hereby is, utterly taken away, extinguished, and forever abolished." *Commonwealth* v. *Holloway,* 2 Sergeant & Rawle 305 (Pa., 1816); "An Act to Explain and Amend An Act, Entitled 'An Act for the Gradual Abolition of Slavery,'" Act of March 29, 1788, Pennsylvania Acts, 1788, § II.

80. William R. Leslie, "The Pennsylvania Fugitive Slave Act of 1826," *Journal of Southern History* 18 (1952): 429–445.

81. Leslie, "Pennsylvania Fugitive Slave Act," 440; Pennsylvania Act of 1826, Sec. 1.

82. Story, ed., *Life and Letters,* 2:392.

83. *Prigg,* at 615–616; Story, ed., *Life and Letters,* 2:393; *Prigg,* at 622; Paul Finkelman, "*Prigg v Pennsylvania* and Northern State Courts: Antislavery Use of a Pro-Slavery Decision," *Civil War History* 25 (1979): 5–35.

84. Newmyer, *Joseph Story,* 182.

85. Newmyer, *Joseph Story,* 101; *United States* v. *Hudson and Goodwin,* 11 U.S. (7 Cr.) 32 (1812); *United States* v. *Coolidge,* 25 F. Cas. 619 (CCD Mass., 1813) reversed at 14 U.S. (1 Wheat.) 415 (1816).

86. Story to Nathaniel Williams, October 8, 1812, reprinted in Story, ed., *Life and Letters,* 1:243; Story to Daniel Webster, January 4, 1824, reprinted in Story, ed., *Life and Letters,* 1:435, at

437, 439–441; see also Story, ed., *Life and Letters*, 2:401, 403–404; Newmyer, *Joseph Story*, at 103. "An Act more effectually to provide for the punishment of certain crimes against the United States, and for other purposes," Act of March 3, 1825, 4 Stat 115; Story to Berrien, Feb 8, 1842, reprinted in Story, ed., *Life and Letters*, 1:402–403; See Story to John Macpherson Berrien, April 29, 1842, in John Macpherson Berrien Papers, Southern Historical Collection, University of North Carolina. This letter is quoted at length in James McClellan, *Joseph Story and the American Constitution* (Norman: University of Oklahoma Press, 1971), 262n–263n.

87. *Van Reimsdyk* v. *Kane*, 28 F. Cas. 1062 (CCD R.I., 1812); and *Swift* v. *Tyson*, 41 U.S. (16 Pet.) 1 (1842).

88. *Prigg*, at 612.

89. *Prigg*, at 611–612.

90. Finkelman, "*Prigg v Pennsylvania* and Northern State Courts," 5; Thomas D. Morris, *Free Men All: The Personal Liberty Laws of the North, 1780–1861* (Baltimore: Johns Hopkins University Press, 1974).

91. See Robert M. Cover, *Justice Accused: Antislavery and the Judicial Process* (New Haven: Yale University Press, 1975), 241.

92. *Prigg*, at 625.

93. *Prigg*, at 622.

94. Story to Berrien, April 29, 1842.

95. Ibid.

96. Story, ed., *Life and Letters*, 2:404–405.

97. Story to Ezekiel Bacon, April 1, 1844, and Story to Harriet Martineau, January 19, 1839, reprinted in Story, ed., *Life and Letters*, 2:481, 139.

98. Story, ed., *Life and Letters*, 2:386; *Prigg*, at 616.

99. *An Article on the Latimer Case From the March Number of the Law Reporter* (Boston: Bradbury and Soden Company, 1843), 8 (capitalization in the original.)

100. Story to Stephen White, February 27, 1820, and Story to Jeremiah Mason, June 25, 1820, reprinted in Story, ed., *Life and Letters*, 1:361–363, 365.

5 · ROGER B. TANEY: SLAVERY'S GREAT CHIEF JUSTICE

1. *Dred Scott* v. *Sandford*, 60 U.S. (19 How.) 393 (1857).

2. Charles Sumner, *Congressional Globe* 38 Cong. 2nd Sess, 1012–17 (Feb. 23, 1865). See Carl Brent Swisher, *Roger B. Taney* (New York: Macmillan, 1935), 581–582.

3. Don E. Fehrenbacher, *The Dred Scott Case: Its Significance in American Law and Politics* (New York: Oxford University Press, 1978), 3, 311.

4. *Dred Scott*, at 404–405.

5. U.S. Federal Census, 1810, Calvert, Maryland, microfilm #M252–15, Stmp pg. 541, HW pg. 149, line 10; note that in this transcription, Michael Taney is rendered as "Michel Tancy"; available at http://us-census.org/pub/usgenweb/census/md /calvert/1810/pgs-514-to-545.txt. For more details see, "Michael Taney (b. 1780–d. 1820), *Archives of Maryland* (Biographical Series), found at http://msa.maryland.gov/megafile/msa/speccol /sc5400/sc5496/050700/050789/html/050789bio.html.

6. National Register of Historical Places, Nomination Form, Roger Brooke Taney House, available at http://msa.maryland.gov/megafile /msa/stagsere/se1/se5/012000/012200/012222/pdf/msa_se5_12222 .pdf.

7. Swisher, *Roger B. Taney*, 93.

8. Swisher, *Roger B. Taney*, 93–96.

9. Speech by Taney, quoted in Swisher, *Roger B. Taney*, 97.

10. Swisher, *Roger B. Taney*, 99.

11. Timothy Huebner, "Roger B. Taney and the Slavery Issue: Looking Beyond—and Before—*Dred Scott*," *Journal of American History* 97 (2010):17–38, quote at 18; David Martin, ed., *Trial of the Rev. Jacob Gruber, Minister in the Methodist Episcopal Church, At the March Term, 1819, in the Frederick County Court, For a Misdemeanor* (Fredericktown, Md., 1819); Paul Finkelman, *Slavery in the Court- room: An Annotated Bibliography of American Cases* (Washington, D.C.: Library of Congress, for sale by GPO, 1985), 158–161.

12. Edward S. Corwin, "The Dred Scott Decision, in the Light of Contemporary Legal Doctrines," *American Historical Review* 17

(1911), 68; Charles Evans Hughes, "Roger Brooke Taney," *American Bar Association Journal* 17 (1931), 785; Alexander M. Bickel, *The Supreme Court and the Idea of Progress* (New Haven: Yale University Press, 1978), 41.

13. Henry J. Abraham, *Justices and Presidents: A Political History of Appointments to the Supreme Court*, 3rd ed. (New York: Oxford University Press, 1992), 76, 72. This language remains unchanged in the most recent (fifth) edition of this book published 2007.

14. G. Edward White, *The American Judicial Tradition: Profiles of Leading American Judges*, 3rd ed. (New York: Oxford University Press, 2007), 66.

15. *Dred Scott v. Sandford*, at 404–405 (1857); "Unpublished Opinion of Attorney General Taney," quoted in Swisher, *Roger B. Taney*, 154.

16. White, *American Judicial Tradition*, 69.

17. Henry F. Graff, "The Charles River Bridge Case," in *Quarrels That Have Shaped the Constitution*, ed. John A. Garraty (New York: Harper and Row, 1962), 72.

18. Kenneth M. Holland, "Roger B. Taney: A Great Chief Justice?" in *Great Justices of the U.S. Supreme Court: Ratings and Case Studies*, ed. William D. Pederson and Norman W. Provizer (New York: P. Lang, 1993), 74.

19. One example of Frankfurter's lack of sympathy for minorities is his dissent in *West Virginia Board of Education v. Barnette*, 319 U.S. 624 (1943), where he supported expelling children from school if they refused to salute the flag because doing so violated their religious beliefs.

20. Felix Frankfurter, "Taney and the Commerce Clause," *Harvard Law Review* 49 (1936): 1286–1302, at 1288 and 1291.

21. Ibid., at 1288.

22. Ibid., at 1299, 1300.

23. *Mayor of New York v. Miln*, 36 U.S. (11 Pet.) 102 (1837).

24. Harold M. Hyman and William M. Wiecek, *Equal Justice Under Law: Constitutional Development, 1835–1875* (New York: Harper and Row, 1982), 60.

25. Fehrenbacher, *Dred Scott Case*, 3, 311.

26. Miller, quoted in White, *American Judicial Tradition*, 67–68.

27. *Charles River Bridge Co.* v. *Warren Bridge Co.*, 36 U.S. (11 Pet.) 420 (1837); see generally, Stanley I. Kutler, *Privilege and Creative Destruction: The Charles River Bridge Case* (Philadelphia: Lippincott, 1971).

28. *New York* v. *Miln*, at 142–143.

29. License Cases (*Thurlow* v. *Commonwealth of Massachusetts; Fletcher* v. *Rhode Island; Pierce* v. *New Hampshire*) 46 U.S. (5 How.) 504 (1847); *Cooley* v. *Board of Wardens*, 53 U.S. (12 How.) 299 (1852).

30. *New York* v. *Miln*, at 102; *Passenger Cases* (*Smith* v. *Turner; Norris* v. *Boston*), 48 U.S. (7 How.) 283 (1849).

31. *Bank of Augusta* v. *Earle*, 38 U.S. (13 Pet.) 519 (1839).

32. *The Thomas Jefferson*, 23 U.S. (10 Wheat.) 428 (1825); *Propeller Genesee Chief* v. *Fitzhugh*, 53 U.S. (12 How.) 443 (1852). Hyman and Wiecek, *Equal Justice Under Law*, 75.

33. In 1787 free blacks voted in New Hampshire, Massachusetts, New York, Pennsylvania, New Jersey, and North Carolina. Some also apparently voted in Maryland. David Bogen, "The Maryland Context of *Dred Scott:* The Decline in the Legal Status of Maryland Free Blacks 1776–1810," *American Journal of Legal History* 34 (1990): 381–411. Blacks were later able to vote in Vermont, Tennessee, Maine, and Rhode Island. By the 1830s they had lost the right to vote in New Jersey, Pennsylvania, North Carolina, and Tennessee. Some people of mixed ancestry were allowed to vote in Ohio. By 1860 blacks had held public office in New Hampshire, Vermont, Massachusetts, Maine, Rhode Island, and Ohio.

34. "Unpublished Opinion of Attorney General Taney," quoted in Swisher, *Roger B. Taney*, 154.

35. Bogen, "The Maryland Context of *Dred Scott.*"

36. *United States* v. *The Garonne*, 36 U.S. 11 Pet. 73 (1837).

37. *Garonne*, at 77.

38. *United States* v. *The Amistad*, 40 U.S. (15 Pet.) 518 (1841); *Groves* v. *Slaughter*, 40 U.S. (15 Pet.) 449 (1841).

39. For a full discussion of *Amistad*, see Chapter 4 of this book.

40. *Groves*, at 508–509.

41. For a more complete discussion of *Prigg*, see Chapter 4 of this book.

42. This holding was consistent with prevailing notions of federalism and states' rights, and Taney should have applauded it. Indeed, later in his career, Taney would argue that the federal courts could not order state governors to enforce the criminal extradition clauses of the same 1793 law. *Kentucky* v. *Dennison*, 65 U.S. (24 How.) 66 (1861).

43. *Prigg* v. *Pennsylvania*, 41 U.S. (16 Pet.) 539, 628 (1842).

44. *Prigg*, at 634.

45. *Prigg*, at 628.

46. *Prigg*, at 629.

47. *Strader* v. *Graham*, 51 U.S. (10 How.) 82 (1851).

48. *Strader*, at 93.

49. Fehrenbacher, *Dred Scott Case*, 311.

50. Sanford spelled his name S-a-n-f-o-r-d, but the clerk of the United States Supreme Court added an extra "d" to his name, thus making the case *Dred Scott* v. *Sandford*. It is impossible to determine whether Sanford actually owned Scott, or was merely acting as an agent for his sister, Irene Emerson, the widow of Dr. Emerson. It is also probably irrelevant. Sanford never denied he owned Scott, and he acknowledged this in all court papers and proceedings after 1853.

51. *Dred Scott*, at 396–397.

52. *Strader*, at 93.

53. See Paul Finkelman, "Was Dred Scott Correctly Decided? An 'Expert Report' for the Defendant," *Lewis & Clark Law Review* 12 (2008): 1219–1252.

54. By 1857, blacks had been admitted to the bar in Maine, Massachusetts, Ohio, and New York. It seemed only a matter of time before a black lawyer from one of those states brought a case into federal court. In a few fugitive slave cases in Massachusetts the black lawyer Robert Morris had sat at the counsel table before a federal commissioner. Taney wanted to prevent this from spreading to other courts. Paul Finkelman, "Not Only the Judges' Robes Were

Black: African-American Lawyers as Social Engineers," *Stanford Law Review* 47 (1994): 161–209.

55. *Dred Scott*, at 404–405.

56. *Dred Scott*, at 451.

57. *Dred Scott*, at 432.

58. *Dred Scott*, at 436–437.

59. *Dred Scott*, at 407.

60. *Dred Scott*, at 410.

61. *Dred Scott*, at 417.

62. Paul Finkelman, "Slavery and the Constitutional Convention: Making a Covenant with Death," in *Beyond Confederation: Origins of the Constitution and American National Identity*, ed. Richard Beeman, Stephen Botein, and Edward C. Carter II, 188–225 (Chapel Hill: University of North Carolina Press, 1987).

63. *Ableman* v. *Booth*, 62 U.S. (21 How.) 506 (1859); *Kentucky* v. *Dennison*, 65 U.S. (24 How.) 66 (1861). For a full history of *Ableman*, see Robert Howard Baker, *The Rescue of Joshua Glover: A Fugitive Slave, the Constitution, and the Coming of the Civil War* (Athens: Ohio University Press, 2006).

64. One exception to this might be the Court's decision in *Ex parte Gordon*, 66 U.S. (1 Black) 503 (1862). Gordon was convicted of piracy under the slave trade prohibitions and sentenced to death by the U.S. Circuit Court in New York, in 1861. He asked the Supreme Court to intervene on his behalf, through both a writ of prohibition, to prevent his execution, and through a writ of certiorari to bring the record of his case to the Supreme Court. Speaking for a unanimous Court, Chief Justice Taney held that the Supreme Court had no power or jurisdiction to issue either writ after a criminal conviction in the circuit court. Taney noted that "the only case in which this court is authorized even to express an opinion on the proceedings in a Circuit Court in a criminal case is, where the judges of the Circuit Court are opposed in opinion upon a question arising at the trial, and certify it to this court for its decision." *Gordon*, at 505. Because there had been no disagreement between the two judges hearing the case, the Supreme Court was powerless to act and so the holding was "motion refused." *Gordon*, at 506. The

Court did not rule on the conviction or the laws prohibiting the slave trade, but only on the impossibility of granting either of Gordon's motions. He was subsequently hanged in February 1862, becoming the first and only person to be executed under the law prohibiting the slave trade. The only book-length study of this case is Ron Soodalter, *The Hanging of Captain Gordon: The Life and Trial of an American Slave Trader* (New York: Washington Square Press, 2007).

65. *Ex parte Merryman,* 17 F. Cas. 144 (C.C.D. Md. 1861).

66. Fehrenbacher, *Dred Scott Case,* 556; *Prize Cases,* 67 U.S. (2 Black) 635 (1863).

67. *Dred Scott,* at 450.

68. Paul Finkelman, "John McLean: Moderate Abolitionist and Supreme Court Politician," *Vanderbilt Law Review* 62 (2009): 519–565.

CODA

1. Paul Finkelman, "The Proslavery Origins of the Electoral College," *Cardozo Law Review* 23 (2002): 1145–1157.

2. *Scott* v. *Negro Ben,* 10 U.S. (6 Cr.) 3, 6 (1810).

3. *Mima Queen* v. *Hepburn,* 11 U.S. (7 Cr.) 290, 293, 296 (1813).

ACKNOWLEDGMENTS

THIS BOOK began as part of the 2009 Nathan I. Huggins Lectures, sponsored by the W. E. B. Du Bois Institute for African and African American Research at Harvard University. I am grateful to Skip Gates and Evelyn Brooks Higginbotham for inviting me to give those lectures, for their gracious hospitality, and for providing such a stimulating intellectual setting for the lectures. Many members of the Harvard community attended and asked hard questions. In particular, Morton J. Horwitz, Orlando Patterson, and Stan Engerman, as well as Skip and Evelyn, pressed me with their questions and comments. All five have been good friends and colleagues for much of my career, and Mort was also my teacher when I was a Fellow in Law and Humanities at Harvard Law School.

Kent Newmyer, who wrote superb biographies of both Marshall and Story, and Charles Hobson, the longtime editor of the Papers of John Marshall, were enormously generous with their time and knowledge. Both are incredible scholars, sharp critics, and good friends. They have both read parts of this book, given me extraordinarily useful comments, and saved me from a number of errors. They probably do not agree with all the arguments and analysis in this book, but their engagement with my work has been critical in shaping my ideas. Both Kent and Chuck exemplify the mind and spirit of the academic community at its best. I have learned much from them. This book is better because of their criticism. It is also a better book because of their important scholarship on Marshall and Story, cited throughout.

My friend and collaborator on other projects, Tim Huebner, provided excellent comments on Taney and, more generally, useful, and supportive conversations on the Court. Tim's own work on Taney has been enormously helpful to me, as has been his friendship and good humor.

Many colleagues and friends have discussed this book with me, and read parts of it. Staff members at various archives and institutions have also contributed in various ways. I particularly want to thank the following: Joni Albrecht, Gill Berchowitz, Richard B. Bernstein, Ken Bowling, John Deal, Raymond T. Diamond, William C. diGiacomantonio, Graham Dozier, Seymour Drescher, Bob Emery, Dennis Hutchinson, Herbert Johnson, Stanley N. Katz, Donald Kennon, David T. Konig, Alysa Landry, John A. Ragosta, Ashley Ramsey, Jeffrey Rosen, Stephen M. Sheppard, Lance J. Sussman, Peter Wallenstein, Kevin Walsh, Alyson Taylor-White, William M. Wiecek, Brendan Wolfe, Conrad Edick Wright, and my late friend Judith K. Schafer. Finally, this book is at least in part an answer to questions raised by Owen Fiss, Stan Katz, and the late Harry Kalven Jr. many years ago in a seminar on the law of slavery at the University of Chicago—especially about the nature of Justice Story's opinion in *Prigg* v. *Pennsylvania* and Chief Justice Taney's opinion in *Dred Scott.*

I worked on parts of this book while I was a scholar-in-residence at the National Constitution Center. I presented some of this work at the University of Saskatchewan College of Law, where I was honored to hold the Ariel F. Sallows Chair in Human Rights, and at the Boston Area Seminar in Early

American History. I thank those who raised good questions and simply allowed me to think out loud about this project. I owe a debt, as all scholars do, to the librarians and staffs at the institutions where I have taught and done research, including reference librarians at Albany Law School, Duke Law School, Houghton Library at Harvard, the John Marshall House, the Library of Virginia, the Virginia Historical Society, the University of Saskatchewan Law Library, the University of Pittsburgh Law Library, and the University of Ottawa Law Library. Writing this book was made much easier with the help of assistants, including Fredd Brewer, Sherri Meyer, Chris Harris, and Amy Change.

I also owe a special debt to the staff at William S. Hein & Co., and particularly to the company's president, Kevin Marmion, and senior vice president, Daniel Rosati. While writing this book I worked with Kevin and Dan in developing HeinOnline's digital library: *Slavery in America and the World: History, Culture & Law*. The project gave me (and now gives all scholars) easier access to many rare documents and books on slavery and antislavery. In the course of that work, Dan helped me do comprehensive searches on all federal cases involving slavery.

Candace Gray Jackson, currently a Ph.D. student at Morgan State University, helped me track down enormous amounts of previously unknown census and tax data pertaining to John Marshall's slaveholding and Roger B. Taney's slaveholding. Candace understands how to use census and tax records better than anyone else I know.

I put the finishing touches on this book while holding a Fulbright Research Chair in Human Rights at the University of Ottawa College of Law. I thank Frederick John Packer at the Human Rights Centre and Brad Hector at Fulbright Canada for their support of my work.

My copy editor at Harvard University Press, Julia Kirby, has become a friend and intellectual collaborator. She has not merely saved me from errors—as any good copy editor does—but has also batted ideas back and forth.

My final thanks goes to my editor at HUP, Joyce Seltzer. She is smart, tough, wise, and demanding, and tempers all these qualities with humor. She has also been enormously patient with this book, which came in later than either of us wanted. Having worked with Joyce, I now understand why she is, in the world of academic publishing, truly "a legend in her own time."

INDEX OF CASES CITED

INDEX